Studies in Celtic History XI

EARLY MONASTERIES IN CORNWALL

STUDIES IN CELTIC HISTORY
General editor   David Dumville

Already published

I · THE SAINTS OF GWYNEDD
Molly Miller

II · CELTIC BRITAIN IN THE EARLY MIDDLE AGES
Kathleen Hughes

III · THE INSULAR LATIN GRAMMARIANS
Vivien Law

IV · CHRONICLES AND ANNALS OF MEDIAEVAL
IRELAND AND WALES
Kathryn Grabowski & David Dumville

V · GILDAS: NEW APPROACHES
M. Lapidge & D. Dumville (edd.)

VI · SAINT GERMANUS OF AUXERRE AND
THE END OF ROMAN BRITAIN
E. A. Thompson

VII · FROM KINGS TO WARLORDS
Katharine Simms

VIII · THE CHURCH AND THE WELSH BORDER
IN THE CENTRAL MIDDLE AGES
C. N. L. Brooke

IX · THE LITURGY AND RITUAL OF THE CELTIC CHURCH
F. E. Warren
(2nd edn, by Jane Stevenson)

X · THE MONKS OF REDON
Caroline Brett (ed. & transl.)

Forthcoming

XII · IRELAND, WALES, AND ENGLAND IN
THE ELEVENTH CENTURY
K. L. Maund

In preparation

GILDAS IN THE MIDDLE AGES
David Dumville (ed.)

NAVIGATIO SANCTI BRENDANI
Giovanni Orlandi

AN INTRODUCTION TO *VITAE SANCTORUM HIBERNIAE*
Richard Sharpe

UNDERSTANDING THE UNIVERSE IN SEVENTH-CENTURY IRELAND
Marina Smyth

ISSN 0261-9865

EARLY MONASTERIES IN CORNWALL

LYNETTE OLSON

THE BOYDELL PRESS

First published 1989 by
The Boydell Press
an imprint of Boydell & Brewer Ltd
PO Box 9, Woodbridge, Suffolk IP12 3DF
and of Boydell & Brewer Inc.
Wolfeboro, New Hampshire 03894-2069, USA

ISBN 0 85115 478 6

British Library Cataloguing in Publication Data
Olson, Lynette
 Early monasteries in Cornwall.—(Studies in
 Celtic history, 0261-9865; v. 11).
 1. Cornwall. Monasteries to ca. 1200
 I. Title II. Series
 271'.0094237
 ISBN 0-85115-478-6

Library of Congress Cataloging-in-Publication Data
Olson, B. Lynette
 Early monasteries in Cornwall / Lynette Olson.
  p.   cm. — (Studies in Celtic history ; 11)
 Bibliography: p.
 Includes index.
 ISBN 0-85115-478-6 (alk. paper)
 1. Monasticism and religious orders—England—Cornwall (County)—
History. 2. Christian antiquities—England—Cornwall (County)
3. Cornwall (County)—Church history. I. Title. II. Series.
BX2594.C67045 1988
271'.009423'7—dc19   88-8611
                                                          CIP

♾ Printed on long life paper
made to the full American Standard

Printed in Great Britain by
St Edmundsbury Press, Bury St Edmunds, Suffolk

This book is dedicated to
the Institute of Cornish Studies
in recognition of the importance of
studying Cornwall – in Cornwall

CONTENTS

GENERAL EDITOR'S FOREWORD

're-Norman Cornwall has been a subject of study finding few practitioners
utside the modern county. Written sources are scarce and a framework of
nterpretation has never been easily won. Yet in recent years academic
pproaches to Cornish history and culture have multiplied fruitfully. The
ate middle ages have received new attention, for example, in much work
levoted to Middle Cornish literature and, on the historical side, Dr John
latcher's important study of rural economy and society in the Duchy. The
reation of the Cornwall Archaeological Society twenty-five years ago gave
urther impetus to study of the area's material remains, not least those of
he early middle ages. The foundation, by Cornwall County Council and
he University of Exeter, of the Institute of Cornish Studies has generated
nuch important activity, resulting not least in Mr Oliver Padel's superb
ook, *Cornish Place-name Elements*, recently published by the English
'lace-name Society. New and fruitful work in mediaeval Breton studies
lso has implications for Cornwall. Now comes the present investigation of
he ecclesiastical history of earlier mediaeval Cornwall: Dr Lynette Olson's
ook, begun as work towards the Ph.D. degree of the University of
'oronto, has the merit of combining close study of all the relevant Cornish
vidence with a broader approach to Church-history. Although she is
either Canadian nor Cornish, her researches bring credit to both countries.

Anglo-Saxon conquest of Cornwall began only in the seventh or eighth
entury and was completed (in the military and political senses) only in the
inth and tenth. Cultural assimilation, very visible already in tenth-century
ources, took hundreds of years to achieve, however. The lateness of the
rocess, by comparison with Anglo-Saxon settlement of most of the rest of
hat came to be England, to some extent allows it to be studied with a
egree of subtlety unattainable for other regions where the transition was
ffectively pre-historic. Dr Olson's particular contribution is to demon-
trate, from very fragmentary and disparate source-materials, something of
he rich variety of Cornish Church-life in the earlier middle ages. In this she
; a worthy successor to Canon Gilbert Doble and to Charles Henderson
ho, in the generation between the World Wars, did so much by their
xample to establish the study of mediaeval Cornish history as a serious
cademic discipline.

A potentially unfortunate tendency of the last generation's work, on the
istory of Britain's South-west peninsula in the earliest phase of the middle
ges, has been the frequent treatment of the whole region as a single unit.
The Kingdom of Dumnonia' can hardly be defined thus from any contem-
orary sources. And by the time when, in the ninth century, Anglo-Saxon
ources speak of *Cornwalas* or *Westwalas*, Latin texts refer to *Cornubia*,

and the Old Welsh form *Cerniu* is found, the names of Dumnonia and the Dumnonii have passed from view save through the Old English derivative *Defnascir* and *Defnas*, '(the territory of) the people of Devon'. It is with the people of *Cornouia*, *Cornubia*, that Dr Olson is concerned. From the precision of a definable unit her study gains significant strength.

Among the Churches of the Celtic-speaking peoples in the pre-Norman era, that of the Cornish has been studied largely archaeologically for the last half-century. Dr Olson's book is the first for more than seventy years to consider this subject in the round. It is greatly to be hoped that her book will inspire, and soon be followed by, one on the secular organisation of Cornwall in the same period: such a work is greatly needed by Celtic historians.

David Dumville
Girton College, Cambridge
August 1987

PREFACE

The subject of this study was suggested to me by Professor Charles Thomas. It needed doing, yet sufficient groundwork had already been undertaken that one would not need to start from scratch. Indeed, if the Cornish historian Charles Henderson had not died at a tragically young age more than fifty years ago, the present study probably would not have needed to be carried out. This is not to say that the subject would not have been in need of reassessment. Henderson, like his contemporaries Thomas Taylor and G. H. Doble, saw the early Cornish Church as entirely monastic. Large foundations were cenobitic, small ones eremitic; parish-churches were late and intrusive. The present study does not make these assumptions.

Research confirmed that the area had been too little studied. Rather to my surprise, 'standard' documents such as are found in Haddan and Stubbs's Cornish section well repaid careful examination. At the same time, the difficulties of determining the monastic nature of a site on archaeological grounds were becoming obvious. Thus my emphasis shifted heavily to written evidence: its testimony to the presence of a religious community is regarded as crucial at this stage in the identification of an early monastery in Cornwall.

More important than recording my debt to past scholarship is acknowledging the help which people have given me in preparing this book. Three especially must be thanked: first and foremost Oliver Padel, for innumerable suggestions and discussions – and for many a field-trip – as the work progressed, for his unfailing interest in it which was so supportive and encouraging, and for time taken from his own important researches into Cornish language and history; Charles Thomas, for the topic and always answering my questions about it and for making the facilities of the Institute of Cornish Studies available to me for extended periods of time; and Michael Sheehan, for his care and patience as my thesis-supervisor in first turning this difficult material into a coherent study. Other thanks to record are to Leslie Douch as curator of The Royal Institution of Cornwall Museum and to Angela Broome, librarian; other staff at the Institute of Cornish Studies, Margaret Bunt, Pat Johnstone, and Myrna Combellack Harris; Wendy Davies, David Dumville, Leonard Boyle, John Hayes, Neil Wright, Simon Keynes, Roger Reynolds, Jonathan Wooding, Ann Preston-Jones, Elisabeth Okasha, W. M. M. Picken, J. H. Adams, Mary Henderson, Peter Sheppard, Mary Irwin, J. A. Buckley, and the late L. C. Penna for advice and information generously given; Gail Pryor and Wilma Sharp for typing earlier drafts; the late Edgar Ford for drawing the maps; and, finally, the many people in Cornwall who kindly answered my enquiries and often had me into their homes both great and small during background fieldwork on prospective sites of early monasteries in Cornwall.

THE MAPS

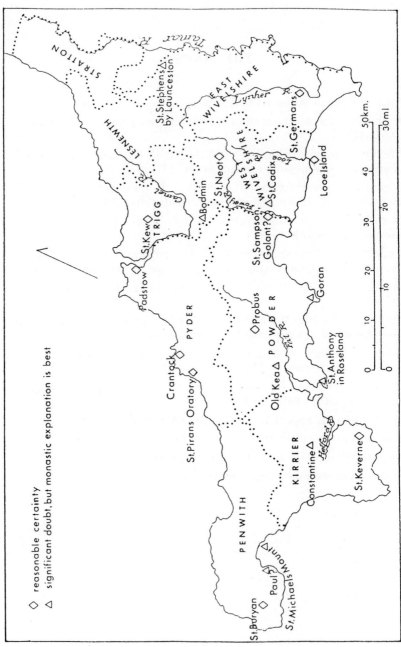

A. *Sites of early monasteries in Cornwall*

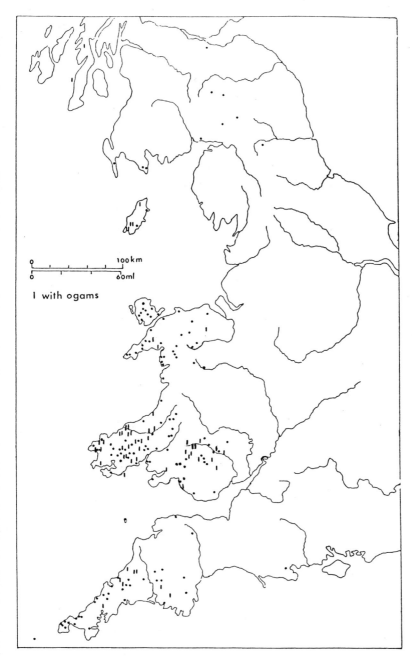

B. Early christian memorial stones (after Ordnance Survey, Britain in the Dark Ages*)*

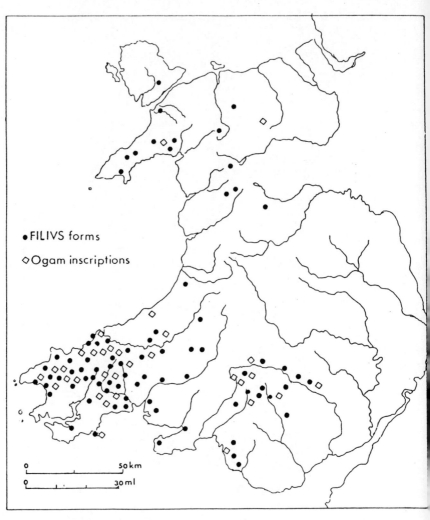

C. *Memorial-stone distribution in Wales, Irish features (after Bu'lock, 'Early christian memorial formulae', p. 137)*

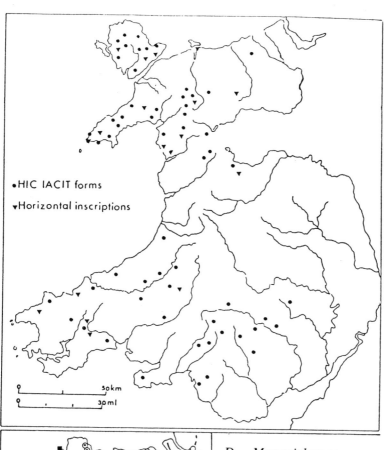

- HIC IACIT forms
- Horizontal inscriptions

50 km
30 ml

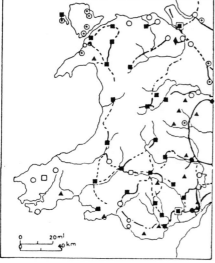

0   20 ml
    40 km

D.   Memorial-stone distribution in Wales, Continental features (after Bu'lock, 'Early christian memorial formulae', p. 138)

E.   Roman activity in Wales (after Nash-Williams, The Early Christian Monuments, fig. 2)

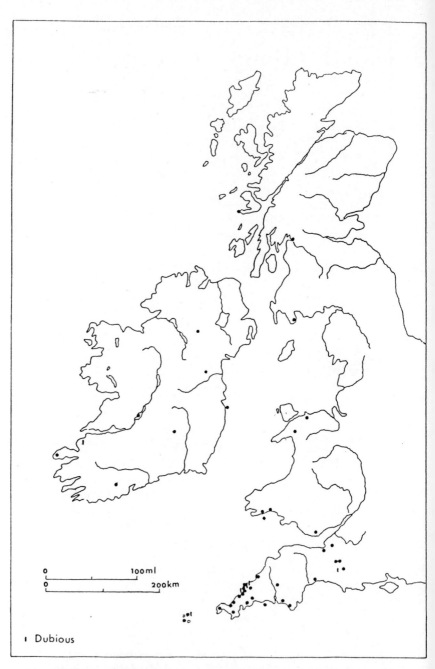

0 ——————— 100ml
0 ——————— 200km

ı Dubious

F. Imported Mediterranean pottery: African and Phocaean Red Slip Wares, Insular Class B i, ii, misc. amphorae, iv two-handled jars

xviii

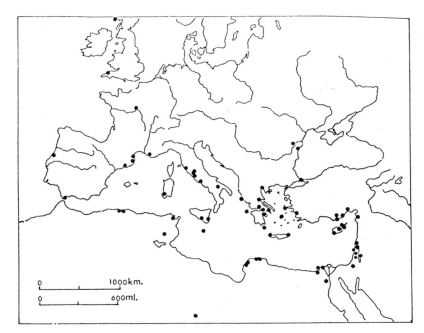

G. African Red Slip Ware: sixth century (after Hayes, Late Roman Pottery, *p. 458)*

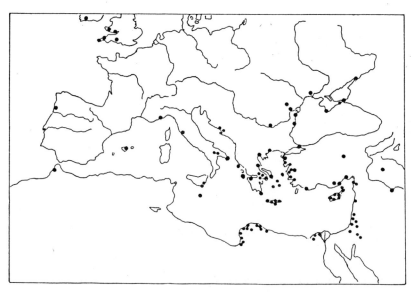

H. Phocaean Red Slip Ware: mid-fifth to mid-sixth century (after Hayes, Late Roman Pottery, *p. 460, as Late Roman C Ware)*

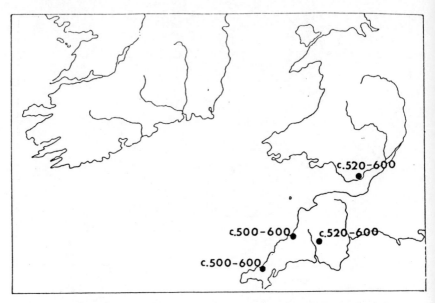

I.   Some dated finds of African Red Slip Ware (after Thomas & Hayes in 1966; obtained from Dr Hayes)

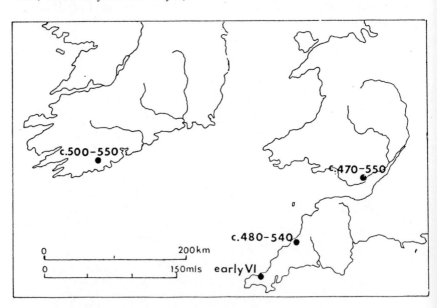

J.   Some dated finds of Phocaean Red Slip Ware (after Thomas & Hayes in 1966; obtained from Dr Hayes)

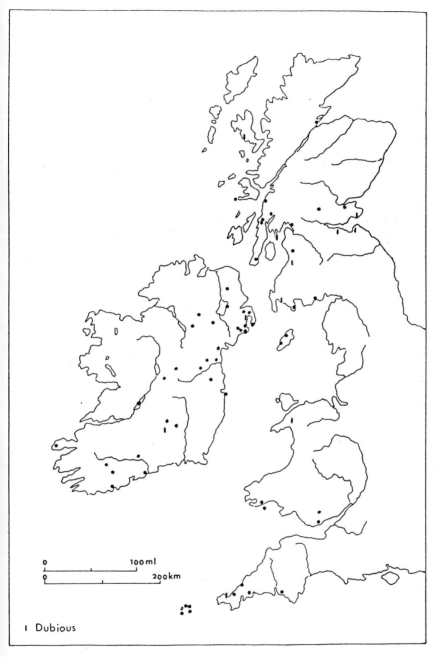

K. Insular Class-E imported pottery, probably from Atlantic France

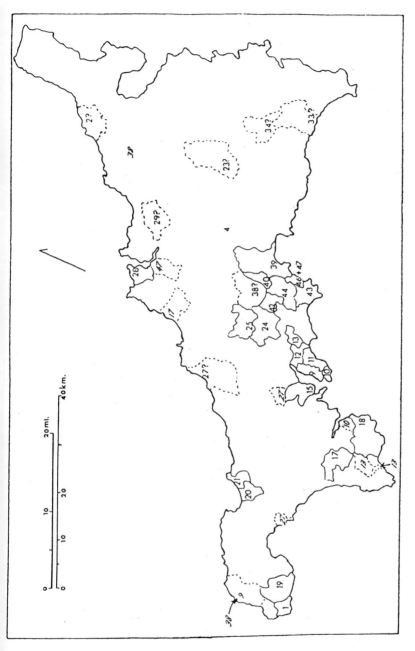

M. *Geographical correlation of saints' names in MS. Vat. Reg. lat. 191*

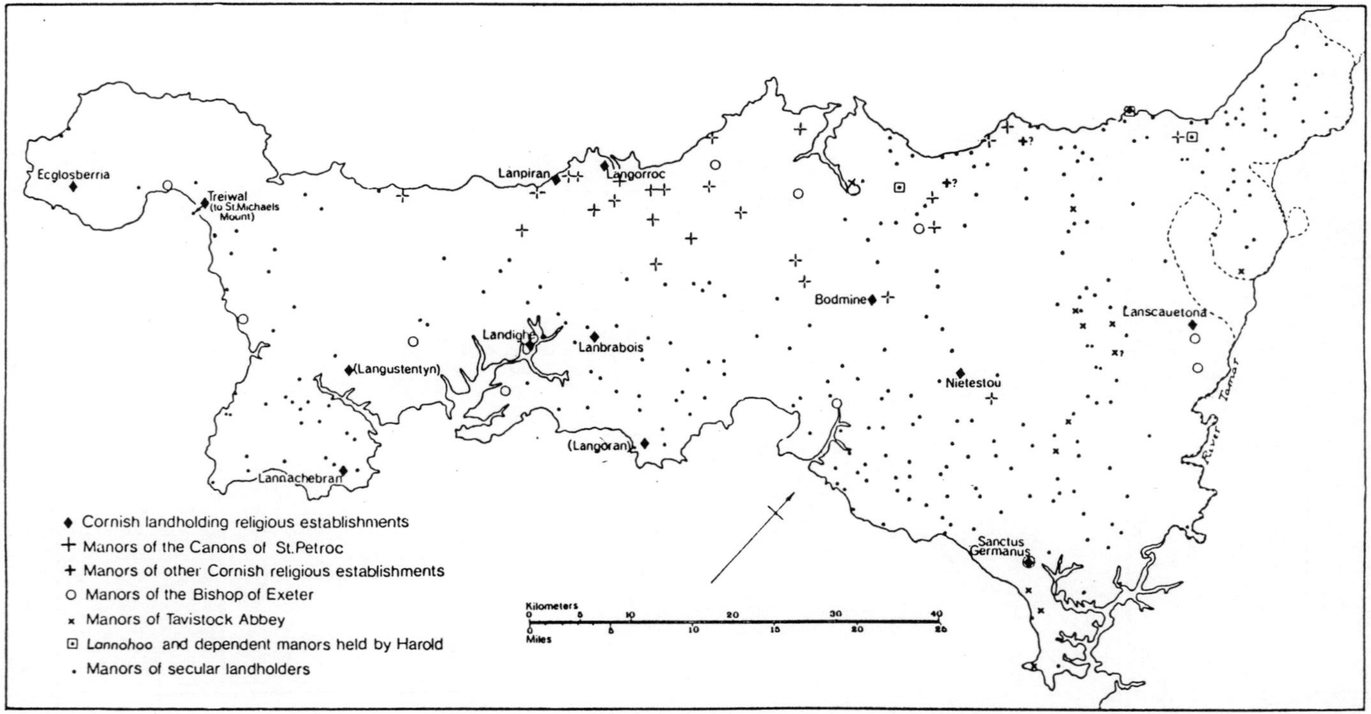
Ecglosberria
Treiwal (to St.Michaels Mount)
Lanpiran
Langorroc
Landighe
Lanbrabois
(Langustentyn)
Lannachebran
(Langoran)
Bodmine
Nietestou
Lanscauetona
Sanctus Germanus
River Tamar
Cornish landholding religious establishments
Manors of the Canons of St.Petroc
Manors of other Cornish religious establishments
Manors of the Bishop of Exeter
Manors of Tavistock Abbey
Lannohoo and dependent manors held by Harold
Manors of secular landholders
Kilometers
0 5 10 20 30 40
Miles
0 5 10 15 20 25

N. Cornwall in the time of Edward the Confessor

I

INTRODUCTION

Christian monasticism had and has its basis in the activity of the individual christian who renounces the things of this world in fact and endeavours to imitate Christ perfectly.[1] At first, such individuals physically isolated themselves from normal society, but often placed themselves under the guidance of masters of what they sought.[2] In the first part of the fourth century, Pachomius, who had begged and received informal counselling from the elderly hermit Palamon, dealt differently with his own disciples: he put them under his authority, gave them a rule, and thereby constituted a community. This is the first known instance of successful cenobitic monasticism; several monasteries under the Pachomian constitution came into existence, and the idea spread.[3] Although the common life was given paramount importance in attaining christian perfection in the eventually very influential teachings of Basil (*ob.* 379),[4] the idea that the solitary life was the highest stage, for which the cenobitic life might be a preparation, was very widespread. It was not until long after monasticism had been introduced to the British Isles that the rule of one master, Benedict of Nursia, came to be adopted by or imposed on the previously heterogeneous cenobitic monasteries of western Europe.[5] Anomalously, its establishment in the Insular Celtic areas began at a remarkably late date.

It is correct, and indeed important, to recognise an early monastic movement. The spread of monasticism from about A.D. 300 was accompanied and accomplished by enthusiasm. Not only propaganda[6] but the actual spread of monasteries bear witness to this monastic movement. Monasteries were not founded gradually, one by one, in the ancient world: whether we look at the inception of cenobitism under Pachomius, who was eventually head of nine monasteries, or at monasticism in Gaul in the era of

[1] Ryan, *Irish Monasticism*, pp. 3–8.
[2] For the role of the abbot and the origins and character of communal monasticism, see de Vogüé, *La Communauté*, especially pp. 533–7.
[3] See Boon & Lefort, *Pachomiana Latina*, pp. 13–74, for Jerome's translation of the rule of Pachomius.
[4] de Vogüé, *La Communauté*, p. 534n: 'Chez Basile . . . la communauté est un terme, sans au-delà érémitique'.
[5] Knowles, *From Pachomius*, pp. 1–9.
[6] Cf. Augustine, *Confessiones*, VIII.14–15, and Sulpicius Seuerus, *Postumianus*.

Martin of Tours, John Cassian, and Honoratus of Arles, we observe an idea catching on rapidly and a resultant burst of activity. By the time when Benedict wrote his rule, about 535–545, the period of vigorous foundation in the British Isles was under way. There is no reason to doubt that this phenomenon was a product of the early monastic movement under discussion – its 'outermost ripple', to use the apt words of Nora Chadwick.[7]

The circumstances in which monasticism was introduced to the British Isles are unknown. Of the Britons in the late Empire who appear as monks in contemporary or near-contemporary sources – Pelagius, Constans, Faustus, Riochatus – none can be shown to have lived in a monastery in the British Isles.[8] The traditional role of Ninian as a pioneer monastic founder in Britain does not stand up to modern criticism.[9] Patrick speaks for himself, but scarcely in monastic terms;[10] nevertheless, he and his converts display an impressive enthusiasm for asceticism. The presence of monasticism in the British Isles in the sixth century is attested by the writings of Gildas and Uinniau[11] and the careers of Columba and Columbanus.[12] These provide strong support for hagiographical and annalistic traditions of a sixth-century burst of monastic activity typical of the movement as a whole,[13] suggesting that it had recently spread to the British Isles. The appearance there of contemporary Mediterranean pottery is noteworthy and, since most of it has been found in southwest Britain, should be kept in mind for future discussion.[14]

Insular monastic expansion, well documented by the seventh century, is more easily traced than are subsequent developments. One of these was 'the tendency, common in every country and century of the early Middle Ages, for the monastic life to lose its regular character, and for houses to

---

[7] *The Age*, p. 60.

[8] See Hanson, *Saint Patrick, His Origins and Career*, pp. 29–71 and (especially 140–70, although his conclusion is different.

[9] Chadwick, 'St Ninian'; MacQueen, *St Nynia*; Wilson, 'St Ninian'.

[10] Mohrmann, *The Latin of St Patrick*, pp. 47–8 and 26–7.

[11] *De Excidio*, II.28 and 34, and Bieler [& Binchy], *The Irish Penitentials*, pp. 74–95; probably also by the 'First Synod of St Patrick' (*ibid.*, pp. 54–9) and four penitentials with British associations (*ibid.*, pp. 60–73). Cf. W. H. Davies, 'The Church', pp. 137–42, and Hughes, *The Church*, pp. 43–56.

[12] See *ibid.*, pp. 67–8 and 57–64.

[13] Summarised by Kenney, *The Sources*, pp. 288–371.

[14] Thomas, *The Early Christian Archaeology*, pp. 22–8, makes this connexion in order to argue for direct eastern Mediterranean influence as the original source of monasticism in the British Isles: this argument is couched in terms requiring considerable modification. The proposal of Mayr-Harting that monasticism spread from the Loire valley via trading contacts to Ireland is plausible, but the archaeological evidence which he has cited in support is now out of date (*The Coming*, pp. 84–6; James, 'Ireland and Western Gaul', pp. 381–2, is still slightly misleading). Late fifth- to sixth-century ceramic wares imported from the Mediterranean miss out the west coast of Gaul; importation of E-ware does seem to have been from this area, but began later. See pp. 41–50 below.

become merely clerical establishments or to fall wholly under lay control'.[15] Yet groups of priests serving major churches represented 'the normal priestly organisation of the early church' and such clerical establishments were themselves open to monastic influence.[16] Categories blurred behind the application of *monasterium* where it need not imply the presence, predominance, or even former existence, of abbot, monks, and rule constituting a monastic community in search of christian perfection apart from society. Monastic reform was possible at any point but is undocumented in pre-Conquest Cornwall.

Monasticism was a dynamic force in early mediaeval christianity and nowhere more so, it would seem, than in the Celtic regions of Atlantic Europe. Our knowledge of monastic development is rather uneven over these regions: as for Cornwall, the usual academic reaction would be to infer that of course it had monasteries, by analogy especially with the (too overwhelming) Irish model, but to allow that we do not know what and where they were. In the circumstances, establishing the location of early Cornish monasteries becomes the main goal, although discovery of particles of information about what these monasteries were like may be anticipated in the course of investigation.

As will be seen, there are certain criteria which render a site liable to early monastic interpretation. These basically rely on evidence which demonstrates or leads one to suspect the presence of a religious community. One piece of evidence not deemed here to give necessary or sufficient indication of monastic status, though commonly so regarded, is a place-name containing the element *lan*. Archaeological investigation has pointed to the existence of a rather open-ended site-category which Charles Thomas has termed the 'enclosed developed cemetery'.[17] A cemetery on sacred ground set off by a surrounding bank and ditch would be said to be 'developed' if associated with a special grave, shrine, chapel, hermitage, or cenobitic monastery. A site might go through progressive stages of development. *Lan* originally meant 'enclosure' but, used as it clearly is in christian religious contexts and in association with recognisable saints' names, it must have acquired a specialised meaning of 'sacred enclosure'. The saint's name combined with *lan* is presumably connected with some stage of development on the site. So a monastery was only one of several sorts of ecclesiastical sites to which a name containing *lan* might refer.[18]

A word about the geographical and chronological boundaries of this study is required. Its focus on Cornwall within southwest Britain is straightforwardly justifiable. The eastern border of Cornwall, formed in very large part by the River Tamar, is a real boundary in so far as survival of evidence of early christian religious foundations is concerned, as comparison of the

---

[15] Knowles, *The Monastic Order*, p. 23.
[16] See the discussion by Blair, 'Secular minster churches'. I am very grateful to Dr Blair for having allowed me to use this study prior to its publication.
[17] *The Early Christian Archaeology*, pp. 48–90.
[18] See Padel, *Cornish Place-name Elements*, pp. 142–5, *s.v.* **lann*.

3

Domesday-entries for Cornwall and Devon and the place-names of the two areas will show. The proportionately far greater amount of groundwork on the subject which had been done in Cornwall and the resources of the Institute of Cornish Studies have significantly facilitated research. The vague term 'early' has been deliberately employed for the monasteries in question. Our concern begins with the advent of the monastic movement in the British Isles, arguably *ca* A.D. 500. The later limit for the survival of such foundations is obscure but in any case falls before the Norman conquest.

In the wider field of scholarship, there is a lack of consensus about what to call the period within which this study falls.[19] The label preferred here is 'early mediaeval', not in the older, restricted British sense which seems to begin with the Norman conquest and continue through the twelfth century, but in the wider sense of approximately the first half of the middle ages, extending from the mid-fifth to mid-eleventh centuries. 'Early christian' is widely favoured, even though its religious connexion may not suit every situation, and the terminal date of such a period is very ill defined. Yet the term certainly seems appropriate for the fifth- to seventh-century inscribed memorial stones of Britain, which continue what is customarily called the early christian epigraphy of the Continent. This particular usage will be employed here, and the term will occasionally be extended to other familiar contexts.

Turning to nomenclature of regions and peoples, perhaps the best procedure would be to refer separately to British, Irish, Breton, Pictish, English, and so forth; but often it is not convenient to do so. 'Insular' will be used to distinguish the British Isles from the Continent (including Brittany), except in the specifically palaeographical usage of 'Insular' to refer to script with certain characteristics, regardless of origin. Furthermore, a legitimate ethnological meaning is accepted for 'Celtic'[20] and the term used accordingly for peoples and regions where such culture was predominant. Considering the general cultural continuity in Cornwall over the Roman period,[21] application of the term 'Celtic' to the region after that period seems acceptable, bearing in mind the increasing Anglo-Saxon influence and settlement there.

A detailed study of the subject of early monasteries in Cornwall has never been made. It received general treatment, based on sound scholarship, in Thomas Taylor's *The Celtic Christianity of Cornwall*;[22] it is upon that work that the present study is founded. In addition, the subject has been treated in studies of specific ecclesiastical sites in Cornwall, but has suffered from lack of a wider perspective and the tools of interpretation which it supplies.

[19] Cf. Laing, *The Archaeology*, p. xxvi, where he makes the wrong choice.
[20] Following the arguments of Powell, *The Celts*, pp. 16–20, based on the acumen of Classical observers (cf. Tierney, 'The Celtic ethnography', pp. 189–275), and on linguistic and archaeological evidence.
[21] Thomas, 'The character'.
[22] Especially pp. 104–21.

Models and concepts for studying early monasteries in Cornwall have
been provided by more general works about christianity among the Celtic
peoples of early mediaeval Europe. John Ryan's *Irish Monasticism* is useful
for bringing together in an organised (but woefully uncritical) presentation
a mass of literary evidence, including some about British monasticism
which he regarded as parent to that of the Irish and little different from it.[23]
The previously orthodox assumption of an entirely monastic Church has
been effectively questioned by Wendy Davis for Wales[24] and by Richard
Sharpe for Ireland.[25] Charles Thomas in *The Early Christian Archaeology
of North Britain* dealt judiciously with written evidence and also drew upon
a considerable body of archaeological material which coalesces into models
of what early ecclesiastical sites, including monasteries, would have been
like.[26] Thus the material remains are seen to be essential in understanding
other types of evidence.

The sources for a study of early monasteries in Cornwall are of two kinds:
written and material. Haddan and Stubbs's *Councils and Documents relating
to the Ecclesiastical History of Great Britain and Ireland* conveniently
assembles material – incomplete, not necessarily in the best edition and
with dated commentary – concerning the church in early mediaeval Cornwall. The *Monasticon Dioecesis Exoniensis* compiled by George Oliver in
the middle of the last century, a sort of expanded local counterpart to
Dugdale's *Monasticon Anglicanum*, furnishes documents, with the same
limitations as in the previous item, pertinent to the mediaeval religious
houses of Cornwall. Most of the material dates from after the Norman
Conquest, but sometimes helps one to work back to the existence of earlier
religious houses on these sites. A few Anglo-Saxon charters are relevant to
this study; a useful survey is offered by H. P. R. Finberg in *The early
Charters of Devon and Cornwall*, while the critical judgments of Pierre
Chaplais in an important article are still of great value.[27] Domesday Book is
a most important source for our purposes, offering a survey of mid-
eleventh-century Cornish religious houses unparalleled in Wales or any
other Celtic region. Work by Oliver Padel on the identification of Cornish
Domesday manors has been very helpful.[28] Finally, there are vast numbers
of mediaeval documents transcribed, if not with flawless accuracy, and

Hughes, *The Church*, gave a more realistic account of how monasteries actually
functioned in the world. Yet a theme running through her book is the development of ecclesiastical institutions in a course specific to Ireland. On the dangers of
generalisation from one Celtic region to another, cf. Davies, 'The Celtic Church',
and Hughes, 'The Celtic Church'.
Wales, pp. 141–68 and 237–42.
'Some problems'. I am indebted to Dr Sharpe for having made this paper
available to me in advance of publication.
Cf. Rahtz, 'Monasteries', on the difficulty of distinguishing monastic from secular
settlements on archaeological grounds alone.
'The authenticity'.
See Thorn *et al.*, *Domesday Book: Cornwall*.

studied by Charles Henderson: manuscripts in his own hand are preserved and indexed in the Royal Institution of Cornwall Library in Truro.

Turning now to hagiographical sources, particular mention may be made of a small group of early Breton *uitae* which have some relevance to Cornwall and to southwest Britain as a whole. In general these are in need of re-editing and further study. The extensive works of G. H. Doble on the saints of Cornwall originally appeared as separate pamphlets, often including articles by Henderson and others;[29] when the most recent editions (by Donald Attwater) of Doble's treatment of many of these saints were conveniently combined in the five volumes entitled *The Saints of Cornwall* this additional material (and much relating to Brittany) was omitted Doble's strengths were familiarity with Cornwall and attention paid to Brittany, his primary weakness the unsophisticated use of dedication evidence to deduce the saints' actual movements.

The archaeological sources are best dealt with in two groups according to technique of recovery. In one are the results of field-survey and general compilations of archaeological data, comprising the following: Ordnance Survey index-cards of antiquities in Cornwall; notes by Charles Henderson on antiquities;[30] J. H. Adams's unpublished compilation of information on mediaeval chapels in Cornwall; Mary Henderson's unpublished compilation of information on mediaeval carved-stone crosses in Cornwall; early christian memorial stones in Cornwall recorded by R. A. S. Macalister *Corpus Inscriptionum Insularum Celticarum*; and imported pottery catalogued and discussed by Charles Thomas and others.[31] Otherwise there are the results of archaeological excavation, which as will be seen[32] have thus far been frustratingly disappointing where early monasteries are concerned for the excavations have been improperly reported or not reported at all

The evidence of place-names will be referred to, time and time again Their usefulness is enhanced by the Cornish habit of locking into the landscape toponyms comprising diagnostic terms for types of sites in combination with a personal name, natural feature or descriptive adjective Here the main sources have been J. E. B. Gover's typescript 'The Place names of Cornwall' and ongoing work by Oliver Padel, Place-name Research Fellow at the Institute of Cornish Studies.[33]

Thus the reader may find it useful to know something of the Cornish language in place-names. These names may be single nouns, but are often phrases of a noun followed by a qualifier (whether adjective or noun) *Landochou* is the *lan* of Dochou. Individual Cornish words nearly always have penultimate stress – however, place-names are a special case, being

[29] A reasonably complete account of these is provided by Catling & Rogers, *G. H. Doble*.
[30] Chiefly in 'The ecclesiastical antiquities'. This and the next item contain abundant information from written sources.
[31] See pp. 41–8 below.
[32] Pp. 34–6 below.
[33] See now his *Cornish Place-name Elements*.

phrases normally of two words: in these phrases the stress always falls on the qualifying adjective or noun. In the case of a noun of one syllable qualified by a two-syllable name, the result is the same as ordinary penultimate stress (like *Landochou*), but it will be different with a place-name like Egloshayle, 'church of the estuary', where the stress falls on *hayle* (pronounced like English 'hail'), 'estuary'. Similarly, Penzance should be stressed on the second syllable, being composed of *pen*, 'headland', and *sans*, 'holy'. There is no need for an excursus on pronunciation, but it may be helpful to know that *c* is always a hard consonant, 'k'. A possibly puzzling feature is that the beginning of the second elements of compound place-names may undergo lenition, that is, their initial letter may change according to fixed rules: so Trevean, 'small farm', is a compound of *tre(f)*, 'farm', and the adjective *byghan*, where the initial *b* has lenited to *v* in the place-name.

In what follows, the early progress of monasticism in southwest Britain will be examined in chapters 2 and 3. Then in chapter 4 attention will be directed towards identifying additional early monasteries, to some extent by working backward from the evidence of later sources.

II

EARLY MONASTICISM AND SOUTHWEST BRITAIN:
THE LITERARY EVIDENCE

At the beginning of the middle ages, according to what is known of other Celtic-speaking areas, the monastic movement should have been expanding in southwest Britain. This chapter will examine written sources for evidence that such was the case. The region in question constituted what is conventionally thought of as the post-Roman kingdom of Dumnonia, roughly corresponding in the early part of our period to modern Cornwall, Devon and western Somerset (but its fullest extent being in fact unknown), and contracting from the second half of the sixth century in the face of West Saxon advance.[1] Its ecclesiastical organisation is obscure, until between 833 and 870 there is brief notice of a bishop among the Cornish in a *monasterium* called *Dinuurrin*.[2]

The earliest reference to monasticism in southwest Britain is probably Gildas, *De Excidio Britanniae*, II.28, relating that Constantine, ruler of Dumnonia, murdered two royal youths 'under the cloak of a holy abbot' in a place of worship.[3] This occurred in the year in which Gildas wrote, in other words sometime in the sixth century;[4] the location is not specified. When Aldhelm, in the late seventh or beginning of the eighth century, warned King Gerent and all *sacerdotes* of Dumnonia that even cenobitic practice and eremitic contemplation are worthless outside the catholic

---

[1] See Thomas, 'The end'; Hoskins, *The Westward Expansion*; Pearce, *The Kingdom*.
[2] Profession of Kenstec to Ceolnoth, archbishop of Canterbury: see pp. 51–6 below.
[3] 'Hoc anno, post horribile iuramenti sacramentum, quo se [Constantinus] deuinxit nequaquam dolos ciuibus, Deo primum iureque iurando, sanctorum demum choris et genetrice comiantibus fretis, facturum, in duarum uenerandis matrum sinibus, ecclesiae carnalisque, sub sancti abbatis amphibalo, latera regiorum tenerrima puerorum uel praecordia crudeliter duum totidemque nutritorum quorum brachia nequaquam armis, quae nullus paene hominum fortius hoc ei tempore tractabat, sed Deo altarique protenta in die iudicii ad tuae ciuitati portas, Christe, ueneranda patientiae ac fidei suae uexilla suspendent – inter ipsa ut dixi, sacrosancta altaria nefando ense hastaque pro dentibus lacerauit, ita ut sacrificii caelestis sedem purpurea ac si coagulati cruoris pallia attingerent.' I am indebted to Neil Wright for pointing out to me that it is the youths rather than Constantine who were *sub amphibalo*.
[4] Sims-Williams, 'Gildas and the Anglo-Saxons', pp. 3–5.

Church, one would expect that he was referring to monasticism within Gerent's realm.[5]

The *Vita (Prima) Sancti Samsonis*[6] provides information about two monasteries in Cornwall: that called *Docco* and one established by Samson of which we are not told the name. Regarding the latter, we have the first-hand testimony of the author of the *uita*. Although the date of this seventh-, eighth- or ninth-century saint's life is much debated,[7] investigation can begin on firm ground with the author's whereabouts. He writes in the monastery of Dol in Brittany,[8] but he has travelled outside Brittany in Wales and Cornwall. He adds to a mention of Samson's master Illtud the remark, 'in whose magnificent monastery I have been';[9] with reference to the wilderness-retreat of three of Samson's associates near the River Severn, he tells us that 'the place in which the above-mentioned three brothers were has always up to the time when I was in Britain been venerated by a great adoration';[10] and, strikingly, he says, when describing an incident in Cornwall, 'on which hill I indeed have been, and I have reverenced and touched with my hand the sign of the cross which St Samson carved by his hand with a certain iron tool on a standing stone'.[11] Such declarations of personal experience seem very unlikely to be mere hagiographical fabrications; moreover, the *Vita (Prima) Sancti Samsonis* is geographically informed about Britain in a way in which the other early Breton *uitae*, which make no such claim for their authors, are not.

[5] *Epistolae*, § 4 (ed. Ehwald, *Aldhelmi Opera*, p. 481): 'Quid enim prosunt bonorum operum emolumenta, si extra catholicam gerantur ecclesiam, etiamsi aliquis actualem rigidae conuersationis regulam sub disciplina coenubii solerter exerceat aut certe cunctorum mortalium contubernia declinans in squalida solitudine remotus contemplatiuam anachoreseos peragat uitam?' The sentence is placed prominently towards the beginning of the letter; Aldhelm specifies when he is writing about Dyfed across the Severn in a later passage. Cf. Lapidge & Herren, *Aldhelm: The Prose Works*, pp. 140–3, although Ms C. Coutts kindly informs me that Herren's narrower dating of the letter does not take into account all possible Anglo-Saxon synods.

[6] Ed. Fawtier, *La Vie*; see also the review by H. Delehaye, *Analecta Bollandiana* 32 (1913), 362–4. A critical edition of this work is very badly needed.

[7] See de la Borderie, *Histoire*, I.560–1; Fawtier, *La Vie* and 'Saint Samson'; Duine, *Saints de Domnonée*, pp. 5–12, 'La Vie de Saint Samson', *Origines bretonnes*, and 'S. Samson'; Loth, 'La Vie la plus ancienne'; Burkitt, 'St. Samson'; Guillotel, 'Les origines'; Poulin, 'Hagiographie et politique' and 'À propos du diocèse de Dol'; Hughes, 'The Celtic Church', pp. 4–5, with whose findings I concur.

[8] *Citra mare* for the author is the Continent (see, for example, *Vita Sancti Samsonis*, I.52). For his location at Dol see *ibid.*, II.10, together with II.15.

[9] I.7: 'in cuius magnifico monasterio ego fui'.

[10] I.41 (see n. 13 below).

[11] I.48: 'intendensque in his qui idolum colebant, uidit ante eos in cuiusdam uertice montis, simulacrum abominabile adsistere; in quo monte et ego fui, signumque crucis quod sanctus Samson sua manu cum quodam ferro in lapide stante sculpsit adoraui et mea manu palpaui'.

In the author's account of his sources, he says that he has written according to information received from an old man living in a monastery across the sea which the saint had founded.[12]

In the first place, however, I want you to believe me that these words have been assembled not according to disordered and disarranged hearsay, but according to this from a certain religious and venerable old man, in whose house beyond the sea which Samson himself alone had founded, he leading a catholic and religious life for almost eighty years, and very nearly in the times of the same above-mentioned St Samson, affirmed to me veraciously that his (Samson's) mother had recounted [information] to his (the old man's) uncle, a most holy deacon, which same deacon was a cousin to St Samson, and compassionately relating to me many things concerning his wonderful deeds; and not only this, but also the above-mentioned holy deacon, Henoc by name, conveyed beyond the sea elegantly by harmonious compositions very many and delightful words concerning his (Samson's) more marvellous acts which he performed most wonderfully on this side of the sea in Brittany and in Roman parts, and that venerable old man about whom we have formerly spoken dwelling always in that monastery before my time [or 'before me'] read [them] piously and diligently.

The only monastery which Samson is said in the *uita* to have founded in Britain is the one in Cornwall.[13] We can have some confidence in the

---

[12] 'Primo autem omnium credi a me uos uolo quod non iuxta adinuentionis meae temeritatem, nec iuxta inordinata et incomposita audita haec uerba collecta sunt, sed iuxta hoc a quodam religioso ac uenerabili sene, in cuius domo, ultra mare, quam ipse solus Samson fundauerat, ille, per octogenarios fere annos, catholicam religiosamque uitam ducens, propissimeque temporibus eiusdem supradicti sancti Samsonis, mater eius tradidisse auunculo suo sanctissimo diacono, qui et ipse diaconus consobrinus esset sancto Samsoni, mihi ueraciter affirmabat, multaque de eius admirabilibus gestis ad me misericorditer referens; et non solum hoc, sed etiam quamplura ac delicata de eius prodigioribus actibus, quae citra mare in Britannia ac Romana mirabiliose fecit, uerba, supradictus sanctus diaconus, Henocus nomine, congruis stilis polite ultra mare adportauit, et ille, de quo nuper praefata sumus, uenerabilis senex semper ante me in istud monasterium commanens pie legere ac diligenter faciebat.' *Quam* is lacking in the text of Fawtier's edition: cf. Loth, 'La Vie la plus ancienne', pp. 303–4.

[13] After disposing of a cave-dwelling serpent on the site, Samson 'pro uirtutis ostensae honore, iussit suis ut monasterium prope antrum fundarent' (I.50; the context is explained below, pp. 11–12 and 17) and put his father at the head of the completed monastery before leaving for the Continent: 'ac monasterii illum perfecte constructum suo patri praesulatui praecipiente [*sic*]' (I.52). In Wales Samson and three companion-monks left the island-monastery of Piro for wilderness-retreats, which his companions made in an old fortified site near the River Severn and which he made in a cave (I.40, and cf. I.42). These ascetic arrangements do not seem to have had any permanence, for Samson is called from the wilderness to be made abbot of an important monastery (I.42) and his three companions are eventually shown accompanying the saint on his southern pilgrimage (I.45). As for the author's day, 'locusque in quo tres fratres supradicti fuerant usque ad tempus quando ego fui in Britannia magno semper uenerabatur

integrity and internal consistency of the *uita*. The author appears to have his narrative fairly well in hand: it is not confused and does not suffer from gaps. He seems conscientious in his task and attentive to it, and was thus unlikely to omit from the saint's deeds the founding of a monastery (clearly regarded by him as a signifiant undertaking) to which he has referred in the prologue. Although he several times says he is limiting his account of Samson, in so doing he gives some idea of what he is leaving out. There is not the slightest indication in the text that Samson founded more monasteries in Britain than the author has specifically mentioned.[14]

We learn several things about this monastery in Cornwall at the time when the author was there and spoke with the old man. It had been in existence for at least eighty years. Its founder was there held to have been a man named Samson who subsequently went to Brittany. The monastery possessed at least one written work, an account of the deeds of the founder by 'Henoc'. There was contact between the monastery and various regions: before and/or after his stay there the author was in other parts of Cornwall, Wales, and Brittany. We also note that Henoc is said to have earlier brought written information about Samson's deeds on the Continent from Brittany to the Cornish monastery, as well as the still earlier movement of Samson himself from his new foundation to Brittany. We see that, more than eighty years after the death of its founder, his kinsman, the old man, was a member of this monastery, over which Samson had placed his own father before departing for Brittany. The old man's uncle, Henoc, the cousin or relation of Samson, may also have been a monk there after he came back across the sea from the Continent.[15] Such relationships are especially interesting in view of the role played by the founder's kin in the abbacy of Celtic monasteries,[16] to which the author in fact refers in book I, chapter 16 of the *uita*.

In the narrative of Samson's life the monastery is said to have been established by order of the saint in honour of a manifestation of God's power which had enabled him to rid the countryside of a destructive serpent or dragon. Samson had been led to where the serpent's cave could be seen across a river, and had crossed to the cave and disposed of the reptile, throwing it down from 'a certain great height'.[17] While his followers set up the monastery, the saint lived as a hermit in the serpent's cave where his

cultu, oratoriumque, inibi est componentes ubi sanctus Samson per cunctos dominicarum dies ad missam cantandam et ad Christi communionem ueniebat' (I.41). At no time is the word *monasterium* used in connexion with this site. Cf. Davies, *Wales*, pp. 147–8 and 151–2.

[14] As there is for Brittany (I.52). Only between his consecration as bishop and departure from Wales is Samson's career rather unaccounted for (I.44–5). A story from Samson's episcopacy in Wales is included in the homily (II.7–9).

[15] Perhaps only the writings of Henoc reached the monastery. On these, cf. a later passage in the prologue, I.38, II.8, and I.1.

[16] See Hughes, *The Church*, pp. 76–7, 160–6.

[17] I.50: 'de quadam grandi altitudine'.

prayers produced a miraculous spring, an inevitable miracle in Celtic hagiography. The cave is described in some detail, and may represent a real place, possibly a minor religious *locus* near the monastery in Cornwall. As the author had spent time in this monastery, one might think that he has reproduced its house-traditions here, giving an example of an early monastic foundation-legend from Cornwall which would be of interest in itself. A suspicious feature, however, is provided by the parallel circumstances of Samson's foundation of the monastery of Pental in northern France. This time it is King Childebert asking Samson to rid the country of the serpent, which the saint then banished to the other side of the River Seine, 'commanding that it remain under a certain stone'.[18] While two monasteries claiming Samson as their founder could have had similar foundation-stories when the author wrote, he may have applied a Pental legend to Cornwall or adapted the story from some source unrelated to either monastery, simply because it was a good tale. Samson is said to have placed his father, Amon, in charge of the Cornish monastery, but no more information is provided about that house in the *uita*, which immediately proceeds with Samson's departure for the Continent.[19]

It remains to try to identify the site of this monastery in Cornwall. The impression given by the *uita* – that Samson took ship directly after making the foundation – suggests that the monastery was on or near the south coast. A few other geographical details in the *uita* may assist in determining its location, as will be seen. The lack of a name is a handicap, although the author in any case only designates religious foundations in Britain by the name of the founding(?) saint, which we can in any case supply in this instance. Samson would have continued to be venerated on the site where he had founded, or was held to have founded, a monastery; and he might well appear later, like Docco, as the patron-saint of a mediaeval church or chapel there.

There are three mediaeval dedications to Samson in Cornwall: typically, none is attested before the eleventh century. The chapel of St Samson at the mouth of the Camel estuary on the north coast of Cornwall lay along the route by which Samson entered Cornwall, according to the *uita*, but the site receives no mention therein.[20] The parish church of South Hill and the chapel, now parish church, of St Sampson, Golant, are located in southern Cornwall. In later times at least, South Hill had a church of some importance, with an extensive parish and glebe. Most significant is the presence of a sixth- or seventh-century monogram chi-rho carved on a stone pillar,

---

[18] I.58: 'ultra quoddam flumen, quod uocatur Sigona, ire eum iussit, mandans ut sub quodam lapide maneret'. This story is known in the mid-ninth-century *uita* of St Germer, who had been a monk at Pental (cf. Fawtier, 'Saint Samson', p. 154).

[19] I.52.

[20] Earliest reference in the first (eleventh-century) *Vita Sancti Petroci*, § 5 (ed. Grosjean, 'Vies et miracles', p. 490). Cf. Doble, *The Saints of Cornwall*, V.96–7.

'discovered on a rockery in the rectory garden' near the church in 1891.[21] This indicates christian activity in the time of the author or of Samson.

Yet this place, considered in the context of Samson's travels from the Camel estuary across the Cornish peninsula to the southern coast, does not correspond well to the topography of Cornwall and in particular of the monastic site, with which the author was familiar. South Hill, far to the east in Cornwall, would be on only a circuitous route to the Southern Sea, perhaps around Bodmin Moor and down the River Lynher. Such a journey would entail extensive travel through the *pagus Tricurius*, a region in northern Cornwall where, it is implied in the *uita*, one of Samson's miracles took place. Contrary to another impression from the *uita*, however, South Hill is hardly near the sea, 11½ miles away at the closest point, and farther by the nearby navigable river. There was a holy well at South Hill, located, until the surroundings were drastically altered, in what G. H. Doble described as 'not a fearsome cavern . . . a pretty grotto full of lovely ferns'.[22] The small River Lynher flows more than a mile to the west of the height on which the church of South Hill stands. In present conditions it is difficult to be certain, but the holy well there is very unlikely to have been visible from the other side of the river.

The earliest reference to a religious establishment at St Sampson, Golant, is the *mostier Saint Sanson* at *Lancien* in the *Roman de Tristan* written by Beroul in the second half of the twelfth century.[23] His utilisation of Cornish topography has been confirmed by Oliver Padel who sensibly suggests a parallel exaggeration in the author's description of the local manor of Lantyan as a city with four thousand inhabitants and the manorial church as a minster with 'evesque, clerc, moine, et abé' in attendance.[24] From the first official record *ca* 1280 until the early sixteenth century, St Sampson, Golant, was only a chapel of Tywardreath parish-church and without right of burial. On the other hand, a religious foundation of importance there might have been overshadowed later on by its neighbour at Tywardreath, site of a Norman priory and perhaps a significant pre-Conquest secular estate.[25]

The site at St Sampson, Golant, certainly suits the topography of the *uita*. It overlooks the Fowey estuary: Samson would thus have followed the prehistoric transpeninsular route between the Camel and Fowey.[26] Further-

---

[21] Macalister, *Corpus*, I, no. 486, quotation from p. 464. Cf. Hencken, *The Archaeology*, p. 242, and Thomas, *The Early Christian Archaeology*, p. 108. On South Hill see Charles Henderson *apud* Doble, *Saint Samson in Cornwall*, p. 32.

[22] *The Saints of Cornwall*, V.95, in contrast with the 'horribile antrum' of *Vita Sancti Samsonis*, I.50.

[23] Lines 2972–96 (ed. Ewert, *The Romance*, p. 89). *Mostier* or *moutier* has a range of meanings like 'minster'; in line 1509 it is synonymous with *chapele*.

[24] 'The Cornish background', p. 60, and 'Beroul's geography', p. 87.

[25] Charles Henderson *apud* Doble, *Saint Samson in Cornwall*, pp. 27–8. *Ty*, 'house', in Cornish place-names appears to have designated substantial settlements.

[26] Bowen, *Saints, Seaways*, pp. 3, 5 (map), 7, 21, and the references cited there.

more, the area by the Fowey corresponds to the narrative in details, having a cave down by the river, one-half mile from the church, with water dripping from its roof like the spring in Samson's miracle.[27] The only known holy well is up by the church, not in the cave.

All things considered, the church of St Sampson, Golant, has a better claim to mark the site of the monastery which Samson founded in Cornwall than does the church at South Hill.

The other Cornish monastery is referred to in the *Vita (Prima) Sancti Samsonis* at the point where Samson, abbot and bishop, had left Wales with a group of monastic companions, including kinsfolk, and sailed across the Severn Sea to Cornwall. Samson and his party arrived at the 'monastery which is called Docco'.[28] This establishment or its successor comes to light in a tenth-century Anglo-Saxon charter recording a grant of land 'in the monastery [or 'minster'] which is called by the inhabitants Landochou', this being its full Cornish name which survives today as Lanow in St Kew parish.[29] Its site is near the north coast of Cornwall by a small river flowing south into the Camel estuary. This estuary is the middle of three major havens and avenues to the interior along the formidable north coast of the southwest peninsula of Britain. The small river was, until fairly recently, navigable to about 1¾ miles below the monastic site.[30] The witness of the *Vita Sancti Samsonis* to the existence of this monastery, combined with the tenth-century charter-reference mentioned above, is crucial for understanding Cornish monastic history, as will become clear in chapter IV.

The *Docco* episode is intriguingly original in Celtic hagiography.[31] Samson never got inside the place. The brethren there heard of his arrival and, at his request, sent one of their number to speak with him. This was Iuniauus: the *Vita (Prima) Sancti Samsonis* provides the earliest named Cornish

[27] I inspected the cave in the company of Oliver Padel and a Cornish miner, Mr John Allen Buckley, to whom I am indebted for their time and observations. Our survey in most respects corroborates Doble, *The Saints of Cornwall*, V.95, n. 30. For about the first thirty feet of the passage its walls are uneven, but after a last irregularity it assumes characteristic adit-shape and is driven straight in for about another hundred feet, marks of manual drilling being evident from this point on. Veins of quartzite, analysed as containing traces of iron and copper, are occasionally seen. The feature is located opposite, and is probably geologically related to, Penpoll Creek. It would seem that action of water through a fault in the rock had washed out material to form a small cave. Although this is not a mining area, the promising quartzite would have been spotted as an outcrop on the surface above or within the cave which was then deepened by miners. Caves beside rivers are rare in Cornwall, and it is hard to doubt that this was the place which the author of the *uita* had in mind.

[28] I.45: 'monasterium quod Docco uocatur'. The form of this name represents a pronunciation archaic after the sixth century (Loth, 'La Vie la plus ancienne', pp. 294–5; Jackson, *Language and History*, p. 569).

[29] 'in monasterio quod ab incolis Landochou uocitatur' (see pp. 81–2 below).

[30] Doble, *The Saints of Cornwall*, IV.105; Loth, 'La Vie la plus ancienne', p. 330.

[31] I.46–7.

monk, as well as monastery, of which we have notice. Samson asked to 'rest with them for a little period',[32] but Iuniauus replied that it would not be meet for him to stay with them, lest discord arise between the brethren and Samson, their better. 'For,' he said, 'I want you to know that we are now become lax in our former practices.'[33] Samson was impressed, sent away his ship, and set off overland for the Southern Sea.

We are told little about the nature of this religious establishment other than that it is a *monasterium* occupied by *fratres*, Iuniauus being described as the 'wisest' without being designated by the title of abbot or by any other monastic office or ecclesiastical order.[34] Nevertheless, it seems clear that the author is portraying a cenobitic monastery. Discipline has slipped, but at least there is recognition of the proper standard represented by Samson and his monks. A word about that standard would perhaps be worthwhile. In the *uita*, Samson is trained in a Welsh cenobitic monastery, apparently of large size. He later displays a taste for eremitism, but is recalled from the wilderness and made abbot of what sounds like another large-scale communal establishment. His personal regimen is rigorous, albeit without extreme asceticism about drink.[35] His monks appear to follow less strict practices,[36] but he is able to maintain the community above a level where thoroughgoing reform is required as at *Docco*. A final point about the monastery of *Docco* is that it would not have been of very recent foundation, as there had to be some time for discipline to have relaxed; however, this could have happened within a few years after the death of an abbot whose fervour had founded the monastery and whose authority and example had guided its monks.[37]

The source of this episode is far from clear. The author does not say that he has been to the monastery of *Docco*, as he does of several other sites in the *uita*. (An origin in the traditions of that house – in view of the tenor of the story – seems in any case rather unlikely!) Perhaps the episode was in the work by Henoc, or alternatively was part of the oral tradition of Samson at the monastery which he founded in Cornwall. Another possibility, less

---

[32] I.46: 'aliquantulum spatii cum illis requiesceret'.

[33] I.46: 'Hoc enim scire uolo quod iam in nostris prioribus institutis laxamur'.

[34] He is *sapientissimus* and *sanctus*.

[35] I.15, also I.10, 14, 21, 36 and II.12. Cf. Ryan, *Irish Monasticism*, p. 163, and the ninth-century Breton *Vita Sancti Winwaloei*, II.12 (ed. de Smedt, p. 226).

[36] Especially I.36.

[37] Cf. Annals of Ulster 473.2 (edd. & transl. MacAirt & MacNiocaill, I.50): 'Quies Docci episcopi sancti Britonum abbatis' (see Binchy, 'Patrick and his biographers', pp. 70–5, on the unreliability of such an early date) and *Catalogus Sanctorum Hiberniae* (ed. Grosjean, 'Édition et commentaire', p. 209): 'A David et Gilla et a Doco Britonibus missam acceperunt', with comments *ibid.*, pp. 293–5; Kenney, *The Sources*, p. 479; Hughes, *The Church*, p. 72; and Morris, 'The Dates', p. 373. A saint of the name has Welsh associations: Llandough (Llandocha Fawr) and Llandocha Fach occur in Glamorganshire, south Wales. Doble suggested that Samson might have chosen to come to a monastery founded from his native south Wales (*The Saints of Cornwall*, V.90).

happy with regard to the accuracy of information about early monasteries in Cornwall in the *uita*, is that the author might be filling in space between specific reports, bringing Samson from Wales into Cornwall by a commonly travelled route,[38] past a monastery known to him at least by name, and on to sites with which Samson was traditionally associated in Cornwall and Brittany. One might expect, however, that such a 'filler' would be made up of pious and vague hagiographical commonplaces, which the *Docco* episode is not.

The journey of Samson and his followers across Cornwall provides a picture of a Welsh pilgrim-monk in action, and of ecclesiastical conditions there as well. Given the relatively early date of the *Vita (Prima) Sancti Samsonis*, the possibility that it might be based on even earlier work by Henoc, and the personal experience and contacts in Cornwall of the author of the *uita*, this portion of it warrants consideration here. Samson and his party, then, set off across the country. Interestingly, 'his spiritual utensils and books' conveyed in a cart on this journey[39] represent influence in ecclesiastical, intellectual, and material – in other words, monastic – culture from Wales into Cornwall, although the *uita* does not indicate that any of these items were left in Cornwall.

We soon see Samson exercising pastoral care in Cornwall. 'On a certain day, when he was walking through a certain district which they call Tricurius',[40] Samson came upon some people and their leader Guedian, apostates, performing pagan rites. He approached the people, bade them to stop, and convinced them with a miracle. They destroyed the idol, and 'then the prudent count made all come to have their baptisms confirmed by St Samson';[41] the good bishop obliged. It is at this point that the author tells us that he has been on the hill where the idol had stood, and has reverenced and touched with his hand a cross which Samson had carved on a standing stone.

A tentative suggestion may be made which would imply that the author was also familiar with the site at South Hill: the cross on the standing stone which he says he saw and touched could have been the chi-rho there.[42] From early christian southwest Britain the only carvings on standing stones which could be described as crosses known are chi-rhos, and they are no more than four in number, rare enough to make this suggestion not totally far-fetched.[43] The South Hill chi-rho stone, assuming that it has not been moved far from its original site, would have stood on a hill like the

[38] See n. 110 below.
[39] I.47: 'spiritualia utensilia sua atque uolumina'.
[40] I.48: 'Quadam autem die, cum per quendam pagum quem Tricurium uocant deambularet'. The place-name survives in Trigg Hundred.
[41] I.50: 'Tunc comes prudens omnes ad confirmanda eorum baptismata a sancto Samsone uenire fecit'.
[42] So Fawtier, *La Vie*, p. 61.
[43] See pp. 37–8 below. The free-standing stone-crosses of Cornwall are ninth-century or later, the vast majority later (Hencken, *The Archaeology*, pp. 266–8; Thomas, *Christian Antiquities*, p. 98).

monument which the author of the *uita* described, but, to judge from later territorial divisions in Cornwall, South Hill was not in the *pagus Tricurius*, where the author implies that the cross was located.[44] Perhaps he had been impressed by the chi-rho, and fitted it into his narrative at what seemed an appropriate point. In general, the author appears to have had real information about Cornwall at his disposal, but we must not expect too much of the way in which he uses it.

Following the conversion-episode in the *uita*, the count and people asked their spiritual mentor for assistance in the earthly problem of the serpent ravaging their land. Samson helped them as has been described. When the count and people learned of his success, they wished to make Samson their bishop.[45] Samson refused, for reasons not given, and it is at this point that he ordered his followers to establish the monastery near the cave.

A few points emerge from these episodes. Samson's action in reclaiming the apostates is typical of Celtic pilgrim-monks.[46] The *uita* offers not the slightest indication that Samson left Wales to missionise; however, Samson, like Columbanus, would do his christian duty by people whom he came across. The Cornish apostates were discovered in the interior of the peninsula by Samson on his way between one monastery certainly near the north coast and another which, as we have seen, may have been near the south coast. Possibly, in view of the tendency for early religious centres in Britain and Brittany to be coastal, less pastoral care was provided to inland folk. Like the monastery where discipline had relaxed, these apostates represent a decline from some period(s) of more vigorous christian activity before Samson arrived on the scene. The request made by lay people to Samson to be their bishop is interesting. As Samson is ever associated with monasticism in the *uita*, we have reason to project a picture of him as bishop of these people, settled in a monastery or eremitical retreat within their territory. Samson did not accept their invitation, and pursued his pilgrimage. Provision of pastoral care is not the reason given for foundation of the monastery which he left behind him in Cornwall.

Again there is the question of the author's source of information. These episodes may fairly accurately represent actual conditions in Cornwall in Samson's time, but we do not know that they do. The conversion-scene is of a standard type in early European hagiography.[47] We may ask whether a

---

[44] See Thomas, 'Settlement-history', pp. 70 and 75.

[45] I.50.

[46] See Ryan, *Irish Monasticism*, pp. 214–15, 261–3 (and especially p. 262[-3], n. 4).

[47] Resemblances have been detected between this episode in *Vita Sancti Samsonis* on the one hand and, on the other, Venantius Fortunatus's *Vita Sancti Paterni*, § 5 (Fawtier, 'Saint Samson', p. 165) and Sulpicius Seuerus' *Dialogi*, II.4, and *Vita Sancti Martini*, § 3 (Duine, *Origines bretonnes*, p. 30). According to Fawtier, *Vita Sancti Paterni* is the source of the episode, whereas Duine commented (*ibid.*): 'Le procédé littéraire du Breton est ici très sensible: il trouve une scène originale, il essaie alors de la développer en rivalisant avec un écrivain en vogue, à qui il ne se fait pas faute de dérober quelques couleurs'. Cf. Poulin, 'Hagiographie et politique', pp. 6–8 and 20–6.

17

Cornish bishopric could have originated in such a way, or whether the author is drawing here upon his Breton experience.[48]

The portion of the *Vita (Prima) Sancti Samsonis* dealing with Cornwall inspires some confidence in its portrayal of conditions in that area. The account contains certain details, including names. *(Lan) Docco* is a real place, and Samson's subsequent journey through the *pagus Tricurius* conforms to Cornish topography. The Iuniauus-*Docco* episode, as mentioned above, is not standard hagiographical fare, although it fulfils a familiar hagiographical function of explaining why the saint did not stay at a particular place where his travels had taken him. For the remainder of this discussion of the *Vita Sancti Samsonis*, concern will be with the place of Samson and Cornwall in the wider monastic and ecclesiastical setting of early mediaeval Celtic lands.

The subject of Samson himself and his connexions with monasteries in Cornwall has been approached with caution in this study of his *uita*. The author lived in a Breton monastery which traced its foundation to Samson and possessed his body[49] but apparently not very much information about him. The author found traditions of Samson in Wales and Cornwall. It is possible in these circumstances for an incorrect identification of individuals of the same name to have been made. All of the sources cited by the author were obtained in Britain; however, the written work of Henoc, which (the author of the *uita* specifically says) had brought back to Britain information about Samson's deeds on the Continent, links the Insular to the Continental figure. The author's statements about this source are sufficiently credible for us to accept that Samson was a Welshman who travelled to Brittany via Cornwall and had some effect on monasticism there. The point has important ramifications. Many saints with dedications in Cornwall bear the names of patrons of Welsh and Breton churches. There are various ways of accounting for this: activities of the saints concerned, spread of their cults, mis-identification of different homonymic saints. According to the *Vita (Prima) Sancti Samsonis*, Samson actually travelled between these regions.[50]

The author is himself evidence of communication between these areas. In view of his relatively wide geographical experience, including a stay in a

---

[48] Encounters between saints and secular rulers occur widely in early Breton *uitae* (although contemporary Welsh and Cornish *uitae* for comparison are largely lacking – but see St 'Germanus' in the *Historia Brittonum*: Dumville, 'Sub-Roman Britain', pp. 185–7, and 'The historical value', p. 22), and we have also the historical examples of the mid-ninth-century Breton rulers Nominoi and Salomon intervening in ecclesiastical matters (see Smith, 'The "archbishopric" of Dol').

[49] I.61.

[50] The *uita* also shows him going to Ireland in an account which is specific regarding one place-name and one episode only (I.37–9). If it has a factual basis, for which the evidence is not compelling, then reality would underly in at least one case the number of 'pan-Celtic' saints associated with Wales, Cornwall, Brittany, and Ireland.

18

Cornish monastery, and his early date (not later than the mid-ninth century), it is worth looking at what he records of Samson's career overall in our search for a general picture in which to place the more limited Cornish material. For example, the author mentions only monasteries in Samson's tour across Cornwall and, surveying the *uita* as a whole, we can see that he usually speaks of organised christianity in terms of monasticism. Mention is occasionally made of churches for which no monastic associations are specified,[51] but never of non-monastic priests.

For the author, bishops are very important figures in the Church, presumably in no small part because of the interests of his see of Dol. Samson's episcopal status receives repeated stress in the account of his career.[52] A key role in that career in Wales was played by Bishop Dyfrig (Dubricius) as well as Abbot Illtud. The only personnel at Dol mentioned by name are bishops: Samson of course, Tigernomalus who asked the author to write the *uita*,[53] and Loucherus who together with the monks at Dol had a fire extinguished through the saint's intercession.[54] The bishops in the *uita* perform the expected functions of ordaining clergy, confirming baptisms, and consecrating churches. Episcopal supervision of monasteries is indicated when the author says that Samson, abbot of the monastery of Piro, went to Ireland 'episcopo permittente',[55] and when Bishop Dyfrig brought about Samson's election as abbot[56] and even his appointment as cellarer of that monastery.[57] Episcopal responsibility for the laity is envisaged in the request of 'Count' Guedian for Samson to be the bishop of his people. The testimony of the *uita* concerning the territorial aspects of the episcopacy and its relationship to monasticism is interesting. There is some evidence, including that of the *Vita (Prima) Sancti Samsonis*, to suggest that Dyfrig was a territorial bishop on the Roman pattern;[58] however, his see and diocese are never specified in the *uita*. His sphere of operations included the monasteries of Illtud and Piro in south Wales, and also the otherwise unidentified monastery founded by Germanus of which Samson became abbot. Dyfrig was accustomed to spend most of Lent in retreat at the island monastery of Piro;[59] this might suggest that he was not

---

[51] A prediction is made that Samson will be a founder of churches (I.9). Members of Samson's family build churches as well as found monasteries (I.31: 'monasteria quae nobis suggeres fundanda et ecclesias construendas non solum desidero, ueram etiam et amanter amplector, sed quoniam promissione de te destinatae tempus venturum est, nostras ecclesias a te consecrandas, Deo adiutore, speramus') and later Samson consecrates them (I.45). Reference is made to the churches which he has built in Brittany (I.61).

[52] I.4–5, 9, 43–44.

[53] Prologue and II.1–2.

[54] II.15.

[55] I.37. Cf. Hughes, *The Church*, pp. 72–3.

[56] I.36.

[57] I.34. Abbot Piro is still alive at that point.

[58] Bowen, *The Settlements*, pp. 35–9 and 44; Davies, *An Early Welsh Microcosm*.

[59] I.33.

19

normally associated with a monastery. Samson is portrayed as abbot of a Welsh monastery when ordained bishop.[60] He continues to reside in a Welsh monastery, presumably the same one.[61] In Brittany his centre of operations is the monastery which he founded at Dol, of which he must have been abbot, where Bishops Tigernomalus and Loucherus are later found, although whether they were abbots is not known. The author appears to have had little regard for the territorial aspects of the episcopacy, and certainly not where Samson is concerned. Samson leaves Wales with nothing said to account for a bishop leaving his diocese or to register that this has even occurred. He brings his episcopate to Dol in Brittany, where his monastic foundation constitutes the see. The author of the *Vita (Prima) Sancti Samsonis* may be said to have a frame of reference of a Church permeated and perhaps structured by monasticism and yet under episcopal authority. The above-mentioned conditions and attitudes may indeed have obtained in early christian Cornwall.

To return to the question of the monasteries revealed in the *Vita Sancti Samsonis*, we can say that these (like the work itself) were in existence no later than the ninth century. The monastery called *Docco*, or its successor, subsequently comes to light in a tenth-century charter. The monastery which Samson founded in Cornwall cannot be said to be heard of again.

The *Vita Sancti Pauli Aureliani*[62] traces the career of the first bishop of the diocese of Léon in northern Brittany, associating him with monasteries in his native Britain and in Brittany. It was composed in 884 by Uurmonoc,[63] priest and monk at Landévennec on the west coast of Brittany. He appears to have had access to some material from Britain, but to have used it imprecisely and perhaps inaccurately, not least because of his geographical distance from the subject. Uurmonoc had clearly not been overseas, and his British geography is so vague that it is uncertain whether some of his narrative is set in Wales or southwest Britain. Accordingly, analysis of the *Vita Sancti Pauli Aureliani* for evidence of early monasteries in southwest Britain will begin with the Insular episode which definitely belongs to that region.

Paul and his disciples, pilgrim-monks en route to Brittany, came to the house (*domus*) of his sister, 'a most holy virgin dedicated to God' named

---

[60] I.42–44.
[61] I.45 and II.8–9.
[62] Orléans, Bibliothèque municipale, MS. 217 (tenth century, provenance Fleury), ed. Cuissart, 'Vie de Saint Paul de Léon'; Paris, Bibliothèque nationale, MS. lat. 12942 (eleventh or beginning of the twelfth century), ed. Plaine, 'Vita Sancti Pauli'. Citations are from the Fleury manuscript unless otherwise specified.
[63] Prologue. He gives us to understand that he has reworked an older account of the deeds of Paul but, as Kenney remarked, 'it does not seem to have been of any great antiquity' (*The Sources*, p. 176); lack of information is admitted in §§ 1 and 11.

Sitofolla,[64] 'who was living on the farthest borders of that country, that is, on the shore of the British sea', viz. the English Channel.[65] She provided hospitality while a ship was fitted out for their voyage. Further indications of her surroundings are given in the account of a miracle which Paul performed there. Sitofolla asked his assistance on behalf of 'us and the inhabitants of the same place'[66] in a situation about which the text is rather specific:[67]

that place, most beneficent brother, in which now at this hour you have deigned to receive hospitality, is discovered to be as suitable for serving God to him who wishes this as it is remote from the society of worldly men. But, evil co-heirs hemming it in on one side, the waves of the sea indeed destroying the borders on the other, it is kept very much excluded from earthly inheritance and straitened in the work of agriculture.

And she asked Paul to pray God to restrain the sea and enlarge the land. Paul asked his sister to put pebbles along the boundary between sea and shore, which when exposed by low tide extended out for 'eight *stadia*, that is a mile, or a little more' at that point.[68] He and his disciples knelt down at the edge of the water at lowest ebb, and prayed that the sea not cross the line of stones or destroy *nostra territoria*. The pebbles became 'stone columns of wonderful size'; the author says that these were still to be seen in his day, and that 'the way, moreover, where they walked along the edge of the same shore, running in the middle between the aforesaid columns, is called "Paul's path" (*semita Pauli*) by the *transmarini*'.[69]

[54] § 9: 'sacrosancta uirgine Deo dedicata'. Her name is given in §§ 1 and 10 in the Fleury manuscript; the Paris manuscript has 'Sicofolla' in § 1 and omits the second. On this saint see Förster, 'Die Heilige Sativola'.

[55] 'quae in illius patriae extremis finibus, id est, in litore maris Britannici degebat' (§ 9); that the *mare Britannicum* is the Channel is clear from 'citra mare Britannicum ad Armoricam regionem processerit' (§ 10).

[66] *Ibid.*: 'saltem in uno bonitatis tuae monimentum ac uirtutis nobis eiusdemque loci incolis, te quaeso, impendere digneris, in quo uenerabilem semper tui nominis mentionem habere possimus, et quod futurae posteritati non parui emulumenti [*sic*] censum conferat'. Cf. *Vita Sancti Samsonis*, I.46.

[67] § 10: 'Iste, frater benignissime, locus in quo nunc ad horam suscipere dignatus es hospitium, quam semotus a consortio mundialium hominum, tam aptus ei qui uoluerit, repperitur ad Deo seruiendum; sed illum coercentibus ex uno latere malis coheredibus, ex altero uero pelagi fluctibus confinia uastantibus, hereditate terrea ualde seclusis et in opus agriculturae habetur angustus'.

[68] *Ibid.*: 'octo stadia, quod est mille passus uel paulo amplius'. The Roman mile of eight *stadia* was ninety-five yards less than the English mile.

[59] *Ibid.*: 'calculos quos eadem Sitofolla suis manibus iactauerat, lapideas mirae magnitudinis columnas in prospectum habuerunt; quae usque hodie in testimonium eius ['eiusdem', Paris MS.] uirtutis sic remanserunt. . . . Litus uero praedictum quod mare exhaustum reliquerat, in opus agriculturae monasterii praefatae feminae omnium seminum fructiferax permansit. Uia autem ubi per ambitum eiusdem littoris peragrarunt inter columnas praedictas media incedens,

This miracle is a variant, often recounted in the same words, of another already performed at the monastery of Illtud.[70] Unique to the Sitofolla version, however, are Sitofolla, her *domus* by the *mare Britannicum*, the stone columns and *semita Pauli* (Illtud drew a trench with his staff as the boundary for the sea to observe), a 'certain place situated in the vicinity'[71] where Paul met his sister for prayer and she requested the miracle (the place is probably a literary device to bring brother and sister into conversation but just possibly a specific site near the *domus*), the mention of inhabitants who would benefit from Paul's miracle, the description of the place as being 'as suitable for serving God to him who wishes this as it is remote from the society of worldly men', the presence of evil co-heirs (the island monastery of Illtud was attacked by the sea on all sides), and Paul's reference to the lands of the place as *nostra territoria*.

The training of Paul Aurelian at the monastery of Illtud is almost certainly adapted from the training of Samson there in the *Vita (Prima) Sancti Samsonis*,[72] a work to which Uurmonoc actually refers at this point. The author's dependence on at least a memory of the *Vita Sancti Samsonis* is strongly indicated by his error in locating the monastery of Illtud on an island mentioned in that work as the site of a different monastery.[73] In a situation designed to enhance his prestige, Paul – together with Samson, David, and Gildas – assisted Illtud in the land-reclamation miracle, following which Paul performed a miracle on his own in related circumstances.[74] Variants of both are found in the twelfth-century *Vita Sancti Iltuti*,[75] where

---

semita Pauli a transmarinis uocitatur'. The seventeenth-century Breton hagiographer Albert Le Grand gave the name of the path as *Hent-Sant-Paul*, according to Doble, *The Saints of Cornwall*, I.42, n. 94. Oliver Padel has informed me that this name is Breton, not Cornish, where one would expect *forth pol* for *semita Pauli*. Also, he doubts the derivation of two field-names, 'Aunt-Saint-Levan', from *Hent Selevan* proposed by Henderson *apud* Doble, *The Saints of Cornwall*, I.9, n. 8.

[70] § 3.

[71] § 10: 'in quodam cum praedicta sorore orationis gratia, in proximo posito interesset loco'.

[72] 1.7 and 9–11. Our author's master, Uurdisten, imitated the *Vita Sancti Samsonis* rather closely in telling of the education of St Guénolé, save that the setting is a Breton monastery rather than that of Illtud (*Vita Sancti Winwaloei*, I.3–5). The account of Paul more nearly resembles Uurdisten's treatment in details than it does the original concerning Samson.

[73] § 2: 'Erat autem quaedam insula Pyrus nomine Demetarum patriae in finibus sita'. Cf. *Vita Sancti Samsonis*, I.20: 'Erat autem non longe ab hoc monasterio insula quaedam nuper fundata a quodam egregio uiro ac sancto presbitero Piro nomine'. Ynys Pyr or Caldey Island lies off the southwest Welsh mainland, the *Demetarum patria* or Dyfed. Samson according to his *uita* was from *Demetia*. *Demetarum* was used by Gildas, *De Excidio*, II.31.

[74] § 4.

[75] §§ 11, 13–15 (ed. & transl. Wade-Evans, *Vitae*, pp. 208–17). The second miracle is here performed by Samson.

that saint has Paulinus, Samson, Gildas, and David as disciples, and his monastery is properly sited at Llanilltud Fawr on the Welsh mainland. A foundation in an older account of Illtud is not indicated for this vague, fanciful, and anachronistic *uita*, and its author has almost certainly adapted these episodes from the *Vita Sancti Pauli Aureliani*.[76] It is doubtful that Uurmonoc had any information about Illtud and his monastery other than what is contained in the *Vita (Prima) Sancti Samsonis*, wherein the land-reclamation miracle is not found: this miracle and the one which Paul performed alone at Illtud's monastery came from elsewhere, and a likely source for the former is local legend about the *semita Pauli*.

Whatever the source of the land-reclamation tale, we are still left with the presence, at some place on the north shore of the English Channel, of the religious settlement of a holy virgin named Sitofolla, inhabitants of an unspecified nature, and an impressive stone feature bearing the name of her brother Paul. This is the setting to which the story has been adapted, if adaptation has occurred. A key-question is whether Sitofolla's establishment was a monastic community or a hermitage. *Domus*, the word by which it is initially described, could designate a monastery or a single dwelling, although the latter might be a cell within a monastery.[77] *Monasterium* is applied to it in a phrase which has a counterpart in the Illtud miracle wherein of course the word refers to a cenobitic establishment. Later in the *uita*, however, the author says that a place where Paul lived alone in Brittany is called in his own time 'monasterium siue uulgato nomine Lanna Pauli in plebe Telmedouiae'. Uurmonoc refers to it in the present as a place for prayer but not as a monastery. The hermitage was occupied, before Paul took it over, by one of his disciples 'who on account of the straitness of his rather severe life and voluntary habitation of a remote solitude was called by all a monk'.[78] It seems, then, that the author might use *monasterium* to refer to a hermitage. Interestingly, most of the monastic activity described in the *Vita Sancti Pauli Aureliani* is of an eremitic or semi-eremitic sort.

There is no undoubted reference to monastic personnel in the *domus* or *monasterium* of Paul's sister other than Sitofolla herself. It is not clear whether the *incolae* are her fellow-religious or tillers of the soil in the locality where she lives and whether she speaks in the first person plural for herself only or for her hypothetical monastic community as well. Specific activities of a monastic community also remain unmentioned.

The author nevertheless may have had a communal monastery in mind in relating this episode. He conceives of the *domus* of Sitofolla as a place

[76] There is a case of verbal similarity between these *uitae* in the account of the first miracle, and several such in the account of the second miracle. For a different view, see Doble, *The Saints of Cornwall*, I.37 (but also 31, n. 65), and his *Lives of the Welsh Saints*, pp. 97–100 and 153.

[77] See *Vita Sancti Samsonis*, I.60 and 33. *Domus*, applied to the religious retreat of the Breton Count Withur, in *Vita Sancti Pauli*, § 18, is ambiguous.

[78] § 13: 'Unus uero ex his qui in remotiora secesserant, fuit Iunehinus nomine, qui propter uitae arctioris angustiam et uoluntariam remotae solitudinis habitationem cunctorum ab ore monachus uocitabatur'.

where Paul and his party could receive hospitality and where sailing preparations could be made. Regarding the miracle, if it is not genuine tradition of the house, one can at least say that Uurmonoc was content to employ it, with implications of land-utilisation beyond the resources of one person, in the context of Sitofolla's establishment.

The reference to co-heirs, to the ownership of neighbouring lands, would be useful if we could be reasonably certain that it had some factual basis. Sitofolla might have been a family-member who followed a religious life-style on a portion of the family-lands, perhaps supported by other kin. She might have attracted followers, and other members of her family have opposed encroachment on their land by the growing monastic community. To this conjecture about the house of Sitofolla may be added two points to note in passing: its coastal location, typical of early British religious settlements, and its communication with Brittany implicit in Paul's voyage. The Sitofolla episode is itself evidence that some information about this place reached Brittany by the author's time. He makes no specific reference to the contemporary existence of the religious establishment there, how-ever, as he does for the monastery which Paul founded in Britain[79] and for the stone-columns and *semita Pauli*.

The author's treatment of the Sitofolla episode is in some respects so vague as to leave us confronting the most basic questions. Was there or was there not a sister of Paul Aurelian named Sitofolla living as a religious on a site on the north shore of the English Channel? It is highly probable that veneration of Sitofolla at the place where she had distinguished herself for holiness lies behind this episode in the *uita*. Even poorly informed saints' Lives have a basis in association of the saints' cults with particular places. Liturgy and sometimes toponymy would preserve knowledge of the saints' names. The obscurity of the saint in question suggests that her cult was confined to the locality where she had lived (and presumably died). There is room for doubt about whether Sitofolla was Paul's sister, but the author of the *uita* gives a little more information about Paul's family.[80] Something must have associated Sitofolla and Paul in the mind of the author of the *uita*, and if it was not family-relationship it must have been proximity of her cult-site to the *semita Pauli* or to some other cult-site of Paul Aurelian. Was hers a monastery or not? Here we are uncertain not only about the extent and accuracy of Uurmonoc's information, but about the meaning of his text. He seems to have intended to portray her establishment to be a cenobitic monastery, but we cannot be sure. In the circumstances, we can

---

[79] See pp. 26–7 below.

[80] He tells us that the saint's father was Count Perphirius and that Paul had eight brothers of whom two were Notolius (*Notalius* in the Paris manuscript) and Potolius and three sisters of whom one was Sitofolla, but continues: 'alia propter temporis inormitatem tam longi ex memoriae thesauro exinanita, aut etiam propter maris spatium terrarumque tam longum inter nostram illorumque distans regionem minus audita nescimus nomina' (§ 1). It is notable that the three named siblings are all associated with religious houses in the text.

only conclude that the *domus* of Sitofolla in the *Vita Sancti Pauli Aureliani* was perhaps based on an actual monastery for women.

An attempt to identify the site in question can be made from the evidence of the *uita* and from mediaeval dedications. The former gives the general location 'in illius patriae extremis finibus, id est, in litore Maris Britannici' as well as a context placing the episode in Celtic Britain; therefore, the site is to be sought on the Channel-coast of southwest Britain. The *semita Pauli*, which sounds like the remains of a field-hedge (as Doble suggested),[81] stone-rows, or even a natural coastal feature, is not now known and (assuming, for the sake of argument, that it existed) has in any case probably been destroyed by man or engulfed by the sea. On the grounds that Sitofolla's establishment may have left a trace in a mediaeval church-dedication to her or to Paul (whose name appears to have been preserved locally at least in association with the stone-feature), attention is directed to two sites.

The first is rather a puzzle. At Exeter there is a dedication to St Sidwell first attested in or after the year 1013 by an entry in Part Two of *Secgan be þam Godes sanctum þe on Engla lande ærost reston* which reads 'ðonne resteð sancte Sidefulla faemne wiðutan Exanceastre'.[82] The name of this saint closely resembles the Sitofolla of *Vita Sancti Pauli Aureliani*, only two vowels being (or appearing) different, and both saints are female. There is also a church dedicated to St Paul located near the churches of the Celtic saints Petroc and Kerrian in the north part of Exeter where the parish of St Davids lies outside the city wall. The proposal has been made that the patron of this church is Paul Aurelian, and that the dedication originated in a Celtic milieu.[83] Exeter ecclesiastical tradition gives no support whatsoever to a double identification of brother and sister in the *Vita Sancti Pauli Aureliani* with the two Exeter saints.[84] It is considered probable that the name of the Exeter female saint is English, being a combination of Old English *sidu*, 'morality' or 'modesty', and *full*.[85] One may wonder if pre-Conquest traditions have not been superseded at Exeter. In question also is whether Sidefulla could represent an adaptation into Old English of an unfamiliar Celtic or latinised Celtic name, or indeed Sitofolla be the result of a reverse-process. Yet Exeter is an unsatisfactory setting for the Sitofolla episode. Though situated near the south coast, it is not on the sea and is a strange place to describe as remote from human society: continuity of settlement in post-Roman Exeter is not proven, but the English had long been installed there by the time when Uurmonoc wrote.[86] It would take

---

[81] *The Saints of Cornwall*, I.42, n. 95.
[82] Ed. Liebermann, *Die Heiligen Englands*, p. 17 (§ 38); cf. Rollason, 'Lists', especially pp. 64, 76, and 92.
[83] Initially by Kerslake, 'The Celt'. For a different view of the origin of the Exeter dedications to Celtic saints, see Pearce, 'The dating', pp. 110–12.
[84] See Doble, *The Saints of Cornwall*, I.40–1, and references given there.
[85] Gover *et al.*, *The Place-names of Devon*, II.437.
[86] Hoskins, *The Westward Expansion*, pp. 12–17; Thomas, 'The end', pp. 211–12.

great ignorance on his part to report legends about the vicinity of Exeter in such terms. Thus, in spite of several coincidences which make it an attractive site, Exeter is hardly to be considered the place of Sitofolla's *domus*.

The church of Paul parish in the far west of Cornwall is a more likely point on which to fix the location of the Sitofolla episode in the *uita*. There the traditional parish-feast is of Paulinus of York, but in this region of dedications to Celtic saints he is most unlikely to have been the original patron; and the influence of his cult is paralleled in Brittany itself.[87] Nothing indicates that a site at Paul on the west side of Mount's Bay beyond Penzance would have been other than remote, and known coastal submergence in Mount's Bay is suggestive in connexion with the miracle-story.[88] On the other hand, no sign of a cult of Sitofolla has been detected in the vicinity. There is convincing evidence of the disappearance of cults and traditions of saints in Cornwall, however, and the replacement of the cult of one saint by another – as conceivably happened with Sitofolla and Paul – is well attested.[89] The author of the *uita* did not write that Paul made any religious foundation where his sister was living, but does indicate that Paul Aurelian was remembered and venerated there. The strength of the identification of Paul near Penzance as the site of the religious settlement of Sitofolla rests in the assumption that the author, when collecting information for the *uita*, looked for places associated with Paul Aurelian, in the soundness of the claim of the Cornish site to have been a *locus* of the cult of that saint, and, in so far as the setting in the *uita* can be relied upon, in that site's topographical suitability. Yet preference for this site is only moderate in view of several uncertainties in the identification.

From the time when Paul leaves the Welsh monastery of Illtud until he arrives on the shore of the English Channel, his geographical whereabouts are obscure; these earlier sections of the *Vita Sancti Pauli Aureliani*, of questionable relevance to southwest Britain, will be dealt with briefly by working back from material already discussed. Paul and his disciples came to his sister's house from 'the place which now is called in their language *Caer Banhed*, the *uilla Banhedos*',[90] where he had been ministering to King

---

[87] Doble, *The Saints of Cornwall*, I.33 and 55–58. The patron was designated Paulus or Paulinus in the middle ages (*ibid.*, p. 33), and appears as *Paule*, etc., corresponding to the former, in Late Cornish forms of the parish-name (Padel, 'Cornish language notes', p. 76).

[88] See Thomas, *Exploration*; cf. Doble, *The Saints of Cornwall*, I.42 and 59.

[89] Cornish place-names in *lan* many times provide the only trace of a former cult-site, and the list of saints' names discussed on pp. 56–60 below suggests that some cults have completely vanished. At a place to which we have referred, veneration of Docco was superseded first by Kew and then by James.

[90] 'locum qui nunc lingua eorum Caer Banhed, uilla Banhedos, nuncupatur' (§ 8; from the Paris manuscript, the Fleury manuscript having only the Latin *uilla Bannhedos* and omitting *nunc*).

Marcus 'whom they called by another name Quonomorius'[91] and his people. The site has not been identified, but was probably in southwest Britain.[92] Although ultimately unsuccessful in persuading Paul to become bishop of his region, the king, seeking a spiritual leader for the newly converted realm and learning of Paul's holiness, had summoned him from an eremitical monastery where he dwelt with twelve disciples who were priests like himself. The term 'eremitic(al)' is used advisedly in as much as Anthony of Egypt is cited as a model for Paul's way of life, which is presented as a step up from the communal monastery of Illtud to a higher level of monastic life in a wilderness-retreat. Uurmonoc writes of it as a substantial monastery in his day, bearing the names of two of Paul's brothers.[93] Doble made a fairly good case for identifying this place with Llanddeusant in south Wales.[94]

Of some interest is the picture of a group of monks, master and disciples, exercising pastoral care at the demand of a secular ruler concerned about the spiritual welfare of his realm, and the leader of the monks being offered the episcopacy by that ruler. Assuming that reference in the *uita* is to southwest Britain, there is still doubt as to whether such a situation might derive from the author's Breton background, a caution which has already been expressed about the story, in some respects similar, of Samson and

[91] § 8: 'quem alio nomine Quonomorium [Quonomonum, *Paris MS*] vocant'. The episode occupies §§ 8–9.

[92] Cf. Doble, *The Saints of Cornwall*, I.39–40; Bromwich, *Trioedd*, pp. 445–6. The interpretation by Bromwich of the phrase describing the place to which Paul journeyed from the king's court, 'in illius patriae extremis finibus, id est, in litore maris Britannici', as indicative of travel from Wales down to the south coast of southwest Britain entails a Welsh perspective. Instead, the author with his Breton perspective probably meant by his phrase the south coast of the vaguely perceived transmarine land, without respect to the point at which Paul began his journey. Attention has focussed on locating King Marcus alias Quonomorius and his realm: see the very full note *ibid.*, pp. 443–8, (cf. also pp. 25–6); see further Bromwich, 'The character', p. 122[–3], n. 6, and Chadwick, *Early Brittany*, pp. 212–14, 219–24. One name of the king occurs on an early christian inscription in the parish of Fowey in south-central Cornwall, reading 'DRUSTAυS HIC IACIT CVNOMORI FILIUS' (with D reversed and M inverted on the stone): see Radford, 'Report', pp. 117–19, and Bromwich, *Trioedd*, p. 445, citing Kenneth Jackson. When the author of the *uita* writes of *Caer Banhed*, 'ubi nunc eiusdem regis ossa diem resurrectionis expectantia pausant' (§ 8), it is just possible that he is referring to this stone, as suggested by Bromwich, *ibid.* Nearby Castle Dore, where the stone perhaps originally stood (Macalister, *Corpus*, I.465–7, no. 487), an earthwork which upon excavation yielded doubtful evidence of early medi-aeval occupation (Radford, 'Report and Romance'; cf. Rahtz, 'Castle Dore') could be *Caer Banhed*, although a Cornish name for the place may be present in Carhurles, a tenement near the site (Charles Henderson, *apud* Doble, *Saint Samson in Cornwall*, pp. 25 and 28).

[93] § 7; the episode occupies §§ 6–7.

[94] *The Saints of Cornwall*, I.33–6, and *Lives of the Welsh Saints*, pp. 150–3 and 156.

'Count' Guedian in Cornwall.[95] Yet even if the *uitae* were not informed on this point for southwest Britain, such conditions may have been present as factors impinging on monks and monasteries in that region, closely linked as it was in culture and communication with Brittany.

Vita Sancti Pauli Aureliani appears to relate the career of a holy man who travelled from his native Wales through southwest Britain to Brittany. The reality behind its account is more doubtful, however, than in the case of Samson of Dol. Paul the founder of the see of Léon, Paulinus of Wales, and the eponym of the *semita Pauli* in southwest Britain are not necessarily to be taken as the same person – even though Uurmonoc thought that they were when he composed the *uita* towards the end of the ninth century in Brittany. Paul may have come to Brittany by the route outlined above or have been a southwest British migrant across the Channel or even have been a native Breton. It is likely, however, that some simple house-tradition of his origin, at least, was preserved at Léon; if that point be admitted, migration from Wales still has the edge among the possibilities.

Vita Sancti Pauli Aureliani is of far less value to our inquiry than the *Vita (Prima) Sancti Samsonis*, owing to its greater remoteness in space and time from the subject and its imprecision on points of interest to us. It provides evidence that a monastery for women associated with Sitofolla and Paul Aurelian perhaps stood on the Channel-coast of southwest Britain. Paul parish near the southwest end of Cornwall is a rather likely, and Exeter a rather unlikely, site for this.

There are no overt references to southwest British monasteries or monks in the other early Breton *uitae*. What little does concern the region in these sources, briefly summarised, will fill in the background to concluding remarks on the contribution of the Breton *uitae*, as a group, to an understanding of monastic conditions in southwest Britain. *Vita Sancti Turiaui*, written in the second half of the ninth century about one of Samson's successors as bishop of Dol,[96] mentions the exemplary 'Constantinum, regem ultramarinum, filium Peterni, in decoruio',[97] the original reading probably having been '. . . filium Peterni, de Cornouio', viz. 'of Cornwall'.[98] Hagiological tradition of a saintly King Constantine of Cornwall is found elsewhere. Constantine has five surviving dedications in southwest Britain: three in Cornwall and two in Devon.[99] Later evidence suggests the existence of an early monastery at one of the Cornish sites.[100] There are also two dedications to Paternus in the Southwest.[101] Turiau had a vision of the death of 'his friend, Geren by name, whom he had across the

[95] See pp. 16–18 above.
[96] Ed. Duine, 'Vie antique'; see his pp. 6–12 on dating.
[97] § 5.
[98] Duine, 'Vie antique', p. 36, n. 21. Cf. Doble, *The Saints of Cornwall*, III.78, n. 9.
[99] *Ibid.*, II.15–23.
[100] See pp. 90, 92–4, 96 below.
[101] Cf. Doble, *Saint Patern*, pp. 41–2.

sea'.[102] Sailors sent by the saint for proof of the matter met in the middle of the sea others coming to tell Turiau about the death of Geren. A saint of this name, in its Cornish form Gerent, is the patron of one church at Gerrans on the south coast of Cornwall.[103] Mixing of hagiographical traditions has probably taken place in *Vita Sancti Turiaui*, with its Constantine and Geren being the Cornish saints. There is evidence here for Breton-Cornish ecclesiastical contacts which, since the author admits that he has no earlier source about Turiau,[104] are apt to relate to his own time.

The *Vita Sancti Brioccii*, probably eleventh-century but from its author's comments in the epilogue clearly based on a somewhat older account of Brioc, has some southwest British content.[105] This *uita* is highly derivative of *Vita (Prima) Sancti Samsonis*, never more so than in the relevant episode. Advised to leave his native Wales in a manner reminiscent of the latter work, Brioc crossed an unnamed sea to an unnamed region and we next see him, like Samson, in a chariot accompanied by his monks. Along the way a pagan *regulus* named Conan was converted by Brioc: the story is different, but the pattern is clearly that of *Vita (Prima) Sancti Samsonis* and is continued by the departure of Brioc and his party for Brittany.[106] Brioc is, then, another saint whom hagiographical tradition brings from Wales across southwest Britain to Brittany. He is patron of a church in Wales, apparently of another in Gloucestershire, of St Breoke church in Cornwall not far south of the Camel estuary, and of several churches in Brittany including the cathedral of Saint-Brieuc.[107] There appear to be elements of Welsh legend in the *uita*, and the story of the converted ruler Conan could incorporate southwest British legend, but too inextricably mixed with material about Samson of Dol to warrant further attention here.[108]

These early Breton *uitae*, of which our survey is now concluding, give the histories of notable persons associated with Breton bishoprics and principal monasteries, generally as their founders. With one exception, these works do not pay much heed to Insular British matters. The author of the *Vita (Prima) Sancti Samsonis* had had personal experience of Britain, and his text has in fact a dearth of information about the saint's activities in Brittany which remains extremely puzzling. The *Vita (Prima) Sancti*

---

[102] § 9: 'amicus eius, Geren nomine, quem habebat trans mare'.

[103] There was formerly an ecclesiastical site in Monmouthshire called *Merthir gerein* (Doble, *The Saints of Cornwall*, III.74, n. 1).

[104] Prologue; cf. remarks by Duine, 'Vie antique', pp. 10–11, pointing out that a little information would have been in liturgical documents.

[105] Edited from one manuscript by Plaine, 'Vita S. Brioci' (without the epilogue, which was translated by Doble, *The Saints of Cornwall*, IV.83–4). For the date of the *uita*, see *ibid.* p. 84, citing Duine, 'Mémento', pp. 326–8, no. 62; for the date of its source, Doble, *The Saints of Cornwall*, IV.85, n. 20.

[106] §§ 38–39.

[107] Doble, *The Saints of Cornwall*, IV.99–101.

[108] For the suggestion that the Conan episode, found in only one of the existing manuscripts of the *Vita Sancti Brioccii*, is an interpolation, see *ibid.*, pp. 90–1; however, its style and content are harmonious with the rest of the *uita*.

Samsonis is, then, by far the most helpful of the Breton group about monasteries in southwest Britain. It exerted a strong influence on later Breton hagiography, providing subsequent *uitae* with considerable material for the British portions of their subjects' careers. There is evidence of independent incorporation of Insular, including southwest British, material in these *uitae*, however. One could not, for example, soundly suggest that stories of Welsh ecclesiastical influence in Brittany can be attributed entirely to the influence of the *Vita (Prima) Sancti Samsonis*. That work in any case shows that such accounts existed at an early date. Southwest Britain is not assigned importance in ecclesiastical matters in these early Breton *uitae*, which indeed give no name to the region.[109] The only hint that the Southwest played an early and formative role in the monastic movement is that, according to the *Vita Sancti Samsonis*, there was monastic activity in Cornwall before Samson's foundation there. Again, the Breton *uitae* in their sources of information, stated or implicit, provide important evidence of unquestionable contact between monasteries in Brittany, Cornwall, and Wales by the ninth century.[110]

From Cornwall, as from Wales, no saint's Life written before the closing years of our period has survived. The eleventh-century *Vita Sancti Petroci* is probably of Cornish origin; certainly most of it is concerned with Cornwall, and it seems designed to serve the interests of the collegiate church of St Petroc at Bodmin where the saint's relics were preserved.[111] We may note that its account of Petroc is set in a monastic world like that in the Breton *uitae* rather than in an eleventh-century milieu of collegiate churches and nascent parishes in the diocese of Exeter. Nevertheless, the *uita* appears informed by little, if any, early hagiographical tradition and its evidence is too distant from the period of this chapter to be considered here.[112]

Also to be abandoned as sources of evidence are the numerous later Lives of Cornish saints. Not only were they written long after the period of their subject and without early material about it, but, as members of a highly imitative genre, they incorporate large amounts of material about other saints and other regions. Eventually a general Celtic hagiographical form came into being, in which the *Vita Sancti Petroci* may have partaken to

---

[109] That is, the *uitae* which we have been examining, those with episodes set in southwest Britain; *Vita Sancti Winwaloei* records that the father of the native Breton saint came from Insular Dumnonia (I.2).

[110] In this connexion, consider the implications of the following from another ninth-century Breton life, concerning St Malo at Llancarfan in south Wales: 'Et ille, cum suo magistro ad monasterium iens, partem fractam sentis quam inuenerat in uia in Nantcaruan, monasterio sui magistri, plantauit. Quam ualidissimam multi ex nostris regionibus ad illam patriam euntes uiderunt' (Bili, *Vita Sancti Machutis*, § 25 [ed. Lot, *Mélanges*, p. 368]).

[111] Ed. Grosjean, 'Vies et miracles'. According to the *uita*, Petroc travelled from his native Wales to Ireland to Cornwall where, except for a pilgrimage to the Far East, he remained.

[112] It will be dealt with in section 4 of chapter IV below.

some extent and towards which the earlier Breton *uitae* were contributing. Aside from information of later mediaeval date about ecclesiastical sites, and the simplest data on the saint, *uitae* of this form are useless on the subject of early monasteries specifically in southwest Britain.

There is a small amount of relevant material in early Irish written sources. The southwest British monastery of Glastonbury (Somerset) may be mentioned in the context of fifth- to sixth-century Irish settlement in Britain in the Glossary of Cormac mac Cuilennáin, which was composed before 908, the date of the author's death:[113]

. . . and not less did the Gael dwell on the east side of the sea *quam in Scotica*, and their habitations and royal forts were built there. *Inde dicitur Dinn Tradui*, i.e. Triple-fossed Fort, of Crimthann the Great, son of Fidach, king of Ireland and Alba to the Ictian sea (the English Channel), *et inde est* Glastonbury of the Gael, i.e. a church on the border [*bru*] of the Ictian sea . . . And it is in that part is *Dinn map Lethain* in the lands of the Cornish Britons, i.e., the Fort of Mac Liathain, for *mac* is the same as *map* in British.

The passage is describing the past phenomenon of Irish settlement and relating to it existing place-names, those of the two forts being British and *Glasimpere* or its variants *Glastimbir* and *Glassdinibir* corrupt but plausible as Irish renderings of an Old English form or forms of Glastonbury.[114] It follows from the passage that the author of the passage thought that the monastery of Glastonbury in Somerset (if the identification be accepted), like the forts, resulted from that settlement. The Irish are known to have had an interest in Glastonbury, considered to be the burial place of Patrick, in the first part of the tenth century.[115] We cannot be at all sure that a reference to Glastonbury in Cormac's Glossary, contemporary or near-contemporary with this interest, represents ancient legend preserved in Ireland rather than antiquarian speculation projected on the past.[116]

[113] '. . . 7 nibaluga dothrebdais Gáedil formuir anair quam in Scotica 7 dorónta anarusa 7 a[r]rigdúinte ann. Inde dicitur Dinn Tradúi .i. Dún Tredúi .i. trédhue Crimthain moir maic Fhidaig rig Erenn 7 Alpan 7 comuir nIcht. 7 inde Glasimpere [nanGáidel .i. cell] forbrú mara nIcht. . . . 7 is[d]inr[a]indsin ata dind map Lethain i tírib Bretan Cornn .i. dún maic Liatha[i]n. Aris mac inní is mabb isin bretnais' (ed. Stokes, *Three Irish Glossaries*, p. 29). The translation used is adapted from that of Stokes & O'Donovan, *Sanas Chormaic*, p. 111; *ibid*., p. 113, Stokes commented that 'Glastonbury is in the heart of Somerset; but the fact that it stands on the river Brue (which, however, flows into St. George's Channel) may perhaps have caused this geographical mistake'. See also Kuno Meyer, *apud* Bergin *et al*., *Anecdota*, IV.xi and 75, for the variants.

[114] I am indebted to Oliver Padel for advice on this identification.

[115] See Finberg, *West-Country Historical Studies*, pp. 74–8 and 81, n. 1; 'The cult of St Indract', pp. 182–3.

[116] The earliest date at which existence of a monastery at Glastonbury is certain is *ca* 670 (Finberg, *West-Country Historical Studies*, p. 71, n. 2). For the archaeological evidence see p. 35 below. Cf. Rahtz, 'Irish settlements', and Thomas, 'The Irish settlements'.

St Cairnech, entered for 16 May in the Irish 'Martyrology of Oengus' (written *ca* 800),[117] is said in the mediaeval notes to the Martyrology to have been 'of the Cornish Britons' and, in another part of these notes, to have brought monks to Ireland.[118] A Cairnech[119] is named with Patrick and Patrick's disciple Benignus among the nine authors of the Irish legal compilation *Senchus mór*. He is identified in the later mediaeval commentary to that text as Cairnech of Tulén.[120] Charles Plummer suggested that the attribution of Cornish nationality 'may be an inference from his name, Cairnech = Coirnech, i.e. Cornish'.[121]

This is probably the extent of references to possible monasteries or monks of southwest Britain in early mediaeval Irish sources.[122] Allowing that the Irish record may be very incomplete, it would still be difficult to argue from the two problematical items cited above that the monastic movement in southwest Britain exercised an early and important influence on Ireland. Support for influence in the opposite direction is forthcoming from an altogether different source. The Anglo-Saxon Chronicle for the year 891 reads in part:[123]

And three Scots came to King Alfred in a boat without any oars from Ireland, which they had left secretly, because they wished for the love of God to be in foreign lands, they cared not where. The boat in which they travelled was made of two and a half hides, and they took with them enough food for seven days. And after seven days they came to land in Cornwall, and went immediately to King Alfred.

---

[117] Ed. & transl. Stokes, *Félire Óengusso*, p. 124.

[118] *Ibid.*, pp. 132–3 ('do Bretnaib Corrnn') and 244–7, respectively. The latter appears to associate Cairnech with the context of Irish settlement in southwest Britain. For a brief comment on the date of the notes to the Martyrology, see *ibid.*, pp. xlvii–xlviii. Plummer described thus the following tale of Cairnech from the Book of Ballymote (*ca* 1400): 'It makes Cairnech son of a king of Britain; he builds an underground monastery in Cornwall, whence he migrates to Ireland, becoming the first Irish martyr!' (*Vitae Sanctorum Hiberniae*, II.390).

[119] See Kenney, *The Sources*, pp. 351–2: 'Cairnech, "the Cornishman", is a hazy and ubiquitous personnage of whom there are many notices but not much clear information. Two or more Cairnechs have been postulated to solve some of the difficulties.'

[120] Binchy, *Corpus Iuris Hibernici*, II.339, 342, 347; III.876; V.1650, 1651, 1658. For the dates of the component parts, cf. Binchy, 'The pseudo-historical prologue', and literature cited there.

[121] *Vitae Sanctorum Hiberniae*, I.cxxv, n. 1.

[122] The identification of the British monastery of *Rosnat* – traditionally in hagiography the school for several sixth-century Irish monastic founders – with a monastery at Tintagel in Cornwall, as suggested by Thomas, 'Rosnat', is pure conjecture (and has now been withdrawn: Thomas, 'East and west', p. 17). The case for *Rosnat* as an alternative name for St Davids in southwest Wales is stronger (see P. A. Wilson, 'St. Ninian', pp. 182–4).

[123] Translated by Whitelock, *English Historical Documents*, pp. 200–1.

This is a contemporary record of an actual incident involving circumstances which would do credit to a saint's Life. As such, it is an important indication of the reality which might at some stage(s) have brought from Ireland founders and occupants of monasteries in southwest Britain. The fact that a boat from Ireland which was left to the will of God in the appropriate manner might drift to Cornwall is of considerable interest. It seems fitting to leave discussion of literary sources concerning the activities of the monastic saints at this point of contact with an actual situation of the sort which could have both inspired and been inspired by the hagiographical genre.

III

EARLY MONASTICISM AND SOUTHWEST BRITAIN: THE ARCHAEOLOGICAL EVIDENCE

This chapter is concerned with physical remains as they relate to the spread of the monastic movement in southwest Britain: settlements, early christian memorial-stones, and imported pottery. Archaeological evidence is specific to sites in a way that the literary evidence which we have been examining is not. There is no doubt that a potsherd, properly stratified, conveys relevant information about the site where it has been found. On the other hand, the association of archaeological evidence with the early monasteries of southwest Britain is more tenuous and difficult to establish than, for example, the direct reference to the monastery called *Docco* in the *Vita (Prima) Sancti Samsonis*. Most useful of all is a coincidence of written and archaeological evidence; however, in the Southwest this has remained an elusive goal, as will be apparent in the discussion of settlement-sites which follows.

For four excavated sites in southwest Britain an early communal monastic interpretation is possible: Tintagel in Cornwall; Glastonbury Abbey, Glastonbury Tor, and Cadbury Hill at Congresbury in Somerset. All have associations of some interest. Tintagel lay within the Domesday manor of *Botcinnii* held by the canons of St Petroc who were successors to one or more early monasteries. Glastonbury Abbey is an early Anglo-Saxon monastery which from the tenth century acknowledged an earlier Irish ecclesiastical link, as we have seen;[1] there was probably a late Anglo-Saxon eremitical monastery on Glastonbury Tor. In a relationship rather similar to that of Tor and abbey, the site on Cadbury Hill overlooks Congresbury where there was a late Anglo-Saxon minster-church and where the patron and eponym (St Cyngar) is a British Celtic saint.

The once widely accepted identification of the site at Tintagel on the north coast of Cornwall as monastic is highly problematical and has been challenged.[2] To be sure, Tintagel on its rocky promontory above the

---

[1] Above, p. 31.
[2] Burrow, 'Tintagel', and especially Rainsbury Dark, 'The plan'. I concur with their findings. No final excavation-report is available. See the following works by Radford: 'Tintagel'; *Tintagel Castle*, pp. 18–27; 'Tintagel in History'; 'Imported pottery'; 'The Celtic monastery'; 'Romance'; Radford & Swanton, *Arthurian Sites*, chapter 2. Important pre-excavation material was given by Henderson, 'East Cornwall', pp. 526–41a, especially p. 539.

Atlantic looks the part of an ascetic retreat; however, the natural protection of the site offers advantages for secular use. A major difficulty with Tintagel as the site of an early monastery is provided by the very restricted number and the ambiguous nature of the funerary remains, which normally abound on early ecclesiastical sites in the British Isles. Tintagel appears to suffer a dearth of graves, but has an ample supply of buildings which have been interpreted as monastic. A second problem, however, is the often imprecise stratigraphic relationship to the buildings of the finds of imported Mediterranean pottery; it is these which provide the late fifth- to seventh-century date-range for the occupation of the site. The available data permit the interpretation that some or all of the buildings represent an occupation-phase later than the deposition of the imported wares on the site. A number of building complexes remains to be excavated, and a major cemetery may of course be discovered. Further excavation and study will probably show the occupation at Tintagel to have been more complex than has hitherto been supposed, as for example by the recovery of traces of wooden structures, and it could prove to have been the site of an early monastery. At present, however, that interpretation must remain doubtful.

At Glastonbury Abbey in Somerset, two sections of a very large ditch and associated bank, considered by the excavator on stratigraphic evidence to have been constructed before 650, suggest by comparison with *ualla* at sites such as Iona and Clonmacnoise the presence of an early monastery. No imported Mediterranean pottery-sherds or other finds were recovered to confirm pre-seventh-century occupation.[3] It is possible that the site on nearby Glastonbury Tor, which did yield the imported Mediterranean wares so crucial for dating, is that of a monastery.[4] The same can be said for a site in a different area, the reoccupied Iron-Age hillfort on Cadbury Hill, Congresbury, from which a large quantity of Mediterranean pottery has been recovered.[5] Yet in neither case has a monastic interpretation been preferred.

Two sites at which from written evidence there were reasonably certainly early monasteries, St Piran's Oratory and St Germans, both in Cornwall, have been subjected to limited and unscientific excavation. Revealed by shifts in Perran Sands at the end of the eighteenth century, the stone-church known as St Piran's Oratory, probably eighth-century at the earliest,[6] was cleared and investigated at various times in the nineteenth and early twentieth centuries. Also discovered were an adjacent cemetery of uncertain

---

[3] Radford, 'Excavations at Glastonbury Abbey, 1956'; note in 'Medieval Britain in 1957', pp. 188–9; Radford, 'The Church in Somerset', pp. 32–3; Radford, 'Glastonbury Abbey'. But cf. Rahtz, 'Excavations on Glastonbury Tor', p. 5.

[4] *Ibid.*, especially pp. 20–2, and 'Monasteries as settlements', pp. 126–7.

[5] Fowler *et al.*, *Cadbury Congresbury*; note in 'Medieval Archaeology in Britain, 1970', p. 133; Rahtz, 'Monasteries as Settlements', pp. 126–7. The latter paper provides a very instructive discussion of the problems of identification and dating of monastic sites.

[6] Cf. Thomas, 'Post-Roman rectangular house plans', pp. 158–9.

extent and, about 100 yards southeast of the church, another stone-building of uncertain function. Only structural remains appear to have been preserved from this site.[7] At St Germans, amateurish excavation in 1928 uncovered, beneath scanty remains of the destroyed chancel of the post-Conquest church, two intersecting walls of an earlier structure of slightly different orientation, probably a church. Again, no finds were preserved.[8] One can conclude little from such archaeological evidence save that religious activity was carried on in simple stone-churches at these sites in the early middle ages. In short, there is no properly excavated and certain instance of an early monastery in southwest Britain.

Memorial stones and the imported pottery date from the period of early monastic expansion in the British Isles.[9] At the minimum they provide visible indications of contacts between the British Isles and those Mediterranean and Continental areas where monasticism was established. The series of memorial stones, which begins a little earlier than the ceramic evidence, reflects the influence of epigraphic traditions, apparently developed in Ireland before the introduction of christianity, which fused with early christian epigraphic traditions in the context of Irish settlements in Britain. The inscriptions are capable of analysis with respect to these traditions.

The incidence of Continental and Irish elements in Welsh memorial stones has been examined by J. D. Bu'lock.[10] From their occurrence, as shown on Maps C and D, distinct areas emerge of predominant Irish or Continental influence in Wales. The distribution in Wales of memorial stones with Irish features clearly reflects their geographic source, while the distribution of stones without these features corresponds fairly well with the concentration of Roman activity in Wales (see also Map E). In addition to providing the distribution-maps, Bu'lock offered a chart in which Irish elements (viz., ogom and formulae of *filius*-type) and Continental elements (viz., formulae of *hic iacit* type and horizontal inscriptions) were examined by counties and grouped in north and south Wales.[11] Bu'lock extended his analysis to other areas of the British Isles where such memorial stones are found, including southwest Britain. The purpose of the following discussion is to examine closely and expand the data for southwest Britain, and ultimately to compare these data with those for other regions.

This survey of the Continental and Irish components of early christian inscriptions in southwest Britain will begin with the features on Bu'lock's

[7] Most useful are: Ordnance Survey Index Cards SW75NE 3 and 31; Peter, 'St. Piran's old church'; W. Michell, *et al.*, manuscripts of correspondence kept at the Royal Institution of Cornwall Library, Truro; Dexter, 'St. Piran's Oratory'; Dexter, 'St. Piran'. The memorial stone reported in Macalister, *Corpus*, II.182, no. 1052, is a modern graffito inverted in restoration of the Oratory.

[8] Henderson, *Records*, pp. 35–6; 'St. German's Church and Port Eliot House', unpublished Port Eliot MS. St Germans, Cornwall, pp. 10, 50, 51, 54, and diagram following.

[9] See pp. 2 and 4 above.

[10] 'Early christian memorial formulae'.

[11] *Ibid.*, p. 136.

chart. Taking his figures for north Britain and southwest Britain and adding these data, with a few minor adjustments,[12] to the chart, one obtains the following.

	Total	% ogom	% FILIUS	% IACIT	% horizontal
N. Wales:					
Anglesey	11	0	10	80	25
Carnarvon	18	5	45	75	35
Merioneth	11	0	30	55	25
S. Wales:					
Cardigan	9	20	45	55	0
Glamorgan	9	20	75	55	0
Brecon	17	40	60	55	0
Carmarthen	22	25	75	20	10
Pembroke	36	45	70	10	10
N. Britain	10	0	20	50	80
S.-W. Britain	38	20	60	25	15

If we focus attention on the bottom line of the chart, we see that inscriptions in the Irish ogom-alphabet have been added to the Latin inscriptions on 20% of the southwestern memorial stones. Filiation of the person commemorated, another Irish feature, occurs in 60% of the southwestern inscriptions. The *hic iacit* formula is Continental and found in 25% of southwestern inscriptions. 15% of the inscriptions are horizontal, while the remainder are placed vertically on the stones in Irish fashion.

Bu'lock called attention also to seventeen occurrences (to which one more from Lundy Island should now be added) of another non-Continental feature in the inscriptions of southwest Britain – the letter *I* written horizontally. Further, he cited four instances of the monogrammatic chi-rho symbol and two of the letters alpha and omega as an accompaniment to

[12] Cf. *ibid.*, p. 140. Two monolingual (non-Pictish) ogoms were excluded by Bu'lock as belonging to a different tradition. He referred to thirty-four inscriptions from Cornwall, Devon, and west Somerset, citing Macalister, *Corpus*, as his source. He made the important qualification that 'some of these inscriptions may be rather later than' the fifth- to seventh-century period covered by the table: no comprehensive classification and chronology of the southwestern monuments exists on the scale of Nash-Williams's work on Wales, although Radford, *The Early Christian Inscriptions*, provides an incomplete survey. Bu'lock however appears to have quietly dropped some items from Macalister (who in *Corpus*, I, records for southwest Britain thirty-nine separate stones, one with three, and another with two, different inscriptions) and his judgment in doing so has been deferred to here. There are eight ogom inscriptions in the southwest – not nine, as given by Bu'lock who perhaps counted both ogoms on the Lewannick stone (Macalister, *Corpus*, I.443–4, no. 467) of which one is a copy and apparently a correction of the other. Four memorial stones from Lundy Island, not given by Macalister, have been added to material analysed on the chart (for these see Selkirk & Selkirk, 'Lundy', pp. 197–9; Thomas *et al.*, 'Lundy, 1969', p. 139).

inscriptions on southwestern memorial stones.[13] The spread of the mono-grammatic form can be traced all over western christendom in the fifth century.[14] Two stones bearing the earlier, Constantinian, chi-rho symbol are also known from west Cornwall.[15] Of course the alpha and omega are another Southern import. The two examples are both devolved forms, suggesting that their source may not derive from direct fifth- or sixth-century Continental influence, but rather from later activity. Another interesting element in southwest British epigraphy is an instance of the *memoria*-formula, otherwise found once each in south Wales and north Britain, this being a common North African and Italian epigraphic type.[16]

Southwest British inscriptions not containing the formulae which we have been discussing consist mostly of names in the nominative or genitive case. The latter is not a Continental feature; nor, according to Nash-Williams,[17] is the former, although one wonders if the name alone in the nominative case might not be based on a Continental formula, as *N. (hic iacet)* or *N. (in pace)*. There are also two instances of formulae of types which, elsewhere in Britain, postdate those under consideration here.

One element on early inscribed stones in southwest Britain which has not so far received attention is a curved line arching over the top of the inscribed part of the monument. This is seen on the Welltown, Cuby, Doydon, and South Hill stones.[18] The latter two also bear the chi-rho symbol: on the South Hill stone there are two parallel arched lines, in the upper of which the chi-rho has its footing, while the chi-rho on the Doydon stone is above (and separate from) a single arch.[19] A comparable feature is perhaps found on one south Welsh inscribed stone.[20] Parallels do not appear to exist in Gaul, but a derivation from Spanish models seems

---

[13] Bu'lock, 'Early christian memorial formulae', p. 140. Stones with chi-rho: Macalister, *Corpus*, I, nos 478, 483, 486, 491. Stones with alpha and omega: *ibid.*, nos 469 and 481.

[14] Leclercq, 'Chrisme', especially cols 1503–15; Thomas, *The Early Christian Archaeology*, pp. 99–101, 106–10. Hamlin, 'A *chi-rho*-carved stone', supplied background and the useful map reproduced as Map L below.

[15] Illustrated in *Victoria History of the County of Cornwall*, I.414 (no. 13 in pl. II) and p. 417 (nos 21 and 21a in pl. III).

[16] 'INGENVI MEMORIA' (Macalister, *Corpus*, I.443–4, no. 466). Bu'lock, 'Early christian memorial formulae', p. 141; Thomas, *The Early Christian Archaeology*, pp. 103, 105–6.

[17] *The Early Christian Monuments*, p. 7.

[18] Macalister, *Corpus*, I, nos 460, 461, 478, 486, respectively. The curved line on the stone at Cuby, apparently hitherto unnoticed, was pointed out to me by Aidan MacDonald (University College, Cork).

[19] One chi-rho at Sourtown may have a short curved base, although Macalister (*Corpus*, I.470–1, no. 491) took this as part of the inscription.

[20] Nash-Williams, *The Early Christian Monuments*, p. 191, no. 335. Cf. nos 348 and 323, seventh- to ninth-century monuments from Pembrokeshire, bearing only crosses.

possible,[21] although the feature may be a local phenomenon. It warrants further study.

From this examination of the inscriptions and other glyptic features of the memorial stones of southwest Britain, it is obvious that the Insular component of putative Irish origin in the epigraphy of the region is very large. This conclusion has wider implications for the existence of intercommunal contacts within the British Isles, in view of the possibility that Irish settlers from Wales were involved.

Let us hypothesise, and test the evidence, that the Continental element in the southwest British monumental inscriptions is small, and Continental influence on the christianity of the region weak. The statistics on the *hic iacit* formula and the horizontal format do tend to this conclusion. One would expect in the case of strong Continental influence that there would have been more than the nine recorded uses of the *hic iacit* formula amid all those stones; the absolute figures for occurrences of this feature in north and south Wales are both in the twenties.

Strictly speaking, there is only one early inscribed monument in the Southwest displaying exclusively Continental features:[22] the memorial to Cunaide at Hayle in western Cornwall, which Thomas has dated to 'the latter part of the fifth century'.[23] The Constantinian chi-rho inscriptions also came from this area where there is some indication of what is, by Cornish standards, a fair amount of Roman activity which apparently went on into a sub-Roman phase during which these stones were produced. The *Optimi* and *Resteuta* stones from Lundy Island may also belong to this category.[24] Thomas has written that the stones 'need be no later than the beginning of the sixth century A.D. and I should have thought the curious use of "Optimi" is more at home in the fifth century'.[25] There is ceramic evidence for third- and fourth-century native British occupation of Lundy; the early mediaeval data are all funerary.[26] Lundy Island may have been especially

---

[21] Cf. Hübner, *Inscriptiones*, no. 11, and Vives, *Inscripciones cristianas*, pl. I, top (but the monument is pre-Constantinian); pl. II, left; pl. V, no. 10; pl. VI, no. 87; pl. VII, nos 489 and 493; pl. XIII, no. 505. The curved line of the Cuby stone looks like an attempt to indicate a smoothly rounded monument.

[22] On the criteria of Bu'lock, 'Early christian memorial formulae', plus 'Celtic' and 'Christian-Roman' formulae as given by Nash-Williams, *The Early Christian Monuments*, pp. 7–10.

[23] Thomas, *The Early Christian Archaeology*, p. 99; Macalister, *Corpus*, I.457–8, no. 479.

[24] Thomas *et al.*, 'Lundy, 1969', p. 139, and photographs given by Selkirk & Selkirk, 'Lundy', p. 197. Thomas interprets 'Optimi' as meaning 'To the best one', but it could represent the Celtic formula '(the stone of) N'. With regard to the other stone, see my remarks on name alone in the nominative case as an inscriptional form, p. 38 above.

[25] Thomas *et al.*, 'Lundy, 1969', p. 139.

[26] *Ibid.*, providing a very instructive account of an excavated early christian cemetery.

open to the seaborne influences which operated in the period with which we are concerned.[27] On the other hand, from north Wales we have five – probably six, and possibly more – inscribed stones exhibiting exclusively Continental features;[28] and from north Britain there are four, perhaps five.[29]

While the Continental content of early memorial stones in southwest Britain is relatively unimpressive in terms of the formulae and layout of the inscriptions, the concentration of the monogrammatic chi-rho symbol on memorial stones in the area is striking. The four occurrences of this symbol in southwest Britain should be compared with its absence from south Wales, two instances in north Wales and three in north Britain.[30] Since this symbol is distributed all over the Southwest and it appears in varied form, we do not have to do here with the products of a single workshop or related workshops; it is not impossible, however, that the occurrence of the motif on one stone inspired someone to include it on another. The alpha and omega, of which there are two examples in southwest Britain, are also found on one stone in north Britain[31] (an area in which the inscriptions are of a more markedly Continental nature than those in north Wales) and, dubiously, on a piece of a lead casket from north Wales.[32] These symbols, it should be pointed out, need not have been borrowed from the iconographic tradition of stone monuments. Charles Thomas has called attention to several possible types of models for cross-design: manuscript-decoration, portable objects, imported pottery with stamped ornament.[33] A chi-rho with pendant alpha and omega occurs on an imported sherd, apparently a roundel from a pottery lamp, found at Dinas Emrys in north Wales.[34] The monogrammatic chi-rho, sometimes with the pendant alpha and omega, occurs among the various stamped ornaments of two types of Mediterranean pottery – the African and Phocaean Red Slip Wares – which are found in the British Isles in our period,[35] but this particular ornament has not so far come to light there. Be that as it may, the occurrences of the chi-rho and

---

[27] 'The position of Lundy, which is accessible and visible from northeast Cornwall, north Devon and parts of south Wales, and which is also athwart the sea-lanes from the Mediterranean to south Wales, and from southern Ireland to north-east Cornwall (an early Irish settlement area) . . .' (*ibid.*, p. 140).

[28] Nash-Williams, *The Early Christian Monuments*, nos 33, 77, 78, 83, 101; in the case of no. 32 (pp. 61–3), the slab bearing the inscription has been trimmed and it is not clear that the inscription is horizontal. This is a problem elsewhere as well.

[29] Macalister, *Corpus*, I, nos 498, 516, 518, 520; no. 517 may comprise two names in the nominative case.

[30] See Map L for distribution of chi-rho-carved stones in the British Isles.

[31] Macalister, *Corpus*, I.493–5, no. 516.

[32] Nash-Williams, *The Early Christian Monuments*, pp. 59–61, no. 27.

[33] Thomas, *The Early Christian Archaeology*, pp. 115–17.

[34] *Ibid.*, pp. 116 and (illustration) 117.

[35] Hayes, *Late Roman Pottery*, pp. 348–9 and fig. 78 on p. 364 (Late Roman C, since renamed Phocaean Red Slip Ware), p. 228 and figs 54 and 55 on pp. 272 and 273 respectively (African Red Slip Ware).

possibly those of the alpha and omega, late though the examples of the last seem to be, suggest a concentration of Southern influence in southwest Britain in the early centuries of the middle ages.[36] Deferring final conclusions about the significance of the memorial stones, we pass on to the other category of evidence in the chapter.

The second body of archaeological evidence to be examined is the pottery. As has been mentioned in chapter I, ceramic imports reached the western British Isles in the late fifth, sixth, and seventh centuries from the Mediterranean and also from some area of western Europe, probably Atlantic France. Unlike the memorial stones, the pottery – table-wares (African Red Slip Ware and Phocaean Red Slip Ware), containers (Class B), kitchen- or domestic-wares (Classes D and E) – does not have an intrinsically religious character, although it seems likely that some wine and oil carried in the amphorae and lagenae of Class B would have enjoyed liturgical use in the British Isles. A significant relationship between finds of any of the imported wares and monastic or indeed religious sites has yet to be proved, however.[37] The possibility of such a connexion, and the solid evidence which this pottery provides of links with areas from which important early monastic influences could have been received, require that we analyse carefully the occurrence of imported pottery in the Southwest.[38]

Mediterranean imports are reported to have been found on the following sites in southwest Britain. (The survey, in which the quantity of pottery will be specified where possible, will begin with the easternmost site in Devon and move clockwise around the peninsula; see Map F.) For Red Slip Ware the following abbreviation-system is employed: RSW; ARSW (African); PRSW (Phocaean).

HIGH PEAK, SIDMOUTH, DEVON – hillfort on the Channel coast. Seven sherds from two vessels B i, seventy sherds from two vessels B ii, one sherd B misc.; a fairly large amount of pottery considering that only a small part of the much eroded hillfort was excavated.[39]

BANTHAM, DEVON – midden on the coast, termed a 'probable trading site' by the excavator. Twenty-one(?) sherds altogether of two(+) vessels B ii and two(?) vessels B misc.[40]

MOTHECOMBE, DEVON – considered by the excavator to be 'the remains of a temporary occupation by traders', coastal site. One sherd B i, four sherds from one(+) vessels B ii, one sherd B misc.[41]

[6] The monogrammatic chi-rho is definitely of later introduction to the British Isles than the Constantinian form, the earliest Insular examples of the former being dated to the late fifth century (Thomas, *The Early Christian Archaeology*, pp. 100–1, 106–7; Hamlin, 'A *chi-rho*-carved stone', p. 24).

[7] See p. 47 below.

[8] The ceramic data to follow have been obtained from Thomas, *A Provisional List*, supplemented as indicated.

[9] Pollard, 'Neolithic'.

[0] Fox, 'Some evidence', p. 61.

[1] Fox, 'Twenty-fifth report', pp. 79–80.

LYDFORD, DEVON – reports on excavation there speak of nothing earlier than a late Anglo-Saxon fortified town; inland site. 'Presumably residual' sherd of ARSW.[42]

LOOE ISLAND, CORNWALL – possible early monastic site on offshore island in the Channel.[43] Single sherd of B i; surface find.

TRETHURGY, ST AUSTELL, CORNWALL – 'round': 'The site seems to be that of a small farming community rather than the seat of a tribal ruler', according to the excavators; inland site about 2½ miles from the Channel. One sherd PRSW, sherds of two(?) vessels B i, one vessel B ii, one(?) vessel B iv, one(?) vessel B misc.; altogether fifty sherds from completely excavated site.[44]

ST MICHAEL CAERHAYS, CORNWALL – foreshore; context unknown. Single sherd of B i, surface find.[45]

GRAMBLA, WENDRON, CORNWALL – Romano-British settlement prolonged after Roman period; site about four miles inland. Sherds of (apparently P)RSW and of one vessel B iv.[46]

SAMSON, SCILLY ISLES – 'presumably domestic' timber-building. Sherds of two vessels B ii.[47]

TEAN, SCILLY ISLES – native homestead. About six sherds of one vessel B ii; about twelve sherds of one vessel B iv.[48]

? MAY'S HILL, ST MARTIN'S, SCILLY ISLES – hut-site occupied second to seventh centuries A.D. Possible sherd of B ii.[49]

CHUN CASTLE, MORVAH, CORNWALL – reoccupied Iron-Age hill-fort; inland, 1½ miles from the sea. Five sherds of one vessel B i.[50]

PHILLACK, CORNWALL – churchyard on estuary near the coast; the find-spot 'seems to be quite low down among graves'. Single sherd of PRSW.[51]

---

[42] Saunders, 'Lydford Castle', pp. 169 (quotation), 170, 136, 151: the find-spot was within the northwest bailey-rampart built on an Anglo-Saxon fortification; cf Radford, 'The later pre-Conquest boroughs', pp. 94–6.

[43] See pp. 98–103 below.

[44] Miles & Miles, 'Trethurgy', p. 147.

[45] In a communication of 30 May, 1977, Thomas wrote to me: '. . . found near beach: I subsequently noted traces of foundations of some structure nearby. Not excavated, no context known'.

[46] Saunders, 'The excavations at Grambla'.

[47] Butcher & Neal, 'Samson'; quotation from Thomas, *Exploration*, p. 186. Late phases of activity included a stone-building and four graves.

[48] Note in 'Medieval Britain in 1956', p. 147; Thomas, 'Imported pottery', p. 108. In a later phase of activity there was a building, probably a chapel, partly overlying christian graves.

[49] Thomas, 'The occupation'.

[50] Leeds, 'Excavations at Chun Castle'; Thomas, 'Evidence'.

[51] Thomas, 'Parish Churchyard, Phillack'; the quotation is from Thomas, communication of 30 May, 1977 (cf. n. 45 above).

GWITHIAN (SITE I), CORNWALL – native homestead by coast. One sherd each of PRSW and ARSW, sherds of two vessels B i, four vessels B ii, one vessel B misc.[52]

PERRAN SANDS, PERRANZABULOE, CORNWALL – area by coast, overwhelmed by sand. Surface-find of one sherd PRSW. Pottery from various periods is rather commonly found on the old land-surface in areas uncovered by sand here. St Piran's Oratory (not the find-spot of the sherd) on Perran Sands is the probable site of an early monastery, but there may have been one or more settlements of other type(s) in the area, which occupies more than two square miles.[53]

THE KELSIES, CUBERT, CORNWALL – midden; coastal. Sherds of one vessel B ii on the surface.

? TREVELGUE, CORNWALL – cliff-castle. There are 'stamped wares comparable with the Tintagel series' (RSW) reported from 1939 excavation; unconfirmed.[54]

MAWGAN PORTH, CORNWALL – late Dark-Age coastal settlement. Residual(?), worn sherd of B i.[55]

CONSTANTINE CHURCH, ST MERRYN, CORNWALL – midden at site of mediaeval chapel and holy well; coastal. Sherds of one(?) vessel B i.

HARBOUR COVE, PADSTOW, CORNWALL – context unknown. Single sherd of B misc., chance-find.[56]

? COASTAL SITE NEAR PADSTOW – Romano-British(+?) settlement. Sherds of what could be stamped RSW reported in nineteenth century; lost.[57]

---

[52] Thomas, *Gwithian*.

[53] Mr L. J. Penna kindly assisted me with local enquiries.

[54] Dunning, 'The Prehistoric Society', p. 111, is the fullest account; the 'alleged B wares' of Thomas, *A Provisional List*, p. 18, represent a misunderstanding.

[55] Bruce-Mitford, 'A Dark-Age settlement', especially pp. 195 and 176.

[56] See next item.

[57] In [Anon.,] 'Proceedings . . . 1849', p. 81, occurs the following notice, in conjunction with comment on a sherd of Samian ware, decorated with a cross, from Catterick Bridge, Yorkshire: 'It does not appear that any other example of a Christian symbol had been noticed on "Samian" ware: Mr. Thomas Kent, of Padstow, Cornwall, discovered some years since in the sands near that place, on a site which he considers to have been occupied by a Roman town or village, some curious fragments of fictile ware, marked with Crosses impressed. Roman coins, fibulae, and other remains were found at the spot. Mr. Kent very kindly sent some of these fragments for comparison with the specimen found at Catterick: they are of a dull red ware, not "Samian", but certainly, as he believes, of the same period. By long exposure to the weather the surface has become decayed, and it is difficult to form any decided conclusion in regard to the ornaments in question, or their claim to be regarded as Christian devices.' [Anon.,] 'Proceedings. . . 1850', p. 403, makes it clear that the site was on the Padstow side of the Camel estuary; therefore, the site may be that at Harbour Cove above, but is not that at St Minver below.

? ST MINVER, CORNWALL – Romano-British(+?) settlement in area of sand-dunes by the Camel estuary opposite Padstow. Sherds of amphorae reported in nineteenth century, now lost, perhaps of B-ware.[58]

KILLIBURY, EGLOSHAYLE, CORNWALL – hillfort; inland, less than eight miles from the sea by a fairly direct route out through the Camel estuary. Two sherds of one vessel B i found in minor excavation.[59]

TINTAGEL, CORNWALL – nature of site uncertain, with preference now for secular over monastic settlement; coastal. Sherds of twenty-six(+) vessels PRSW, ten(?) vessels ARSW, fourteen(+) vessels B i, ten(?) vessels B ii, three vessels B iv, twenty(?) vessels B misc.[60]

CANNINGTON, SOMERSET – sub-Roman cemetery, 'pottery in occupation-material in and among graves'; near coast. Sherds of one(+) vessel B ii and four(?) vessels B misc.[61]

? ILCHESTER, SOMERSET – context uncertain. Sherds of B ware reported; unconfirmed.[62]

SOUTH CADBURY, SOMERSET – reoccupied hillfort; inland. Sherds of one vessel each PRSW and ARSW, sixty sherds of one(+?) vessel B i, nine sherds of one vessel B ii, six sherds of one(?) vessel B iv, eighteen sherds of one(+) vessel B misc.[63]

GLASTONBURY TOR, SOMERSET – defensive secular settlement or monastery (the excavator, who proposes both identifications, prefers the first); inland. Three sherds of three vessels B i, five sherds of two vessels B ii, six sherds of four vessels B misc.[64]

GLASTONBURY MOUNT, SOMERSET – 'occupation layer under ? castle mound'.[65] Single sherd of B ii; other sherds apparently of B ware reported; lost.

CADBURY HILL, CONGRESBURY, SOMERSET – reoccupied Iron-Age hillfort; now about five miles inland, thought to have been closer to sea in sixth-century coastal conditions. Sherds of six(+) vessels PRSW, one vessel ARSW, three(+) vessels B i, eighteen(?) vessels B ii, four(?) vessels B misc.[66]

---

[58] Trollope, 'Roman remains'; Kent, 'Antiquities'; *Victoria History of the County of Cornwall*, V. 6 and 8.
[59] Miles *et al.*, 'Excavations at Killibury'.
[60] See n. 2 above.
[61] Rahtz, 'Pottery in Somerset', pp. 98–9, 101–3, 108–11, and 122 (quotation); Rahtz, 'Excavations on Glastonbury Tor', p. 67; note in 'Medieval Britain in 1962 and 1963', p. 237; Rahtz, 'Sub-Roman cemeteries', p. 194.
[62] Rahtz, 'Pottery in Somerset', pp. 101 and 123; Cox, *Government of the Town*.
[63] Alcock, 'Excavations at South Cadbury Castle'.
[64] See n. 4 above.
[65] Rahtz, 'Pottery in Somerset', pp. 111–12 and 123; cf. Bulleid & Morland, 'The Mound, Glastonbury'.
[66] See n. 5 above.

Occurrences in southwest Britain of E-ware imports, probably from Atlantic France, are as follows (see Map K).[67]

BANTHAM, DEVON – midden on the coast (same site as above). Base-sherd of E 2(?).

TRETHURGY, ST AUSTELL, CORNWALL – 'round' (native settlement); inland (same site as above). One sherd of E (?).

BAR POINT, ST MARY'S, SCILLY ISLES – surface of early field under sand. Sherds of one vessel E 1 and one E 5 lid.[68]

SAMSON, SCILLY ISLES – site as described above. Sherds of four(?) vessels E 1, one vessel E 2, and one vessel E 3.

TEAN, SCILLY ISLES – native homestead (same site as above). Fifty(+) sherds of five vessels E 1, one vessel E 2, two vessels E 3, and one vessel E 4.

MAY'S HILL, ST MARTIN'S, SCILLY ISLES – hut-site (as above). Eight sherds of four vessels E 1.

HELLESVEAN, ST IVES, CORNWALL – native homestead near coast. Single sherd of E 1.[69]

GWITHIAN (SITE I) – native homestead by coast (same site as above). Sherds of four(?) vessels of E 1 and one vessel of E 2.

THE KELSIES, CUBERT, CORNWALL – midden; coastal (same site as above). Surface-finds from one vessel E 1 and one vessel E 2(?).

The imports of Mediterranean pottery and E-ware not only have a different source but, as a glance at the accompanying maps will show, a different distribution-pattern in the British Isles. It is proposed to discuss separately the occurrence of each category in southwest Britain on the basis of material in the catalogue of finds given above.[70] The Mediterranean imports have found their way to a number of points in southwest Britain: twenty-five certain and five possible sites have been accounted for, above. There is a concentration of find-spots of these wares in the western part of the peninsula. The frequency of their recovery – especially as some are surface-finds or the products of very restricted excavation – and the apparently insignificant nature of some of the sites on which they have been found are beginning to suggest that they occur commonly in the region. The number of sites in the British Isles yielding this Mediterranean pottery has more

---

[67] The occurrence of D-ware mortaria and bowls in the British Isles is as yet too sparse to analyse, and will be merely noted here: May's Hill, St Martin's, Scilly Isles – one sherd D 3 or 4; Tintagel, Cornwall – sherds of two(?) vessels D 1 or 2 and two vessels D 5; Cadbury Congresbury, Somerset – sherds of one vessel D 3(?) and another of doubtful D-ware; South Cadbury, Somerset – sherds of one vessel D 3 (or 4?); and one site (Dinas Powys) in south Wales, two sites in Scotland, one site in Ireland.

[68] Ashbee, 'Excavations at Bar Point'.

[69] Guthrie, 'Dark Age sites' and 'Hellesvean'; Barton, 'Excavations at Hellesvean'.

[70] Pp. 41–5.

than doubled since Thomas's survey in 1959.[71] The number of 'new' find-spots of the pottery in the Southwest since 1959 is much greater than in other regions of the British Isles.[72] Doubtless these Mediterranean wares will come to light on more sites, and it would seem that a good many more such await discovery in Cornwall.

Three areas in the Southwest to which imported Mediterranean pottery was brought by sea may be distinguished:

(1) the Atlantic coast of Cornwall (including the Scilly Isles) with a heavy concentration of sites; and one such site, Tintagel, has produced a relatively large amount of pottery;

(2) the coast of the English Channel, with a scatter of sites of which one, High Peak, may have once contained a considerable quantity of these ceramic remains, and another – the carefully and completely excavated 'round' at Trethurgy, which the excavators had not considered to have been a settlement of any great importance – is perhaps instructive regarding volume of importation in that fifty sherds of several different types were found there;

(3) the upper reaches of the Bristol Channel, where pottery in some quantity reached two inland sites and where a relatively large amount has been found at Cadbury Congresbury near the coast (Dinas Powys, a site in south Wales, across the water from Congresbury, is probably also to be placed in this group.[73])

Few of these sites are far from the coast; the suggestion that pottery reached the inland sites by a secondary trade[74] seems a likely one. Not every coastal site need have been a primary point of import, of course. It is not impossible that secondary transportation brought these goods from the Atlantic region to one or both of the others, or to other parts of the British Isles. For the distribution makes it clear beyond question that the pottery was received in the Southwest directly from its Southern sources. On the present evidence, this southwestern region of the British Isles was especially visited by these contacts, containing as it does one half of the certain Insular pottery-producing sites.

---

[71] 'Imported pottery', pp. 107–8. The amount of the pottery found thus far does not testify to much volume of trade. His cautionary comment (p. 105, n. 27) that all of the pots of which there were then remains could have been carried in one ship can still be made, although the wide distribution of this material renders such a circumstance most unlikely.

[72] Such figures should be treated with caution as perhaps resulting from different intensity of excavation of early mediaeval sites, or even of awareness of the presence of these wares. On the last point, the pottery has become widely known and looked for by archaeologists in the British Isles in the past thirty years.

[73] Alcock, *Dinas Powys*.

[74] Thomas, 'Are these the walls of Camelot?', pp. 29–30; Thomas, *The Early Christian Archaeology*, pp. 24–5.

E-ware is of sparser occurrence in southwest Britain than the Mediterranean wares. At the Trethurgy site, to which a possible diagnostic value regarding volume of pottery imported has been attributed above, only one E-ware sherd was found. The distribution of E-ware shows a concentration in the far southwest, where Gwithian and Tean have produced a good number of finds of this pottery by comparison with other sites where it occurs. Compelling negative evidence on this point is provided by the absence of E-ware from Tintagel and the Somerset sites, although at Dinas Powys in south Wales a relatively large amount of it, a minimum of nine pots, was found.[75] A comparison of the occurrence of E-ware in the Southwest with that in the rest of Britain shows at least that material brought from points south need not show a concentration in the southwest peninsula as the first landfall, since E-ware, a Southern import, is mainly found elsewhere.

The implication of these imports for early monasticism in southwest Britain (as for other parts of the British Isles where they occur) is that where the exchange of goods took place the exchange of ideas might also, especially in this period when travel and communication by sea were almost inevitably by cargo-vessel. A link between pottery-importation and early monasticism in southwest Britain would receive some support from the occurrence of finds on ecclesiastical or specifically monastic sites in the region. Although this does not appear to be demonstrable beyond question in a single case,[76] a few of the sites where imported pottery has been found are almost certainly of a religious character, and the nature of a considerable number of sites is sufficiently ambiguous that they might possibly be ecclesiastical. In any case, there would seem to have been an opportunity for the penetration of ideas brought with the Mediterranean pottery all along the coasts of the southwest peninsula except in north Devon, and especially on the western portion of that peninsula. The chances for associated ideological influence are less, and more restricted in area, in the case of E-ware. Nevertheless, the concentration of its find-spots in the far Southwest (with the sites at Gwithian and Hellesvean, St Ives, straddling the Hayle estuary) should be noted. This is the area for which sub-Roman christianity and Continental, perhaps monastic, influence were suggested on epigraphic evidence, and E-ware, probably produced in western France, may be evidence of similar, albeit later, lines of communication.[77] Returning to the

---

[5] Thomas, *A Provisional List*.
[6] The specific context of finds at the undoubted Celtic religious foundations of Phillack and Constantine Church is imprecise; that of the Cannington material is unknown until publication, and there is some question about the identification of christian and pagan graves on this site (most are aligned east–west).
[7] In the rest of the British Isles, the distribution of E-ware does not correlate with a high incidence of Continental features on early christian memorial stones, being almost absent from north Wales and not present to any extent in north Britain. Its overall distribution suggests, if anything, a tendency to occur in Ireland and in areas of Irish influence. See Map K. On the date of E-ware see Thomas, *A Provisional List*, p. 27.

Mediterranean imports, we can take a suggestive example of a setting for possible transmission of monastic ideas in the area of the Camel estuary, with the potsherd(s?) at Harbour Cove, about one mile from the early monastic site at Padstow, and others at Killibury, 2 to 2½ miles from the site of the monastery called *Docco*. Charles Thomas has suggested that cenobitic monasticism was introduced to the British Isles, and first to southwest Britain, via the contacts by which imported Mediterranean pottery was obtained.[78] This assigns to the region an important role at the earliest stage of the monastic movement in the British Isles.

It is time to consider the overall implications of the evidence examined in these chapters in relation to the subject of early monasticism and southwest Britain, using the findings to test Charles Thomas's hypothesis just mentioned. The postponed conclusion about the testimony of the early christian memorial stones claims attention first. Their Irish features attest specifically to influence from Ireland and/or Wales in the commemoration of the dead in the Southwest, and generally to settlement from either area in the region, settlement which could have included monastic foundations. The Continental tradition of christian memorial epigraphy appears to be part of the general influence of the Gallican on the British Church and to have been strongest and longest-operative in areas of Britain where Roman culture persisted; in such regions contact was maintained with the neighbour-Church to the south and there was a receptive audience to Continental developments. In Cornwall there is only one area where these conditions can be seen to have been present: the far Southwest. One might expect any monastic influences from Gaul to have entered in such a context. The concentration of instances of chi-rho-carved memorial stones in the Southwest, on the other hand, suggests an openness to Southern influences, in this case in the sphere of christian iconography. There may be support here for Thomas's view of the Southwest as the area which first received the monastic movement. Should the inspiration for the use of the chi-rho symbol have been by any chance stamped design on imported pots, such use would not be independent evidence for Southern contacts, however.

The saint's Lives examined in chapter II do not support the idea of an important formative role for southwest Britain in Insular monasticism. This having been said, the very restricted nature of this evidence should be emphasised. Most of the material in the early mediaeval *uitae* has only the most tenuous (if any) link with a late fifth- to seventh-century state of affairs. Only the *Vita (Prima) Sancti Samsonis* would seem to have any amount of information relating to the career or time of its subject. Samson, of south Welsh origin, travels by way of Cornwall to Brittany and founds a monastery and a see there. The only thing in the Cornish section of the *uita* which harmonises with the idea of that region being the original *locus* of monasticism in the British Isles is the *Docco* episode. Samson finds a

[78] Thomas, *The Early Christian Archaeology*, pp. 22–7; Thomas, 'Imported Late-Roman Mediterranean pottery', pp. 251–2.

monastery in existence in Cornwall, one at which discipline has grown lax. This could be significant: Samson may be visiting one of the initial monastic foundations in Britain which had been in existence long enough for its observance to have declined. We have previously met with a St Docco who would seem to have held a place in hagiological tradition as a very early figure: his death is entered for the year 473 in the *Annals of Ulster* ('Quies Docci episcopi sancti Britonum abbatis'). Mention has been made of the existence of monasteries bearing the name Dochou in Wales.[79] Loth and Doble suggested that the Cornish monastery was a daughter-foundation of a Welsh house.[80]

Yet the hagiological tradition of the early *uitae* as a whole has south Wales as the area from which monastic influences spread. One gathers from the *uitae*, however, that Brittany was especially in communication with southwest Britain. One may ask why, if the earliest British monasteries were located in the Southwest, these were not involved in the establishment of the Church among the Continental Britons. Possibly foundations such as *Docco* and Tintagel(?) were in contact with Wales (and perhaps Ireland) across the sea which they faced, and had little to do with the hinterland behind them. Possibly the first monasteries were not established on the south coast of the peninsula, whence contact with Brittany would have been likely; then, at a later date, a fresh impetus from the newer Welsh foundations reached Cornwall and Brittany. Possibly the connexion with Wales in the *uitae* is the result of the importance of the Welsh monasteries, and lack of importance of the old Cornish ones, at the time when the *uitae* were composed. The fact remains that a state of affairs such as Thomas has proposed, if ever in existence, has been essentially lost to such of British hagiography as remains to us.

The obscure and traditionally early figure of Cairnech presented in Irish sources – if there is any accuracy in his description as Cornish – could be part of monastic influence on the Irish Church from Cornwall. Of course, if the monastery of *Rosnat* in Irish sources were Tintagel, an important, perhaps *the* important inspiration of Irish monasticism could be traced to the Southwest – but this identification is a fading possibility.

Often the earliest and most important stages of change are obscure: perhaps the first monasteries in the British Isles largely escaped mention in what was written down at a later date. One would have to argue this in order to maintain Thomas's hypothesis in the face of the evidence considered here. An alternative scenario may be set beside that of Thomas, however, while yet allowing that cenobitic monasticism was introduced directly from the Mediterranean via the links which brought the pottery, as he has proposed. It may be outlined as follows. The pottery was given in exchange for commodities, and of these the most desirable to the people at the Mediterranean end of this far-flung trade – perhaps tin and other ores –

See p. 15 above.
Loth, 'La Vie la plus ancienne', pp. 329–30, and p. 22; Doble, *The Saints of Cornwall*, V.90.

49

were in southwest Britain. Thus a good deal of pottery reached that region. While there was a ready market for the pottery and associated goods in the Southwest, it was not fertile soil for monastic ideas, whether these were carried by Thomas's 'returning tourists or pilgrims', in books, or howsoever: in much of the region christianity was feebly established or absent and the Church nowhere well organised. These ideas did take root elsewhere, namely in southeast Wales, where there are traces of a Church then organised on the territorial Roman model, and the monastic movement spread thence westward over Wales (and ultimately to Ireland perhaps) and south to Cornwall and Brittany. This picture is in keeping with the southwestern evidence, which suggests a derivative rather than a primary role for the region in the monastic movement (and to some extent in more general christian practice) in the British Isles.

In chapters II and III we have considered discrete types of evidence, which represent or purport to represent information about monasticism in southwest Britain from the late fifth century to the seventh. The existence of monasteries in the region is established beyond reasonable doubt by that called *Docco* and the monastery which Samson founded in Cornwall, at which the author of the *Vita (Prima) Sancti Samsonis* received much of his information. If monasteries in southwest Britain were important at an early date, for which idea there is singularly little evidence, it is not likely that they remained so for a very long time.

IV

EVIDENCE OF EARLY CORNISH
RELIGIOUS COMMUNITIES

A number of writings relating to Cornwall from the ninth century on provides information about religious communities there before the Norman conquest. Consideration will be given to eight texts or groups of texts, taken up in an order roughly chronological: the ninth-century profession of obedience of a Cornish Bishop Kenstec to the archbishop of Canterbury; a tenth-century list of Brittonic names including many of Cornish saints; tenth-century writings relating to St Germans; others of the tenth and later centuries concerning establishments of St Petroc in Cornwall; two tenth-century charters surviving in later copies; evidences of the tenth century and later about the place known as St Neot; Domesday Book and related materials; and documents of the twelfth century and later relating to the priories of St Carroc, Lammana, and St Anthony in Roseland.

I. A PROFESSION OF OBEDIENCE

Among twenty-nine professions of canonical obedience made by bishops of various English sees to archbishops of Canterbury in the late eighth and ninth centuries is one addressed to Archbishop Ceolnoth between 833 and 870 by a Cornish bishop named Kenstec.[1] In the words of an editor of these texts, 'the episcopal profession was a regular and normal feature in the making of a bishop in the Anglo-Saxon Church at that time';[2] the profession of Kenstec is typical of its counterparts in the formulae which it employs. Obviously the document represents a stage in the assimilation of Cornwall into Anglo-Saxon England, underway in the ninth century.[3]

The description of Kenstec's see is unusual among the professions,

---

Canterbury, Cathedral Library, Register A, fo 292.

Richter, *Canterbury Professions*, p. xlviii; for the text see *ibid.*, p. 24 (no. 27), and Birch, *Cartularium*, II.145, no. 527.

See the Anglo-Saxon Chronicle, *s. aa.* 815 and 838; will of King Alfred (Sawyer, *Anglo-Saxon Charters*, p. 422, no. 1507; ed. & transl. Harmer, *Select English Historical Documents*, no. 11); Asser, *De Rebus Gestis Ælfredi Regis*, §81 (ed. Stevenson, pp. 67–8).

however. He is 'humilis licet ad indignus episcopalem sedem in gente Cornubia in monasterio quod lingua Brettonum appellator [*sic*] Dinuurrin electus'.[4] Nowhere else among these documents is *monasterium* used to designate a see. Whereas reference to Anglo-Saxon bishops in terms of the particular people in their care is paralleled,[5] the style of Kenstec is exceptionally vague: he is not really said to be bishop *of* anything. In these circumstances, we may enquire whether Kenstec might be an example of what has been conceived as a monastic bishop, with authority not over a diocese with fixed territorial limits but wherever the influence of his monastery extended. Caution dictates that the possibility merely be noted, for this dubious status is not necessarily implied by mention of *monasterium* in connexion with an episcopal see.[6]

In any case, the profession of Kenstec indicates the existence in mid-ninth-century Cornwall of a *monasterium* called *Dinuurrin*, which from its Cornish name, the Cornish name of its bishop, and its early date must have been a Celtic establishment. As has been pointed out in the Introduction, the use of *monasterium* need not imply the presence of monks living under the control of an abbot according to a rule, for a group of clergy serving a church could also be meant.[7]

Discussion in the remainder of this section will be devoted to locating the *monasterium* called *Dinuurrin*. The place-name appears to have been lost. Doble undermined the identification with Dingerein Castle in Gerrans parish,[8] which is in any case linguistically impossible without numerous emendations.[9] Identification with Castle Teen-Urne at Lowertown near Helston is linguistically possible, but the site is decidedly unpromising, being without ecclesiastical associations and located in southwest Cornwall:

[4] *indignus*, Birch; *dignus*, Richter, 'the humble Kenstec, elected though unworthy to the [or "an"] episcopal seat among the people in Cornwall in the monastery which in the language of the Britons is called Dinuurrin.' An alternative, even preferable, manuscript-reading is *Dinnurrin*; however, Oliver Padel has advised me that the spelling with *-uu-* is much more likely in a ninth-century Cornish place-name.

[5] Birch, *Cartularium*, I.407–8, no. 292 (cf. Richter, *Canterbury Professions*, pp. 3–4, no. 3): 'Scio enim uere quod me tam indignum aecclesiae quae est in prouincia Huuicciorum cum episcopatus officio praeesse iussisti', with pre-Conquest rubric '. . . Uuicciorum Episcopi'. See also *ibid.*, p. 17 (no. 19) 'Lindisfarorum antistes' (cf. Birch, *Cartularium*, I.596–7, no. 425).

[6] So Duine (reviewing Taylor, *The Celtic Christianity*), *Analecta Bollandiana* 31 (1915/16) 575. An interesting parallel with the language of Kenstec's profession is the following entry at the end of a list of Galician sees and parishes in the late sixth-century Spanish *Parochiale*: 'Ad sedem Britonorum ecclesias que sunt intro Britones una cum monasterio Maximi et que in Asturiis sunt' (ed. David, *Études* p. 44). Both concern fringe British areas of a regular diocesan Church. David (*ibid.*, pp. 57–8) considered that the foregoing refers to a monastic bishopric of Celtic type, but cf. Thompson, 'Britonia', p. 203.

[7] See p. 3 above.

[8] *Saint Gerent*, pp. 8–9; cf. Henderson, *apud* Doble, *ibid.*, pp. 17–19.

[9] Information from Oliver Padel.

there is almost no reason to think that that area was under Anglo-Saxon control in the ninth century.[10]

Siting of *Dinuurrin* at St Germans in southeast Cornwall on the grounds that bishops are known to have sat there in the tenth and eleventh centuries[11] is effectively ruled out by the existence of a Cornish name *Lanalet* or *Lannaled* for the *monasterium* at the latter place.[12] The point is important. A *lan* was the enclosure of sacred ground on which the religious house would stand: if the latter bore a name in *lan*, there is no room for an alternative designation. *Dinuurrin* and *Lanalet* were separate places, each the seat of a bishop in Cornwall for some part of the early middle ages.

An attractive identification of the site of *Dinuurrin* as Bodmin has been proposed, initially because of the similarity of its second element *uurrin* to the name of the holy hermit Uuron whom St Petroc was traditionally held to have replaced at Bodmin.[13] A plausible emendation of-*ri*-to-*o*-would give *Dinuuron*, now correlating perfectly with early forms of the Cornish saint's name.[14] *Din* is a normal Cornish place-name element meaning fortification'.[15] Although it is not common for a saint's name to be combined with a secular place-name element such as *din*, instances are known; from Wales, Caergybi, 'the fortification of (St) Cybi', designating a monastery founded within an earlier Roman fort, provides a suggestive parallel.[16]

Dinuurrin strictly speaking should have reference to a fortified site at Bodmin. Castle Canyke,[17] a large hill-fort located a mile southwest of the

[10] The Anglo-Saxon Chronicle reports that 'King Ecgberht ravaged in Cornwall from east to west' in 815, but this was a military foray, not an extension of permanent control. The battle of *Hehil* in 722 (cf. Hoskins, *The Westward Expansion*, p. 19) is exceedingly unlikely to have taken place at Hayle in west Cornwall. On Castle Teen-Urne see four essays by Charles Henderson: *apud* Doble, *Saint Gerent*, p. 19; 'The ecclesiastical history', p. 479; *The Cornish Church Guide*, p. 100; *apud* Henderson & Coates, *Old Cornish Bridges*, p. 99. In a note to the first of these, Doble remarked that a small earthwork there yielded upon partial excavation in 1936 no 'ecclesiastical remains'. According to Norman Quinnell, Archaeological Field Officer for the Ordnance Survey, no earthworks are visible (report at the Cornwall County Record Office, Truro).

[1] Haddan & Stubbs, *Councils*, III.674–5, 702, 704.

[2] See pp. 60–6 below.

[3] Doble, *The Saints of Cornwall*, III.88, n. 21, and his *Saint Petrock*, pp. 27–8. Cf. Loth, 'La Vie la plus ancienne', p. 280, n. 2. The *Vitae Sancti Petroci* are discussed on pp. 66–9 below.

[4] Suggested by Oliver Padel.

[5] See Padel, *Cornish Place-name Elements*, p. 84, *s.v.* **dyn*.

[6] Even so, we cannot be sure that the Bodmin hermit of later legend was, at the time when the house of St Petroc was established, anything more than a name attached to the site thereof. The equivalent, Guron, is attested as a saint's name with reference to the church of St Goran near the south coast of Cornwall (see pp. 56–60 below); its patron is identified with the Bodmin saint in the second *Vita Sancti Petroci*, § 19 (ed. Grosjean, 'Vies et miracles', p. 163).

[7] Cf. Gover, 'The Place-names of Cornwall', p. 99.

parish-church, would seem too distant to have given its name, assuming that this was ever *Dinuurrin*, to a religious house at Bodmin. On the ridge to the north of the church and the centre of the town are some place-names suggestive of fortification. 'Berry' designated a considerable block of property in the Tithe Award of 1840. The area is reached by Berry Lane, and the valley running westward from Bodmin is called Berrycombe. These names derive from Old English *burh*.[18] The neck of the same ridge, east of the lands called Berry, is reached by Castle Street going up Castle Hill, which has given its name to Castlehill farm on its crest.[19] Neither the Ordnance Survey nor such fieldwork as has been possible in present conditions has identified the fortification(s) evinced by these place-names, although a local antiquary, Mrs M. Irwin, maintains that there is such a site at Castlehill farm. Certainly the ridge is well suited to early settlement by its defensiveness and access to abundant water-supply.[20] A site there would be qualified by location to have given its name to a predecessor of the later Bodmin religious houses.

There is evidence that the fifteenth-century Berry Tower on the top of the ridge, the remains of the Chapel of the Holy Rood, stands on an ecclesiastical site of some antiquity and importance. This is known to have been a guild-chapel, but uncharacteristically to have possessed rights of burial and, apparently, of baptism.[21] J. H. Adams has cogently argued that Berry and its chapel are vestiges of an early mediaeval settlement and its church, which both came into existence earlier than the town and religious establishment in the valley below.[22] In particular, he has called attention to the foundation by Petroc, according to the second *Vita Sancti Petroci*, of 'two habitations, one on top of the northern hill (tumulus) and the other where St Uuron had lived, in the valley by the spring',[23] and identified the

---

[18] Berrycombe, attested in early fourteenth-century forms, is 'valley of the fort or stronghold' (*ibid.*, p. 98). The street is also mentioned in the fourteenth century (Truro, Royal Institution of Cornwall, MS. Henderson 18).

[19] This street also receives fourteenth-century mention, of which one form, Carstret, may be a variant with Cornish *caer* (*ibid.*).

[20] The main spring at Bodmin rises on its southern flank (Ussher *et al.*, *The Geology*, p. 181).

[21] Maclean, *The Parochial and Family History*, I.199–201; Adams, 'Berry Tower', p. 125.

[22] 'Berry Tower.'

[23] The passage reads in full: 'Seruus uero Dei Petrocus, ducatu directus angelico locum adeptus aptatum, inuitatis fratribus, cellam ex lapidibus aggressus construere, permanere ibi disposuit. Est enim uallis inter montes duos media fontibus satis irrigua, aruo quidem sacionali, consitiuo et pascuali idonea, et quia primitus a monachis inhabitata et exculta est, dicitus Bothmenaa, id est Mansio Monachorum. Quo in loco, procedente tempore, multiplicatis fratribus, duo construxit habitacula, unum supra tumulum borealem et aliud, ubi sanctus Wronus habitauerat, in ualle preter fontem. Extat et adhuc, non procul a cella superiore, in montis supercilio, fons eius admodum salubris, in cuius riuulo horis nocturnis interdum cingulo tenus positus orasse dicitur aliquadium' (§ 20; ed Grosjean, 'Vies et miracles', pp. 163–4). Adams also suggested that an episode in

54

site of the former as Berry. Adams proposed that the monks moved from an earlier monastery on the hill down to the valley where we later find their successors, and that eventually a corresponding shift of lay people took place from a settlement on the hill to the neighbourhood of the monastery below.

Such a change of site provides an explanation of why, if *Dinuurrin* is to be located at Bodmin, it bears a different name. Bodmin is now regarded as comprising the secular place-name element *bod*, 'dwelling', and *menehi*, 'sanctuary'.[24] Bodmin, 'the dwelling by the sanctuary', is a name which, as Henderson commented, 'does not suggest an ancient religious establishment but a secular settlement growing up round a church'.[25] Bodmin thus began as the name of the town, not the religious house. The latter, in the identification proposed here, was originally called *Dinuuron*, a name taken from a fortification near which, or possibly within which, it stood on the ridge. Ecclesiastical, perhaps monastic, expansion into the valley attracted a lay settlement which acquired the name Bodmin. Eventually this name was transferred to the religious settlement and, perhaps as the result of a shift of activity away from the higher site, the old name *Dinuuron* was forgotten. The profession of Kenstec was made before the original name fell out of use.

Bodmin is eminently suitable – as the site of the *monasterium* called *Dinuurrin* in which Bishop Kenstec had his seat – in view of the wealth, influence, and episcopal associations attaching to the heirs of St Petroc, as attested in documents to be considered in sections 4 and 7 below.[26] Furthermore, ninth-century Anglo-Saxon participation in ecclesiastical affairs is reputed to have taken place in this part of Cornwall with the grant by King Ecgberht to the bishop of Sherborne of one and probably two large estates west of Bodmin.[27] There can be few reservations about the identi-

the *Miracula Sancti Petroci* in which a woman who had come to Bodmin was cured while praying 'in oratorio supra collem' (ed. Grosjean, *ibid.*, pp. 171–2) refers to Berry.

[24] Henderson, 'Concerning Bodmin Priory', pp. 27–8; cf. Gover, 'The Place-names of Cornwall', pp. 97–8, and Padel, *Cornish Place-name Elements*, pp. 23–5, *s.v.* *bod*, and p. 163, *s.v.* *meneghy*.

[25] 'Concerning Bodmin Priory', p. 28.

[26] A worn inscribed stone at Tawna in Cardinham parish near Bodmin was held by Macalister (*Corpus*, I.437–8, no. 459) to mention a Bishop Titus; however, Elizabeth Okasha has advised me that the inscription cannot be made out, and his reading was also questioned by Henderson, *apud* Doble, *A History*, p. 9, and Radford, *The Early Christian Inscriptions*, p. 7; cf. Hencken, *The Archaeology*, pp. 242 and 244.

[27] The subject of a tenth-century forged document (ed. Birch, *Cartularium*, II.276–9, nos 614–15, and Robinson, *The Saxon Bishops*, pp. 27–8; cf. Whitelock, *English Historical Documents*, pp. 892–3) and the apparently authentic letter of Archbishop Dunstan to King Æthelred the Unready (edd. Napier & Stevenson, *The Crawford Collection*, pp. 18–19 and 102–10, no. VII; cf. Sawyer, *Anglo-Saxon Charters*, p. 374, no. 1296; translated by Whitelock, *English Historical Documents*, pp. 892–4, no. 229).

fication of *Dinuurrin* as Bodmin. No other candidates suggest themselves, leaving the unlikely alternative of traceless disappearance of a religious house important enough to have a bishop in the ninth century. Thus consideration of *Dinuurrin* as an early monastery merges with that of Bodmin and will be continued when texts referring to the latter are taken up in section 4 below.

2. A LIST OF SAINTS' NAMES

The next source is a list of forty-eight Brittonic personal names in Insular script in Rome, Biblioteca Apostolica Vaticana, MS. Reginensis latinus 191.[28] In the following transcription, the manuscript's punctuation and arrangement of the names in lines have been reproduced. A point under a letter indicates an uncertain reading, and a point under a blank denotes an illegible letter; a name designating the patron-saint of a church or chapel in Cornwall is underlined, the line being broken in uncertain cases.

fo iiv salamun ·

guenosa*m* · barmot · cuncar · ¹cioc · guenb .

ruaton · guicmor · iust · entenin ·

gerent · filii · rumon · comet · meler

sibillon · maucan · achobran · berion ·

  en

felec · guidian · erbec · nioth · propus ·

latoc · luidin · pierguin · geuedenoc ·

fo iir ciguai · ..nu · ..... cu · iogarun · gernun ·

lallu · be...en · entr.r. · bie · elenn ·

austoll · megunn · iodechall · crite ·

guron · euai · gu.ai · memai · iti ·

aboel ·

About half of these names are of saints associated with Cornwall, and some, like Felec and Latoc, distinctively so. The name Iodechall designates a known saint apparently unconnected with any Cornish ecclesiastical site. Two others are attested as personal names but not of saints. The connexion of the list with Cornwall can be demonstrated in another and rather impressive way. Map M shows that the order of names of the list, repre-

---

[28] I owe my knowledge of the existence of this text to Oliver Padel, with whom the marked and previously unrealised association of the list with Cornwall was discovered: see now our detailed study – Olson & Padel, 'A tenth-century list'.

sented by consecutive numbers, sometimes correlates with the geographical location of the churches having patron-saints with these names.[29] Especially notable is the occurrence together on the list (numbers 9–13) of the patrons of the four parishes of the Roseland Peninsula and of adjacent Ruan Lanihorne (in south central Cornwall), which would seem to be beyond coincidence. The correlation is continued by three couplets and the association of numbers 39, 40, 42, 43, 44, and 47 within one area. It may also be remarked that, after leaving the Roseland group, following the dedications of identifiable saints takes us on a tour around the far southwest of Cornwall.

Palaeographical and linguistic evidence provide some guidance as to the date and provenance of the list. To texts in Breton Caroline script of the period *ca* 885–*ca* 915 the names were appended in Insular minuscule of that turn-of-the-century period (at the earliest) or perhaps of a somewhat later date in the tenth century.[30] The language of the list is Old Cornish or Old Breton, consistent with this dating.[31] The folios bearing these texts, which subsequently were used as scrap-binding around an earlier, ninth-century, Reims manuscript, attest to the movement of scribe(s) and/or manuscript across the English Channel.

Unless there is some connexion of the names with the Latin text immediately preceding them,[32] a natural assumption is that the bare list is a set of notes of names taken from and/or to be supplied in some text or other. Some negative inferences can be drawn about the nature of the list. The names of the saints are not arranged in the order of their feasts in the ecclesiastical calendar. As much hagiological tradition as has survived does not show these saints to be a group of companions or blood-relations, or of the same regional origin, or all martyrs, all virgins, or all confessors. The

[29] Numbers on the map are placed over the relevant church- or chapel-sites. In cases of uncertain identification of listed names with those of patron-saints, the numbers are followed by a query. In cases in which a name is borne by a saint who is patron of two or more establishments, the geographical correlation of proximate saints on the list suggests that one particular church is meant: its site is indicated by an upright number, the other(s) by that number italicised. Parish-boundaries, while perhaps anachronistic, have also been indicated where appropriate: a broken line indicates cases of uncertainty, as an accompaniment either to a queried number or to the less likely alternative (as just explained).

[30] Professor Bernhard Bischoff has kindly given me his judgment about the Caroline minuscule script and made a suggestion about the date of the Insular script: these views are followed here.

[31] Information from Oliver Padel.

[32] The texts in Caroline minuscule script which come before the list are Pseudo-Seneca's *De Moribus* followed by an extract about Seneca from Jerome's *De Viris Inlustribus*. The latter begins 'Lucius · Bennius · Senica ·' (*sic*; or 'Beninus'), goes on to explain why Seneca is included 'in catalogo sanctorum' and concludes 'Hic ante b[i]ennium antequam Petrus et Paulus martyrio coronarentur a nerone interfectus est'; the first Brittonic name follows on the same line.

only factors common to any sizable number of names on the list are the possession of these by saints and the connexion with Cornwall. One agent for the ordering of the names on the list is identifiable: the location of the churches of which the saints are known patrons. The marked geographical correlation described above leads to the hypothesis that the names of saints might stand for places – that is, for the churches of which they were patrons – and/or, by extension, associated monasteries, properties, or parishes. The idea appeals in a Cornish setting, where saints' names are components of so many place-names. Several possibilities exist for the purpose of the list, viewed in this light. It might record properties belonging to a church, monastery, or episcopal see, or represent a group of daughter-monasteries, or constitute a list of churches or parishes to be used in connexion with some aspect of ecclesiastical organisation.

The list seems unlikely to be a record of properties. While strictly contemporary Cornish material for comparison is lacking, Breton monastic estates in tenth- and eleventh-century charters of the Cartulary of Landévennec are usually designated by place-names in *lan*, *tref*, etc., not by simple personal names. Occasionally, however, a property in the cartulary is referred to by the name of a saint only.[33] The impression received is that these names might designate a *plebs* or *uicarium*, that is, a parish. Possibly such a unit was understood to apply to the list in question. Yet from late eleventh-century Cornwall, Domesday manors such as *Lannachebran* and *Ecglosberria*, belonging respectively to Saints Achebrannus and Berriona who have their counterparts on the list, display names much more likely to have been written in our text if properties were being designated.[34] And in as much as these properties were possessed by no one except the saints in question and the communities serving their churches, such Domesday tenures are incompatible with the theory that the list comprised properties of some unspecified landholder.[35] This problem remains if the names are

---

[33] Edd. Le Men & Ernault, 'Cartulaire': charters no. 10 (Morcat), no. 14 (Sulian and Moelian), no. 19 (Rioc, and cf. nos 11 and 21); nos 17, 19 and 43 (Buduc); nos 26 and 43 (Silin); no. 57 (Creuen). Cf. nos 13 and 14 (Brithiac – not a saint's name but an instructive example of the optional use of *plebs*). There are instances where *plebs* or *uicarium* is granted as property in these charters.

[34] Also *Lanbrabois* (Exon., fo 206r) (Propus), *Languihenoc* (Exon., fo 202r) (Geuedenoc: this name-form is corrupt; cf. *Lan Wethinocke* in the roughly contemporary *Vita Sancti Petroci*), *Lanpiran* (Exon., fo 206v) (Pierguin?). *Nietestou* (Exon., fo 207r) (Nioth) is an English compound; no Cornish place-name is known. A small group of Domesday manor-names includes the counterparts to Maucan, perhaps Guenosăm, possibly Gernun, preceded by Cornish or Latin for 'saint', essentially uncompounded forms paralleled in Landévennec charters.

[35] Also lands of SS. Probus, Niet?, Pieranus?, Germanus?, Goranus (Exon., fo 72r, property not named), and the presence of *Languihenoc* among the lands of St Petroc.

taken to represent proprietary churches belonging to a monastery and/or mother-church.[36]

If the list is meant to indicate a group of daughter-monasteries, the identity of the mother-house becomes a question. A concentration in south-central Cornwall of churches dedicated to the saints listed suggests that a mother-house might have been in this area. There is evidence for the existence of monasteries of St Probus and, more questionably, SS. Goran and Entenin here, but these names are on the list. Additional putative monasteries of SS. Keverne, Buryan, and Neot elsewhere in Cornwall are unsuitable for the same reason. Perhaps the ultimate monastic founder was St Petroc who is conspicuously absent from the list. If so, it is strange that the churches dedicated to the saints listed and the area associated with Petroc (through dedications and Domesday properties which tend to lie farther north in Cornwall) overlap so little.[37] The tendency of the churches whose patrons are on the list to have a southern distribution would better suit a relationship with a parent-monastery at *Lanalet* in southeast Cornwall, where St Germanus was regarded as patron (assuming that Gẹrnụn on the list is not he). There is also the possibility that the head-house has disappeared without leaving any clear trace; however, the closer one approaches the tenth- and eleventh-century documentation, the less likely seems the total disappearance of an important monastery. All things considered, a sibling monastic relationship of which a full or even partial extent is outlined by the list is not easy to perceive in terms of what we know about Cornwall, although we lack a secure basis for its firm rejection.

Concerning the third proposal for the nature and purpose of the list if the names are taken to represent places, Charles Thomas has suggested that it sets out a number of proto-parishes, areas of influence of churches which might or might not pass into the stabilised parochial system which emerged after the Norman conquest.[38] We have seen that the simple name of a saint may have designated parishes in the Cartulary of Landévennec. I have not made an exhaustive search for examples of lists of parishes, but texts of this type appear to be rare. A so-called *Parochiale* drawn up in the Suevic kingdom in the sixth century lists under the proper sees the parishes of which these consist.[39] The parishes are designated by place-names of which the names of saints do not seem to be a part. This document was produced in connexion with diocesan reorganisation, of which it sets forth the results.

---

[36] Cf. the list of the disciples of St Brigid in the Book of Leinster (edd. Best *et al.*, *The Book of Leinster*, VI.1580).

[37] See Maps M and N.

[38] Cf. Henderson, *The Cornish Church Guide*, p. 18: 'The number of Celtic monasteries, churches, chapels and shrines, was very great and only about a third of them were selected for the new parochial system.' Even if Thomas's proposed interpretation is rejected, the list and its geographical correlation suggests that in an area like the Roseland Peninsula the roots of this selection-process may extend back at least as far as the tenth century.

[39] Edited with discussion by David, *Études*, pp. 19–82.

The list in the Vatican codex, Reginensis latinus 191, could be notes for some piece of ecclesiastical administration. Yet if the names on this list represent parishes or churches, written down for whatever purpose, the reason why some are included and many others certainly left out is not apparent.

There are problems with all of the suggestions for the purpose of the list when they suppose the names to stand for places. Explanations of the purpose of the list can be given, however, which take into account the geographical correlation of the order of the names while allowing them to be names of saints and nothing more. If a person were to call to mind a considerable number of local saints, (s)he might proceed, at times anyway, by reference to the location of the places with which the saints were associated as patrons and/or eponyms, that is, where they were buried or where their relics were kept. The haphazard clustering of the names would be understandable as the result of such a mental process. (Such may in fact have been responsible for the order of the names, whatever was the purpose of the list.) Names of saints could be noted down in a number of connexions: litanies, diptychs, the *Communicantes* or *Hanc igitur* sections of the mass, relics, or some hagiographical function. The extant litanies with large rosters of Breton saints show that there was an interest in assembling such names.[40] The concentration of patron-saints of churches in south-central Cornwall could be due to connexions of the author, or of an oral or written source, with this area.

A monastic purpose for the list of Brittonic names is an unlikely possibility. It is of use to the study of early monasteries in Cornwall in providing (with two possible exceptions) the earliest record[41] which we have of the existence of the churches of SS. Achobran, Probus, Berion, Guron, Entenin, Neot(?), Piran(?), and Germanus(?), and of the church at Padstow: all were, more or less arguably, the sites of Celtic monasteries.

3. WRITINGS CONCERNING ST GERMANS

These may be divided into (internal) liturgical texts produced by and for the use of the early ecclesiastical establishment at St Germans in southeast Cornwall and external documents relating to its episcopal status. One of the former, found on folio 1 of the so-called 'Codex Oxoniensis Posterior', is an incomplete *Missa propria Germani episcopi* in which reference is made to the church of a place called *Lannaled* in Cornwall.[42] The first part of the codex has been studied by D. N. Dumville, who has dated folio 1 to the

---

[40] See Loth, 'Les anciennes litanies'.
[41] Documents relating to Berion and Gernun (if for Germanus) could predate the list (see sections 3 and 5 of this chapter).
[42] Oxford, Bodleian Library, MS. Bodley 572 (*S. C.* 2026), a composite codex.

mid-tenth century and argued that it and a number of texts following in the manuscript were copied in Cornwall.[43]

The mass, which is of normal Roman form, has two relevant passages. The alternative collect reads:[44]

Favour, Lord God, all christian people coming together from diverse parts of nations to one place so that they who desire – the more fervently, the more speedily – to visit the very famous and universally known place Lannaled, where the relics of Bishop Germanus are preserved, may certainly be freed from infirmities of soul and body.

The picture of wide contacts of this place is interesting but quite possibly exaggerated in the interests of self-advertisement. Germanus is referred to in the *Missa propria* as bishop and confessor. More information about the saint is given in the proper preface. In the following translation, portions of this text which have been copied from the proper preface for the feast of SS. Abdon and Sennen, falling on the day preceding that of St Germanus of Auxerre, are italicised.[45]

It is truly fitting, Eternal God, *even to praise You, the wonderful Lord, in Your saints, who before the establishment of the world You prepared for Yourself in eternal glory, that through them You might show the light of Your truth to this world. From the company of whom* that Bishop Germanus, sent to us by St Gregory, pope of the Roman city, shone forth, the lamp and pillar of Cornwall and the herald of truth;

[43] '*Codex Oxoniensis Posterior*: manuscripts as evidence for Anglo-British relations in the tenth century' ([unpublished] paper read at the Fifth International Congress of Celtic Studies, Penzance, Cornwall, 9 April 1975, which Dr Dumville was kind enough to make available to me in manuscript).

[44] 'Propitiare, Domine Deus, omni populo christiano ex diuersis partibus linguarum conu[en]ienti in unum; ut hi, qui locum praeclarum atque notum ubique Lannaledensem, ubi reliquiae Germani episcopi conduntur, quanto ardensius tanto cicius uisitare cupiunt, ab omnibus infirmitatibus anime et corporis fideliter liberentur' (ed. Doble, *Pontificale*, p. xxi).

[45] Cf. Deshusses, *Le Sacramentaire*, p. 541. Jenner, 'The Lannaled mass', p. 487, pointed out the borrowing. 'Uere dignum, eterne Deus, et Te laudare mirabilem Dominum in sanctis tuis, quos ante constitutionem mundi in aeternam Tibi gloriam praeparasti, ut per eos huic mundo ueritatis tuae lumen ostenderes: de quorum collegio iste Germanus episcopus, a sancto Gregorio Romane urbis apostolico ad nos missus, lucerna et columna Cornubiae et praeco ueritatis efulsit; qui in Lannaledensis aeclesiae Tuae prato sicut rosae et lilia floruit, et tenebras infidelitatis quae obcecabant corda et sensus nostros detersit [*or* "detrusit"]. Propterea supliciter atque lacrimabiliter deprecamur totis uiribus claementiam Tuam, ut licet meritis non exsigentibus misereri tamen nostri semper digneris; quia priscis temporibus legimus Te irasci magis quam misereri propter uesaniam dementiamque imp[ii] et crudelis regis Guortherni. Idcirco petimus, obsecramus, deprecamur, in his ultimis diebus, indulgentiam pietatis Tuae; ut per Te ueniam peccatorum nostrorum mereamur accipere, et post finem huius seculi. Te interpellante, cum Deo et sanctis Eius immaculati conregnare possimus' (ed. Doble, *Pontificale*, pp. xxi–xxii).

who flourished[46] *in the field of Your church* of Lannaled *as roses and lilies*, and drove away the darkness of infidelity which was blinding our hearts and senses. Therefore we pray humbly and tearfully Your mercy for all men, that notwithstanding [our] merits not requiring [this] You nevertheless deign always to have mercy on us, since we read that in former times You were more angry than merciful on account of the madness and insanity of the impious and cruel King Guorthernus. Wherefore we ask, we beseech, we pray, in these last days, the indulgence of Your compassion; in order that through You we may deserve to receive the remission of our sins, and after the end of this world, by Your interposing, we, spotless, may be able to reign together with God and his saints.

This external figure who was in Britain on a papally inspired mission of spiritual enlightenment is recognisably Germanus of Auxerre. A curious confusion has substituted Pope Gregory for Celestine, perhaps from influence of the story of St Augustine's mission to the Anglo-Saxons.[47] The allusion to divine anger directed at King Guorthernus (that is, Gwrtheyrn or, as he is better known, Vortigern) is interesting in showing some cognisance at *Lannaled* of the distinctively British tradition of St Germanus.[48] Albeit partly in borrowed terms, the *Missa propria* expresses the belief that Bishop Germanus actually came to Cornwall, which is not found expressed elsewhere in written form.[49]

On folios 183r–184r of Rouen, Bibliothèque municipale, MS. A.27 (368), commonly but misleadingly known as the Lanalet Pontifical, is a formula of excommunication beginning as follows: 'The bishop, by the assent of the divinity, of the *monasterium* of Lanalet to all the faithful of the holy church of God: let it be known . . .'.[50] This text has been added at the end of one of the quires of the tenth-century pontifical in a later hand, perhaps in the second quarter of the eleventh century.[51] The description of *Lanalet* as the seat of a bishop clinches the identification of *Lannaled/Lanalet*, a place-

---

[46] In the Abdon and Sennen preface we find the plural here.

[47] As suggested by Jenner, 'The Lannaled mass', p. 489. See also Plummer, *Vitae*, I.cxxiii.

[48] Recounted in *Historia Brittonum*, §§ 32–35, 39, 47–48, and by Heiric of Auxerre, *Miracula Sancti Germani* (edd. Bollandus *et al.*, *Acta Sanctorum*, XXXIV.283). These works and the *missa propria* ('legimus') allude to written source-material. See Chadwick, 'Early culture', pp. 40–3, 106–15.

[49] For oral tradition in Cornwall to this effect, see Whitaker, *The Ancient Cathedral*, I.270.

[50] 'Diuinitatis suffragio · lanaletensis · monasterii episcopis omnibus sanctae dei aecclesie fidelibus notum sit', with *u* written above the second *i* of *episcopis* (ed. Doble, *Pontificale*, p. 130). For Continental parallels see Vogel & Elze, *Le Pontifical*, I.313–17; the Cornish excommunication seems an impressive specimen of its genre.

[51] Doble, *Pontificale*, pp. x, vii–viii, v; and he suggested on pp. xii–xiii that the excommunication-formula was added by the agency of Lyfing, bishop of Cornwall from some time between 1026 and 1043 (perhaps 1027) until 1046, to whom the pontifical appears to have belonged; Leroquais, *Les Pontificaux*, pp. 287–300, especially 298.

name known only from these texts, with St Germans, the seat of the bishops of Cornwall.[52] The meaning of *monasterium* at this time was, as has been pointed out, rather indefinite:[53] reference in the excommunication-phrase could be either to the community of canons of which we have notice in Domesday Book or to a monastic predecessor.

Coming now to the external sources, we read in a letter written by Archbishop Dunstan to King Æthelred the Unready between 980 and 988 the statement, 'Then it happened that King Æthelstan gave to Cunun the bishopric as far as the Tamar flowed', followed by a reference to the seat of the bishop of Cornwall at St Germans in King Eadred's time (946–955).[54] Six centuries later Leland noted from a charter of Æthelstan, the authenticity of which we cannot check, that the king 'raised [or set up] a certain Conan as bishop in the church of St Germanus on the nones of December, A.D. 936'.[55] In fact, Conan occurs among the signatories of authentic charters in the period 931–934.[56] An important document illuminating these matters has recently been identified by W. M. M. Picken. Notes of a charter of Æthelstan dated 936 are entered in a seventeenth-century transcript of the now lost Register of Plympton Priory, featuring the text of all or part of the disposition:[57]

Therefore I restore and willingly bestow *in diocesim perpetuam* all the territory of the episcopate, viz of Blessed Germanus, bishop of the region of Cornwall, with the yoke of servitude of the bondman in part taken off, free from all payment of royal tax, these things excepted, namely expedition against enemies and sea-watches; etc.

[52] On the former erroneous identification with Alet in Brittany see Doble, *Pontificale*, pp. x and xiii; Jenner, 'The Lannaled mass', pp. 489–90; Henderson, *Records*, pp. 3–4.

[53] See p. 3 above.

[54] 'þa gelamp hit þæt æþestan cing sealde cunune bisceoprice ealswa tamur scæt · þa gelamp þæt eadræd cyng het daniel 7 betæhte þa land swa him witan ræddun · inn to scē germane to þam bisceopstole' (edd. Napier & Stevenson, *The Crawford Collection*, p. 19). The former sentence is added over an erasure and above the line in another hand, which Napier & Stevenson (*ibid.*, p. 104, n. 3) described as contemporary but about which Chaplais ('The authenticity', p. 19) had doubts.

[55] 'Ex charta donat. Æthelstani. Erexit in Ecclesiam S. Germani quoddam Conanum Episcopum anno Dni. 936 nonis Decembris' (Leland, *Collectanea*, ed. Hearne, I.75).

[56] Sawyer, *Anglo-Saxon Charters*, nos 412, 416, 417, 425. See also Haddan & Stubbs, *Councils*, I.676, and Napier & Stevenson, *The Crawford Collection*, p. 104[–5], n. 6.

[57] Oxford, Bodleian Library, MS. James 23 (*S.C.* 3680); photograph passed on by Picken to Oliver Padel, who printed the text as an additional note in 'Two new pre-Conquest charters', pp. 26–7. The complete entry is: 'Omne igitur territorium episcopatus uidelicet Beati Germani Cornubiae regionis Episcopi partim abstracto iugo servitutis addicti ab omni censu Regalis fisci, exceptis hiis rebus, scilicet expeditione contra hostes et uigiliis marinis liberum restituo et in diocesi[m] perpetuam libenter offero, Etc. in charta Athelstani Regis, Anno Domini DCCC[C]° xxxvĵ , Ego Adelstanus nutu dei omnipotentis Rex totius Albionis hoc donum confirmo cum titulo sanctae crucis'.

Despite the coincidence of data, this does not seem to be the charter to which Leland referred but rather another granting immunities to the Cornish see, unless the compiler of the Plympton Register saw fit to record only the immunities-section of a document which elsewhere mentioned Bishop Conan. The authenticity of the charter from which the text quoted above derives is strongly suggested by the phrase 'in diocesim perpetuam', paralleled in Breton charter-material but not Anglo-Saxon – except for a newly identified grant by a Cornishman of land in Cornwall, also in the reign of Æthelstan.[58] These evidences reveal English initiative in constituting a recognised bishopric of Cornwall within the West Saxon domains, with Cornish personnel in the shape of Bishop Conan; the language of the last document quoted conveys clearly that this was a pre-existing bishopric, associated with an earlier saint, to which Æthelstan restored liberties.

Three matters – the name, patron-saint, and nature *ab origine* of the *monasterium Lanaletense* – require further discussion with reference to the foregoing documents. *Lannaled* and *Lanalet* are forms of a Cornish name compounded of *lan*, 'sacred enclosure', and a second element: that is far more likely to be *alet/aled* than *naled*, since the first element is properly Old Cornish **lann*. This is probably an infrequent case of *lan* combined with a topographical element rather than with a saint's name.[59]

It has been suggested that the Germanus with dedications in southwest Britain[60] is not Germanus of Auxerre but rather a local or at least British saint, and more generally that the British hagiological tradition of Germanus represents a conflation of the legends of the bishop of Auxerre with those of a native saint or saints.[61] On the last point, a different explanation would see the strong influence of early texts of the Western Church, particularly marked in the case of a subject who actually visited Britain, acting as a basis for elaboration in native legend. One specific argument for a late identification of Germanus of Auxerre with the patron of St Germans in Cornwall is easily disposed of. The phrase in the *Missa propria*, 'ubi reliquiae Germani episcopi conduntur', has been held to indicate that *Lannaled* claimed to possess the body of Germanus, who thus cannot have been the bishop of Auxerre.[62] On the contrary, this expresses in standard terms a

---

[58] See *ibid.*, pp. 20–6, and p. 84 below.

[59] No equivalent personal name is known. Allet (*Aled* and *Alet* in 1284) in Kenwyn parish in Cornwall and Alet in Brittany, standing on their own with no indication that they designate saints, are unlikely to be personal names, and the same is true of the River Aled in Wales.

[60] Also at Rame, a few miles southeast of St Germans, Germansweek in west Devon, and a chapel in Padstow parish recorded in 1415 (perhaps within the parish-church; see Henderson, *apud* Doble, *Saint Petrock*, p. 41).

[61] Henderson, *Records*, p. 2 (he did not comment on the British Germanus legend); Jenner, 'The Lannaled mass', pp. 490–1; Picken, 'St. German'; Rutherford, 'The *Historia Brittonum*', especially pp. 33–6; Radford, 'The church of Saint Germans', pp. 190–2.

[62] Jenner, 'The Lannaled mass', pp. 486–7; cf. the other authors cited in n. 61.

claim to possess relics, corporeal or incorporeal, of Germanus of Auxerre.[63] A second argument for a local Germanus, derived from the charter-text transcribed in the Plympton Register, is more telling: how could Germanus, bishop of the region of Cornwall, be Germanus, bishop of Auxerre? Local hagiological tradition, assuming that it is correctly represented by the charter-phrase, could have developed in this way if the association with Germanus was old, perhaps influenced by an example like that of St Samson, a Welsh bishop who founded the see of Dol. The possibility is still worth considering that Germanus of Auxerre became associated with St Germans in Cornwall at a rather early date, as was the case with Whithorn and Martin of Tours.

The passage quoted above from Æthelstan's charter confirms that the *monasterium Lanaletense* was originally a Celtic religious house. If episcopal claims have been distorted in the interest of ecclesiastical and secular politics, the statement represents an appeal to the past which certainly presupposes a pre-existing centre of veneration for Germanus which became the recognised seat of the West Saxon bishopric of Cornwall. In other words, St Germans would not have originated as an episcopal community planted by Æthelstan conveniently near the eastern border of Cornwall and endowed appropriately with relics of a saint with a marked British cult.

This conclusion receives support from other sources. The place-name in *lan* strongly suggests that a Celtic foundation antedated the institution of a West Saxon bishopric at St Germans in the early tenth century. There may be a few cases where *lan*-names were given equally late or later, but *Lannaled/Lanalet* is unlikely to be among them; it could certainly not be so if the second element were a saint's name, for this would imply a previous dedication superseded by one to Germanus, and it could probably not be so if (as is much more likely) the second element is topographic. *Lannaled/ Lanalet*, which is not known after the eleventh century, looks like an old place-name kept in use by the church and community there, as witnessed by the liturgical texts discussed above. When the church declined in importance, losing its episcopal status and lands to the bishop of Exeter in the mid-eleventh century, the original name fell out of use in favour of the more obvious *aecclesia Sancti Germani* and *Sanctus Germanus* which designate these lands in Domesday Book.[64]

Further support for a Celtic foundation comes from circumstantial evidence for the cultural context at St Germans. The two liturgical items and the corroborating evidence of a number of other texts in 'Codex

---

[63] Cf. the rubric from the Lanalet Pontifical, 'Incipit ordo quomodo in sancta romana ecclesia reliquiae condantur', pertaining to liturgy for placing relics in a church (ed. Doble, *Pontificale*, p. 22). Cf. also Du Cange, *Glossarium*, VII.112: 'Apud Christianos vero alia sunt *corpora*, aliae *reliquiae* Sanctorum: corpora enim integrae sunt Sanctorum exuviae: *reliquiae*, corporum pars tantum'.

[64] Exch., fo 120v and Exon., fo 199v, respectively.

Oxoniensis Posterior' (which may also have come from St Germans)[65] indicate the following characteristics of cultural activity there: a Celtic component (Germanus legend, Cornish glosses, colloquy in Welsh and Latin), Anglo-Saxon influence (glosses, letter-forms such as ð, perhaps the connexion of Pope Gregory with Germanus), and early penetration of Continental influences (liturgical content and Caroline script). The presence of Celtic culture and language, contacts with Wales, and a receptivity to Continental influence which almost certainly reflects the Breton tie, as well as to English culture, form a context suitable to a well established Cornish religious house near the English border rather than to an English outpost inside Cornwall.

The existence of an early Cornish *monasterium* of *Lannaled* or *Lanalet* at St Germans can be safely deduced from the foregoing. Caution is in order regarding the episcopate centred at this place. We know that there was in the mid-ninth century a bishop at a different *monasterium* in Cornwall, *Dinuurrin*; so the picture, of an age-old unified diocese of Cornwall in the name of Germanus, painted by the charter-language is clearly a distortion; and the distortion may extend further than we know. Yet knowledge of at least an episcopate exercised within Cornwall from St Germans must lie behind the charter.

4. WRITINGS CONCERNING ESTABLISHMENTS OF ST PETROC

In this section sources will be consulted for information about the state of Cornish establishments of St Petroc prior to the appearance in Domesday Book of the impressive landholding complex of his clerical community at Bodmin.[66] Nine texts of various types and dates (but mainly of the tenth and eleventh centuries), plus additional place-name data, are involved. Before examining them, it is essential to understand the main issues on which evidence is sought: the existence of early monasteries at Padstow and Bodmin, and of bishops therein.

The existence of an early monastery at Padstow is assumed from the insistence, in the eleventh- and twelfth-century *Vitae Sancti Petroci*, that this was Petroc's original monastic settlement in Cornwall. As mentioned above, the eleventh-century *uita* was probably written in Cornwall,[67] which is the setting for a good deal of it: all of the religious foundations by Petroc

---

[65] An early Caroline minuscule copy of an *Expositio missae*, the Book of Tobit with Cornish glosses, the letter of Augustine to Proba 'de orando Deo', *Epistola Augustine de igne purgatorio* (in fact by Caesarius of Arles), a Cambro-Latin colloquy *De raris fabulis* with Old Welsh, Old Cornish, and Old English glosses. Dumville (see above, n. 43) has suggested that the sections of the manuscript on which these occur were in Winchester by 981 and judged it likely they came thither together. Cf. Jackson, *Language and History*, pp. 54–6, 59, and Jenner, 'The Lannaled mass', pp. 477–81.

[66] See pp. 87–8, 92, 93 n. 199, 96–7 below.

[67] For the date see Grosjean, 'Vies et miracles', p. 478 (language and style consonant with the period of the Norman conquest, give or take a generation).

are in Cornwall and the saint dies there. The *uita* gives details of several names and clearly identifiable places with which the saint was associated in Cornwall and, concluding with notices of some healing miracles performed by the saint while alive and the assertion that miracles continued to be worked at his tomb, seems designed to serve local interests. Certainly the author was informed about the region and its legends of Petroc.[68] His text was known in Cornwall in the second half of the twelfth century: it was used in the composition of the second *Vita Sancti Petroci*[69] whose author, while elaborating and expanding the first *uita* with further local legend, gave essentially the same account of Petroc.

The story – as told in the earlier version, unless otherwise specified – is that Petroc and his band of monks went from Wales to Ireland and subsequently sailed from Ireland to the *amnem Hailem*, the same Camel estuary by which Samson of Dol entered Cornwall. In this area Petroc found a hermit named Samson who had a dwelling by the shore[70] and a Bishop Wethinoc who had a *cella*. This last would seem to mean 'monastery', for Wethinoc departed from it with his people (*cum suis*) after Petroc had asked leave to live with him there, and Petroc and his disciples then entered the *cella*. In making way for Petroc, Wethinoc asked that the place be named after him, and the author gives the name 'in the language of that people' as *Landwethinoch* in his own day.[71] This is an old name for Padstow, on the west side of the estuary about two miles from its mouth, and (as mentioned previously) the site of Samson's hermitage is identifiable nearby.[72]

After several episodes – including a pilgrimage to Rome, Jerusalem, and an island of hermits in the Eastern Ocean and back to western Britain – Petroc appointed a near-namesake Petrus as prior over his eighty monks[73]

and withdrew into the wilderness, twelve only taken with him because he had chosen them to dwell with him in the solitude separately throughout the hollows of the mountains in the coverts of the rocks.

[68] Grosjean wrote (*ibid.*) of the author: 'Aurait-il été moine ou clerc à Bodmin? Ce serait assez naturel'.

[69] *Ibid.*, p. 473. Grosjean edited this later life *ibid.*, pp. 131–88.

[70] § 5: 'Erat cuidam Sansoni, digno Dei famulo, secus littus, iuxta amnem Hailem, habitatio in solitudine'. *Hayl* is the Cornish word for 'estuary', and the Camel estuary is known to have been so called, the name surviving in Hayle Bay.

[71] § 7: 'Unde etiam lingua gentis illius Landwethinoch adhuc usque hodie dicitur'.

[72] See p. 12 above. A chapel of St Sampson at Hawker's Cove by the estuary-mouth appears on a seventeenth-century map (Henderson, 'Antiquities', III.121). Evidence for a chapel of the saint at Place above Padstow is late and doubtful (Ordnance Survey index-card SW97NW 19; Henderson, *apud* Doble, *Saint Petrock*, p. 39).

[73] § 10: 'Inde reuertens, fratribus octoginta, quibus ipse prefuerat, dominum Petrum, summe religionis uirum, quem nuper ad fidem susceperat, collato magistratu priorem constituit, et seccessit in heremum, assumtis sibi solum duodecim quod secum cohabitaturos in solitudine delegerat seorsum per montium concaua in scopulorum latibulis'.

The last phrase suggests that Petroc established a colony of hermits. Certainly the author of the second *Vita Sancti Petroci* took it in this way, and he could have had other sources of information on this point.[74] The saint miraculously caused a spring to flow beside the *cellula*, a spring which still existed in the author's time. This is the place now known as Little Petherick (= Petroc) – and formerly as Nanceventon, 'the valley of the well' – situated on a tributary of the Camel two miles above Padstow.

A final stage of Petroc's activity in Cornwall came after he had lived some years in the *cellula* and left it for a remote wilderness, where he found a solitary named Uuron dwelling.[75] They conversed, and Uuron departed for a new abode. The site of this third settlement of Petroc in Cornwall is Bodmin – with the holy well of Guron (Uuron) near the church – situated in the middle of the Cornish peninsula not far from the River Camel. Petroc's disciples followed him there: according to the second *uita*, as numbers grew the saint founded an additional house on the hill to the north of their settlement in the valley below, and we have seen that the hilltop-establishment is a likely site for the *monasterium* of *Dinuurrin*.[76] The first *uita* ends with a fairly simple account of the saint's death and the statement that miracles continue to be worked at his tomb, without the location of the place of his death or of that tomb being specified in any way;[77] however, the second *uita* makes it clear that Petroc was buried at Padstow.[78]

The first (as well as the second) *Vita Sancti Petroci* chiefly offers explanations of features of Petroc's cult, and miracles to celebrate the same. The content, relating to a monastic church with a peripatetic bishop like Wethinoc and not to the world of eleventh-century Cornwall, is at least in part the product of Cornish monasticism in the early middle ages. Behind it all must be the existence of an early monastery of St Petroc at Padstow. There the saint was buried, where according to a document discussed below his body remained in the tenth century.[79] This suggests that, despite assertions in the *uitae* that Petroc made monastic foundations inland at Little Petherick and finally Bodmin, his primary association (as opposed to secondary expansion of cult) was confined to the coastal monastery at Padstow.

The progression of Petroc from one to the other of his three foundations in Cornwall is couched in terms of the retreat of a monk into a more remote

---

[74] § 11: 'assumptis duodecim de tanto numero (erant enim omnes octoginta), in osculo sancto secedens, mansiones fecerunt ad Uallem Fontis in diuersis cellulis. Ipse habebat cellulam ex lignis contextam et quidam e fratribus similiter, plerique uero in cauernis moncium seu concauis uallium latitabant, solempnes tamen oraciones pariter celebrantes et mense refeccionem.' As I have pointed out, this *uita* appears to incorporate more local traditions than its predecessor.

[75] § 11 (first *uita*).

[76] pp. 54–5 above.

[77] § 13.

[78] § 23.

[79] See p. 70.

olitude so as to be nearer God, a motif present in *uitae* back to that of Anthony of Egypt and an actual phenomenon in early monastic life.[80] What the author of the *uita* is likely to be attempting in describing the retreat of Petroc into the interior of Cornwall – or what the hagiological tradition which he is recording has accomplished – is the association of the saint in his lifetime with prominent *loci* of his cult: this is done by means quite credible within the hagiographical genre. There is neither written nor archaeological evidence to support the account in the *uitae* of an eremitical monastery at Little Petherick near Padstow. Quite conceivably, a simple church and the holy well of St Petroc there (note that it is the latter feature, which does not imply a monastic settlement, to which the Cornish name of the place refers) have been incorporated into the story of Petroc's successive monastic foundations. What would have called for explanation in the *uitae* was the relationship between Padstow and Bodmin. Certainly Bodmin superseded Padstow as a cult-centre, for in post-Conquest documentation the site of the community and tomb of Petroc is Bodmin not Padstow, and the latter was known until the late middle ages as *Aldestow*, 'the old holy place'.[81] This English place-name implies a shift of cult-centre at some much more recent time than that of Petroc.

When and how did the ecclesiastical settlement at Bodmin originate? Modern scholars, rejecting the traditional account of the Bodmin foundation by Petroc, have proposed two alternatives. (1) The community of Petroc moved from Padstow to Bodmin after the viking-raid on 'Sancte Petroces stow' (understood to be the former place) in 981, as recorded in the Anglo-Saxon Chronicle, of which event more below.[82] (2) The move to Bodmin took place after King Ecgberht granted the estates of *Polltun* (Pawton) and *Cællwic* (if correctly identified with the later episcopal manor of *Burnayre*) to the bishop of Sherborne in the first part of the ninth century, leaving a little coastal enclave at Padstow, perhaps depriving the community there of the estates granted and isolating it from extensive possessions beyond.[83] Both alternatives entail a late foundation at Bodmin. The former prompts the question of what kind of *monasterium* would have existed at Bodmin when Bishop Kenstec of *Dinuurrin* made his profession of obedience – over a century before the viking-raid induced the Padstow

A reasonably certain example of actual practice in the British Isles is the withdrawal of St Cuthbert to the island of Farne, described in the anonymous *Vita Sancti Cuthberti*, III.1 (ed. & transl. Colgrave, *Two Lives*, pp. 96–7).
Gover, 'The Place-names of Cornwall', p. 354, the earliest instance being in 1201 (*Ealdestou* in the Petroc genealogy found in manuscript-association with the second *uita* [ed. Grosjean, 'Vies et miracles', p. 188] may be older) and showing the change to forms like *Petrokestowe* occurring *ca* 1300, the old Cornish name persisting as late as *Lanwethenek*, 1351.
Henderson, *apud* Doble, *Saint Petrock*, p. 35; Doble, *The Saints of Cornwall*, IV.150. See pp. 70–3 below.
Henderson, *apud* Doble, *Saint Petrock*, p. 35; Doble appears to have earlier favoured this, *ibid.*, p. 26.

community to move thence. The object of the following discussion will be to examine the relevant sources and see to what extent they compel us to accept either of these alternatives, or suggest or permit new ones.

William of Malmesbury (in the passage quoted below)[84] clearly located the seat of the Cornish bishopric at Padstow, situated as this is by the entrance to the Camel estuary formerly called *Hegelmuðe*. The Old English *Secgan be þam Godes sanctum þe on Engla lande ærost reston* also locates there, in phrases similar to William's, the burial-place of Petroc.[85] This part of the text, completed by the early eleventh century,[86] meant to give contemporary information about where the saints rested. It is unlikely to have been incorrect about a saint whose devotees included tenth-century English kings, except perhaps in the case of a recent transfer of Petroc's remains to Bodmin following the raid of A.D. 981. This is evidence for the later importance of the Padstow foundation.

The entry for 981 in the C-text of the Anglo-Saxon Chronicle reads: 'In this year *Sancte Petroces stow* was ravaged; and that same year much harm was done everywhere along the coast, both in Devon and Cornwall'.[8] Where was this place: Padstow or Bodmin? The raid was very likely on Padstow, but the case for this should not be overstated. Although Padstow is readily accessible by sea, attackers could have gone past it up the River Camel to within easy striking distance of Bodmin, were this by reason of greater wealth or reputation the more desirable target. *Sancte Petroce stow*, 'the holy place of St Petroc', could in theory refer to any church dedicated to the saint, possessing of course some relic of him. There is little evidence that it was for a time applied to Bodmin. In the West Saxon homily *Of Seinte Neote*, composed in the eleventh – probably the late eleventh – century, the place in Cornwall now known as St Neot is said to be 'ten milen fram Petrocesstowe'.[88] This is a far less accurate statement of its distance from Padstow than from Bodmin,[89] lying as it does between St Neot and Padstow; as the site of the most eminent landholding religious

---

[84] See p. 74.
[85] II.40 (S-text) (ed. Liebermann, *Die Heiligen Englands*, p. 17): 'þonne resteð sanctus Petrocus on Westwealum be þære sæ neah þam fleote, þe man clypað Hægelmuða'. Compare the wording of the passage cited below in n. 104: 'Locus est apud aquilonales Britones, supra mare, iuxta flumen quod dicitur Hegelmuðe'.
[86] See Rollason, 'Lists', pp. 64–8.
[87] 'Her on þys geare wæs Sancte Petroces stow forhergod. and þy ilcan gear wæs micel hearm gedon gehwær be þam særiman. ægþer ge on Defenum ge on Wealum' (ed. Rositzke, *The C-text*, p. 51, with substitution here of original punctuation from Earle & Plummer, *Two of the Saxon Chronicles*, I.124).
[88] § 42 (ed. Warner, *Early English Homilies*, p. 130). For discussion of the homily see Stevenson, *Asser's Life*, pp. 256–61.
[89] The direct distance between Bodmin and St Neot churches is just over seven modern miles, but the journey by road adds about another mile; between Padstow and St Neot churches about seventeen-and-a-half miles direct, by water and road over twenty miles. The homilist's mile may have been only about four-fifths of a modern mile (see Grierson, *English Linear Measures*, pp. 27–9).

community in Domesday Cornwall, Bodmin was more likely to have been given as a geographical reference point in the homily. Also, there is record in the Bodmin Gospels of a manumission made *ca* 1100 at *Petrocys stow*.[90] This could have been performed at the (by then) minor church at Padstow, but when Padstow emerges in official documents about a century later it is called *Aldestow*.[91] Any evidence that Bodmin was ever called *Petrocesstowe* is interesting. Of course the usages cited are later than the date of the raid and could represent transfer of the place-name to the new centre of Petroc's cult. Yet there is room for doubt as to whether the name would have been so transferred in a mere century, especially where it was probably not essential to find a name for the new site.

On the other hand, identification of the site of the viking-raid of 981 as Padstow is supported by the above-mentioned near-contemporary testimony of *Secgan be þam Godes sanctum* that here was at least the main shrine of Petroc, sufficiently well known outside Cornwall. This implies material wealth and reputation such as the raiders would be unlikely to ignore and as would merit the attack specifically mentioned in the Anglo-Saxon Chronicle. Also, while an offshoot-foundation at Bodmin would probably possess a relic of Petroc, one might expect his main shrine to be referred to distinctively as *Sancte Petroces stow*.[92]

The establishment of a house of St Petroc at Bodmin only after the viking-raid on Padstow would entail transfer thence of the late ninth- or early tenth-century manuscript known as the Bodmin Gospels.[93] Fifty manumissions, performed from the fourth decade of the tenth century until as late as the early twelfth century, which are recorded on its pages are not particularly helpful in providing evidence for such a change.[94] Only a few contain place-names indicating where the transaction was carried out, of which we have seen that *Petrocys stow* occurs once late and may refer to Bodmin. Two manumissions of the second half of the eleventh century have

---

[90] Ed. Förster, 'Die Freilassungserkunden', no. XXXVII (his numbering is followed in citing manumissions, below); the date is supported by Ker, *Catalogue*, p. 159, Förster, *ibid.*, pp. 94–5, and by clearly late forms in the English text, whereas Finberg, *The Early Charters*, p. 19, dated it 950 × 1000.

[91] See n. 81 above.

[92] At least between Padstow and Bodmin; however, there was a Petrockstow in north Devon as early as Domesday Book.

[93] London, British Library, MS. Add. 9381; cf. Ker, *Catalogue*, p. 159, no. 126, and Jenner, 'The Bodmin Gospels'.

[94] They are often stated to be performed simply on the altar of St Petroc. In one entry (no. XXII) a manumission is made on Petroc's bell at Liskeard, eleven miles east of Bodmin, and then repeated at the *monasterium sancti Petroci*, showing that the site could shift. As the date is early in the eleventh century (Förster, 'Die Freilassungsurkunden', p. 89; Finberg, *The Early Charters*, p. 19; Ker, *Catalogue*, p. 159), the *monasterium* was presumably at Bodmin. There is nothing to indicate that this is a different site from the *mynstre* in a mid-tenth-century manumission (no. XXIX, dated from its being made 'for [the soul of?] Eadwig cyningc' [955–9]). In manumission XXVI (946 × 953) *on tune* is enigmatic.

71

a unique and almost identical phrase – 'at the church-door in *Bodmine*'.[95] This could easily be an alternative place-name or specialised usage, possibly referring to the lower settlement in the area, as suggested above.[96] *Petrocys stow* in two manumissions of the second half of the tenth century and late tenth or beginning of the eleventh century[97] is, on the basis of my argument in the foregoing paragraph, probably Padstow. Given participation of kings, bishops, and nobles in some of the manumissions recorded in the Bodmin Gospels (though not the last two mentioned), any evidence that they were regularly performed at Padstow strengthens the case for the importance until a late date of the religious establishment there.

A final indication of the religious importance of the Padstow site is the existence there in the middle ages of a privileged sanctuary, placing 'land and houses outside the Church' in the area within which asylum could be found.[98] This was probably referred to by Leland when he wrote of Padstow, 'And the toune there takith King Adelstane for the chief gever of privileges onto it'.[99] This privileged sanctuary may in fact have its origin further back in an early monastic past.[100]

The evidence considered compels us to accept that the body of Petroc was still at Padstow in the tenth century. It provides several indications of the tenth-century importance of the ecclesiastical establishment at Padstow, but nothing identifiably relating to Bodmin before the eleventh century. The evidence does not, however, compel us to accept that there was no monastery or collegiate church at Bodmin before the plausible shift of religious activity from Padstow as a result of the raid of 981. It is important to note that evidence for the tenth-century religious significance of Padstow is by and large able to be connected with the presence of the saint's body there. The alternative origins of the religious house at Bodmin, outlined

---

[95] Nos XXX ('æt þære cirican dura on Bodmine') and XXXIII (read *þere* for *þære* and *æt* for *on*). My dating follows Ker, *Catalogue*, p. 159, rather than Förster, 'Die Freilassungsurkunden', pp. 92–3, and Finberg, *The Early Charters*, p. 19, who both make it a century earlier. Comparison of witness-lists suggests contemporaneity of nos XXX and XXXIII with XXXI, dated by Förster 'aus dem Ende des 11. Jhs. oder noch später' (p. 92); cf. Jenner, 'The manumissions', pp. 247–9, for additional support for such a late date.

[96] See pp. 54–5.

[97] Nos XLIX (dated 959 × 981 by Finberg, *The Early Charters*, p. 19, and 959 × 993 by Förster, 'Die Freilassungsurkunden', pp. 97–8) and X (dated 975 × 1010 by Finberg, p. 19, and probably *ca* 1000 by Förster, p. 85).

[98] Henderson, *apud* Doble, *Saint Petrock*, p. 36.

[99] Leland, *Itinerary* (ed. Smith, I.179). *Ibid.*, p. 180, we find a similar statement about Bodmin! 'The toune of Bodmyn takith King Edelstane for the chief erector and gyver of privileges onto it.' In his *Collectanea* (ed. Hearne, I.75), Leland named Æthelstan as the founder, or rather re-founder, of the monastery at Bodmin, information said to have been obtained 'ex antiquis Donationum chartis'. We cannot check the authenticity of his source(s), and the reference is vaguer than that to the St Germans charter (see p. 63 above).

[100] See pp. 106–7 below.

previously, can in fact be combined satisfactorily by regarding the development of ecclesiastical foundations dedicated to Petroc as a step-by-step process.

The theory that development of the religious settlement at Bodmin followed the isolation of the Padstow community by Ecgberht's land-grants to the bishop of Sherborne in the earlier ninth century has considerable merit. If the lands of Petroc in north-central Cornwall had at this time anything like the distribution revealed in Domesday Book, it is easy to see how those grants might have interfered in proprietary and indeed episcopal administration carried out from Padstow.[101] Accordingly, the centre of administration was moved, beyond the estates of the bishop of Sherborne, to a site valued perhaps for its accessibility to northern and southern properties of Petroc and for its more easterly orientation. Here at the *monasterium* called *Dinuurrin* Bishop Kenstec had his seat in the mid-ninth century. These circumstances would not have called for the translation of the body of the patron-saint from Padstow.[102] Probably a religious community continued to exist there until the raid of 981 brought about the removal of community and patron to the inland house.

There is yet another possible history. The *Vitae Sancti Petroci* are clear on the point that Uuron was held to have preceded Petroc on the site at Bodmin. As we have seen, this personal name is thought to be the second element in *Dinuurrin*.[103] Perhaps *Dinuurrin* was originally an independent monastery which was later taken over in some way by the heirs of Petroc, and which, rather incredibly, left no trace beyond hagiological tradition of a forest hermit who gave place to Petroc.

Was there an early monastery at Bodmin or, assuming that they are to be identified, *Dinuurrin*? There are circumstances to suggest that foundation may have come after 800. Bodmin lacks a sign that it was an early monastery: original interment of the saint claimed as the founder, a name in *an* to suggest antiquity, a privileged sanctuary such as Padstow had. On the other hand, there is no reason to rule out the possibility that Bodmin was an early foundation. Bodmin/*Dinuurrin* is nonetheless a questionable case of an early monastery in Cornwall.

We must now turn to the association of bishops with the establishments of St Petroc in Cornwall.

The only specific indication of a bishop's seat at a place dedicated to

---

[101] See Map N. Cf. the statement in a spurious but tenth-century account that the estates were transferred early in the tenth century to the bishop of Crediton 'ut inde singulis annis uisitaret gentem Cornubiensem ad exprimendos eorum errores. Nam antea in quantum potuerunt ueritate resistebant, et non decretis apostolicis oboediebant' (on this text see n. 27 above). This envisages deliberate interference in Cornish religious life, though long after Ecgberht's original grant.

[102] William of Malmesbury may have been led to place the seat of the Cornish bishops at the coastal establishment of Petroc from old information that the saint was buried there.

[103] Above, p. 53.

Petroc is in this passage from the *Gesta Pontificum Anglorum* by William of Malmesbury:[104]

Indeed I neither know nor contrive the successive order of Cornish bishops, except that the seat of the bishopric was at St Petroc the confessor's. The place is among the northern Britons, on the sea, by the river which is called Hegelmuðe. Some say that it was at St Germans, by the River Liner, on the sea in the southern part.

Yet in the foundation-charter of the see of Exeter, written somewhat after 1050, the diocese of Cornwall is said to have been bestowed 'in beati Germani memoria atque Petroci ueneratione';[105] and in the authentic charter of King Æthelred the Unready, dated 994, the liberties of that diocese and power of the bishop over it are granted 'pro amore domini nostri Iesu Christi atque sancti confessoris Germani necnon et beati eximii Petroci'.[106] There can be no doubt that the association of Petroc as well as Germanus with the see is formal and significant. It argues that he and a place of which he was patron had an official role, or were felt to have rights, in the diocese of Cornwall.

The charter of Æthelred requires more discussion regarding the possible existence of a bishopric centred in a foundation of Petroc. As the meaning of the dispositive sentence is obscure it is best given in full.[107]

Wherefore I now make known to all Catholics, that, with the counsel and licence of the bishops and nobles and of all my best men, for the love of our Lord Jesus Christ and of the holy confessor Germanus and also of the blessed excellent Petroc, for the redemption of my soul and for the absolution of my crimes, I have granted that the

---

[104] II.95: 'Cornubiensium sane pontificum succiduum ordinem nec scio nec appono nisi quod apud Sanctum Petrocum confessorem fuerit episcopatus sedes. Locus est apud aquilonales Britones, supra mare, iuxta flumen quod dicitur Hegelmuðe Quidam dicunt fuisse ad Sanctum Germanum, iuxta flumen Liner, supra mare in australi parte.' The term *aquilonales Britones* is odd, for in Anglo-Saxon usage the West Welsh seem to have lived in southwest Britain, the North Welsh in Wales.

[105] Ed. Kemble, *Codex Diplomaticus*, IV.118–21, no. 791; cf. Sawyer, *Anglo-Saxon Charters*, pp. 303–4, no. 1021; date from Chaplais, 'The authenticity', pp 29–31.

[106] Ed. Kemble, *Codex Diplomaticus*, III.275–8, no. 686; cf. Sawyer, *Anglo-Saxon Charters*, pp. 270–1, no. 880; Chaplais, 'The authenticity', pp. 19–21; Keynes *The Diplomas of King Æthelred*, p. 251.

[107] 'Qua de re, nunc patefacio omnibus catholicis, quod cum consilio et licentia episcoporum ac principum, et omnium optimatum meorum, pro amore domini nostri Iesu Christi atque sancti confessoris Germani necnon et beati eximii Petroci, pro redemptione animae meae, et pro absolutione criminum meorum donaui episcopium Ealdredi episcopi, id est in prouincia Cornubiae ut libera sit eique subiecta omnibusque posteris eius, ut ipse gubernet atque regat suam parochiam sicuti alii episcopi qui sunt in mea ditione, locusque atque regimen sancti Petroci semper in potestate eius sit successorumque illius.'

diocese of Bishop Ealdred, that is, in the province of Cornwall, be free, and subject to him and all his successors, that he govern and rule his diocese as the other bishops who are in my dominion, and that the place and governance of St Petroc be always in his and his successors' power.

As far as is known, grants or confirmations of liberties were not made regularly to dioceses on the accession of a new bishop in Anglo-Saxon England; therefore, we are entitled to assume that special circumstances resulted in the charter under consideration. H. P. R. Finberg interpreted the situation as follows: the bishops of Cornwall, back to the initial appointee of the Anglo-Saxon monarchy, Conan, had been *chorepiscopi* of the bishops of Crediton, but now 'Æthelred gave Bishop Ealdred of St Germans a charter establishing a see in Cornwall with full diocesan juris-diction'.[108] This explanation fits the content of the charter reasonably well, with the statement, 'that he govern and rule his diocese as the other bishops who are in my dominion', meaning that Ealdred is to be a full bishop rather than a *chorepiscopus*. It does not, however, fit the facts in so far as these can be gleaned from the documents mentioned in the previous section of this chapter. Æthelstan established a territorial diocese of Cornwall. Dunstan, writing to Æthelred before the charter under discussion was issued, gave no indication that Conan and his successors were *chorepiscopi*. His reference to the incumbent as 'þære scire bisceop' conveys the image of a bishop on equal footing with bishops in other parts of England.[109] We can do better that this in explaining the meaning of Æthelred's charter.

Rather than altering the status of the episcopate of Cornwall in the way proposed by Finberg, the charter of Æthelred could have been drawn up to meet a need for clarification of the status of the bishopric. Dunstan's letter, written only a short time previously, concerns a problem of the bishops of Cornwall regarding their title to three Cornish estates originally given to the bishopric of Sherborne and later passing to that of Crediton before the creation of the Cornish see. Dispute on this point suggests an uncertain or weak status of bishop and diocese. It is not difficult to see how a fairly new episcopate in a fringe-area mainly occupied by an alien people might have had difficulty maintaining its rights, and the charter of Æthelred is under-standable as a remedy putting the episcopate on a firm basis.

Another matter to consider is that of possible problems of authority of the bishops of Cornwall within their diocese. Was the authority of the bishop whose seat was beside the Tamar readily recognised throughout Cornwall? There is no evidence that it was not, but indication of a possible setting for conflict is provided by the existence in the mid-ninth century of a bishop with a seat, not at *Lanalet*, but at *Dinuurrin*. The charter of Æthelred is also conceivable as a remedy for this type of difficulty on the part of the bishops of Cornwall, with the words, 'that he govern and rule his

[108] *Lucerna*, p. 113; cf. pp. 109–10 and 170.
[109] Napier & Stevenson, *The Crawford Collection*, pp. 19 and 110 (note on *scire*); cf. Stenton, *Anglo-Saxon England*, p. 439, on southwestern bishoprics.

diocese as the other bishops who are in my dominion', receiving a different complexion: 'that his diocese be governed in a regular manner'.

Let us now probe the meaning of the phrase, 'locusque atque regimen sancti Petroci semper in potestate eius sit successorumque illius'. The *locus sancti Petroci* would be a particular place, an ecclesiastical establishment distinctively associated with Petroc. An establishment of sufficient importance to have received such mention in the charter would be either Padstow or Bodmin, and in 994 almost certainly the latter. What is the *regimen sancti Petroci*? *Regimen* has been given the meaning of 'governance' in the above translation of the passage, not governance over St Petroc, but governance in some way belonging to St Petroc; however, the word has several specific ecclesiastical meanings: 'episcopal dignity', '(arch)bishopric', 'dignity of an abbot', 'administration of a church'.[110] The penultimate meaning appears to have been adopted in the interpretation of the 'locusque . . . illius' phrase put forward by Henderson and Grosjean. The latter has written:[111]

Until 1043, the bishop of Cornwall was at the same time the abbot of the richest monastery of his diocese. One obtains proof of his frequent residence at Bodmin in the manumissions included in the gospel-book of that house. Bodmin, one can say, was his administrative capital; St Germans, his spiritual capital, where he had his seat and his cathedral.

This is a defensible understanding of the import of the text, and invites comparison with the problems of insufficient endowment of other southwestern sees,[112] but it is hardly borne out by the evidence. Only once, after the charter was issued which is here supposed to have begun the association of Bodmin with the bishopric, was a Cornish bishop recorded as witness in the Bodmin manumissions.[113] A second objection applies additionally to another interpretation of the charter-phrase – as a design to change the episcopal seat from St Germans to the place of St Petroc, explained by Finberg as a move from the coast inland to Bodmin in order to avoid viking-raids.[114] Not only is there no sign that this transfer of the diocesan

---

[110] Niermeyer, *Mediae Latinitatis Lexicon*, p. 901, *s.v. regimen*, from early mediaeval Continental sources; not given by Latham, *Revised Medieval Latin Wordlist*.

[111] 'Jusqu'en 1043, l'évêque du Cornwall sera en même temps l'abbé du plus riche monastère de son diocèse. On tient la preuve de sa fréquente résidence à Bodmin dans les manumissions que renferme l'Evangéliaire de cette maison. Bodmin, peut-on dire, était sa capitale administrative; St. Germans, sa capitale spirituelle, où il avait son siège et sa cathédrale' ('Vies et miracles', pp. 131–2, almost certainly after Henderson, *The Cornish Church Guide*, pp. 26–7).

[112] Stenton, *Anglo-Saxon England*, pp. 439–40.

[113] See Jenner, 'The manumissions', pp. 252–4.

[114] Napier & Stevenson, *The Crawford Collection*, p. 105, n. 1; Finberg, *Lucerna*, pp. 113, n. 4, and 170.

seat took place,[115] unless the above-mentioned statement of William of Malmesbury be such, but also none that the bishops of Exeter, heirs to the lands of the defunct bishopric of Cornwall, either possessed or tried to possess any property of Petroc. It is very doubtful that such a claim on behalf of the see of Exeter would not have been made, had justification been provided by a former attachment of the property of the church of St Petroc to the see of Cornwall.

Both interpretations of the phrase in the charter allow that it gives direct control and use of a monastery or collegiate church of St Petroc, either at Padstow or Bodmin, into the hands of the bishops of Cornwall. An objection would be why a matter of this sort is not expressed in the charter as a direct donation of the *monasterium sancti Petroci* to bishop or bishopric. Why is the curious *in potestate* there?[116] Also, does a meaning for *regimen* of 'dignity of an abbot' or 'administration of a church' adequately suit the combination *regimen sancti Petroci*?

There is another interpretation of the phrase in question, which seems to suit better both its language and that of the passage as a whole, and which is at least conceivable in the situation with which the charter dealt. Let *regimen* have a general meaning of 'governance', and let the *regimen sancti Petroci* be the extent of control of the saint, or actually of the ecclesiastical community by whom he was revered as the founder, over churches, other ecclesiastical communities, and estates. To go one step further, the *regimen sancti Petroci* might be a rendering of what in Irish sources would have been called the *parrochia (paruchia) Petroci*. Be that as it may, the force of the phrase, as proposed here, is to put the church and governance of St Petroc under the episcopal administration and jurisdiction of the bishops of Cornwall.[117] That sense of *in potestate* would follow naturally from the previous phrase, 'ut ipse gubernet atque regat suam parochiam'. As for the provision that the bishop is to govern 'as other bishops who are in my dominion', this would refer at least in part to internal irregularities in the diocese of Cornwall. The other interpretations make this last phrase of the disposition independent of what precedes it, whereas in that under consideration the whole grant would concern the status of the bishopric. What is envisaged here is a situation in which a bishopric centred in the 'place' of St Petroc has become defunct and been replaced by that at St Germans, but

[115] Two charters, dated 1018 but probably forged after the middle of the century (Sawyer, *Anglo-Saxon Charters*, nos 953 and 951), refer respectively to the seat at St Germans and title to episcopal property of Germanus alone.

[116] A meaning for *potestas* such as 'possession', 'the aggregate estates of a landed proprietor', 'an estate', 'l'autorité seigneuriale – lordship' found in Niermeyer, *Mediae Latinitatis Lexicon*, pp. 819–20 (but not Latham, *Revised Medieval Latin Word-list*), would render the charter phrase capable of granting property, but this is not normal Anglo-Saxon diplomatic usage.

[117] Not a new suggestion: cf. Haddan & Stubbs, *Councils*, I.703; and Henderson, 'East Cornwall', p. 142, apparently abandoned by him in favour of the first interpretation above.

77

in which the house there has persisted in asserting (perhaps not all but) some claims of independent administration and jurisdiction over itself and the old bishopric, to the annoyance of the bishops of Cornwall. After all, we can suspect from evidence discussed in the first and third sections of this chapter that the whole territory of Cornwall was unified under a bishop at St Germans only after the first quarter of the tenth century.

The testimony of William of Malmesbury and the charter of Æthelred, for which the most satisfactory explanation is perhaps that outlined in the preceding paragraph, indicates the existence of an episcopate centred in a house of St Petroc in Cornwall. This interpretation is assisted by our knowledge that there was a bishop's seat other than St Germans in ninth-century Cornwall – that at *Dinuurrin*. The well established episcopate at Padstow and/or Bodmin, of which traces have persisted in the above mentioned sources, should have been in existence when there was a Celtic monastery at either of these places.

5. TWO CHARTERS FOR CORNISH RELIGIOUS HOUSES

Two texts purporting to be Anglo-Saxon charters granting lands to ecclesiastical communities in Cornwall concern us here in different ways. The first provides grounds for inferring the existence of an early monastery at St Buryan in the far west of Cornwall. The second supports that inference by showing a similar development from the early monastery called *Docco*, glimpsed in the *Vita (Prima) Sancti Samsonis*. Both, taken together with other evidence within and without Cornwall, indicate that early Cornish religious houses may have secured written records of their landed possessions.

In the St Buryan charter, King Æthelstan declares that he has given[118]

a certain little part of my land, in the place which is called the Church of St Berian that is, I have bestowed into eternal heredity in honour of God and blessed Berian for the redemption of my soul and for the longevity of my days, one *mansa* divided into seven places, with all things pertaining to it – fields, meadows, pastures, rivers fisheries – with this condition, namely that the aforesaid land be free from all worldly payment except prayer which the clerics have promised me, that is 100 masses and 100 psalters and daily prayers.

---

[118] 'Quapropter ego Ethelstanus, rex Anglorum, ceterarumque gencium in circuit persistencium gubernator et rector, pro peticione nobilium meorum ded quandam particulam terre mee, in loco qui dicitur Ecclesia Sancte Beriane, id es unam mansam in septem loca diuisam, in honorem Dei et beate Beriane pro redempcione anime mee et pro longeuitate dierum meorum in eternam heredit atem largitus sum cum omnibus ad se pertinentibus, campis, pratis, pascuis riuulis, piscariis, ea uidelicet condicione ut libera sit illa prefata terra ab omn mundiali censu nisi oracione quam clerice mihi promiserunt, id est .C. missas e .C. psalteria et cotidie oraciones.' See n. 120.

Further on in the document is a coherent account of the property, with its bounds and names of the seven places, which permits us to identify fairly well the lands granted.[119]

The charter has come down to us in a corrupt copy with a rather peculiar background, and its authenticity has been seriously questioned. It is found in the register of John de Grandisson, bishop of Exeter (1327–69), forming part of a document drawn up by a predecessor, William Briwere, on the occasion of his visit to St Buryan in 1238.[120] In this, statements framing the charter record how Bishop Briwere dedicated the church and confirmed the privileged sanctuary there; he saw the charter in the church and ordered it copied word for word into the church's books, 'that the aforementioned privilege and deed of sanctuary and liberty, drawn up of old, might not be able to perish from age'.[121] The document found its way into Grandisson's register because he was contesting a royal claim, initiated at the beginning of the fourteenth century and ultimately successful, that St Buryan was a royal free chapel.[122]

Indications are that the St Buryan charter, despite its problems, derives from a genuine document.[123] To excuses offered by C. B. Crofts (and

---

[119] The bounds of one of the seven places, *Bodenewel* (Burnewhall), are given separately, and enclose an area in the extreme southwest of St Buryan parish (see Crofts, 'St. Buryan', p. 8). These are preceded by another set of bounds, many of which are unidentifiable topographic features; however, identification of *kescelcromleghe* with Caer Bran (near Grumbla; Gover, 'The Place-names of Cornwall', p. 659, *s. v.* Grumbler) and *kacregan* with Crean (*ibid.*, p. 618) indicates that the land covered the northern three-quarters of the parish of St Buryan. Included within the area bounded were the other six places: *Pendre* (Pendrea), *Bokankeed* (Bosanketh), *Botilwoelon* (defunct farmstead; see Henderson, 'Ecclesiastical Antiquities', I.64; cf. the incorrect identification by Gover, 'The Place-names of Cornwall', p. 647), *Treikyn* (name lost; see n. 127), *Bosselynyn* (Bosliven), and *Trevernen* (Trevernen). Cf. map of Domesday manors given by Henderson, 'Topography', I.9.

[120] Exeter, Devon Record Office, MS. Grandison, vol. II, no. 4, fo 25v; for a photograph, see Crofts, *A Short History*, opposite p. 16; the best edition is by Hingeston-Randolph, *The Register of John*, I.84–6; cf. Sawyer, *Anglo-Saxon Charters*, p. 179, no. 450.

[121] 'ne priuilegium et scriptum sanctuarii ac libertatis predicte, ab antiquo confectum, deperire posset propter uetustatem.'

[122] For a history of the controversy, see Henderson, *Essays*, pp. 100–5.

[123] The charter cannot be in exactly its original form, for 'ponsprontiryon' and probably 'peluagerens' in the bounds must be at least twelfth century, before which the *ns* would have been *nt* (cf. Padel, 'Cornish language notes', pp. 57–8, and Jackson, *Language and History*, pp. 507–8). Oliver Padel has remarked to me that also there are no distinctively Old Cornish place-name forms in the charter and that its spellings with *k* for *c* should be seen as post-Conquest. The diplomatic formulae employed would suit a charter a little later in the tenth century than the reign of Æthelstan (924–39), and the St Buryan charter actually bears the date 943.

supported by Finberg), on grounds of miscopying,[124] for faults in the dating clause and witness-list two points can be added and a third foreshadowed here. First, it appears safe to dismiss suspicion that the charter is a fourteenth-century episcopal forgery for use in the above-mentioned controversy about St Buryan, for it was more a liability than an asset to the episcopal cause. Thus we see Bishop Grandisson, writing against the claim the Æthelstan had founded a free chapel at St Buryan, refer to Briwere's document and then maintain on the basis of 'chronicles' that Æthelstan had held nothing in Cornwall;[125] this flatly contradicts the words 'a certain little part of my land' in Æthelstan's charter. The impression received is that the episcopal side is making the best of an existing document, and the royal side perhaps taking advantage of it.[126] Secondly, there is evidence in the bounds – as well as the subscriptions – that the charter was copied from an exemplar in Insular script.[127] Support for authenticity will also be forthcoming in our discussion of correspondences of the St Buryan charter with others originating in a Celtic milieu.[128]

In the charter, the king bestows land in honour of God and St Berian on a

---

[124] Crofts, 'King Athelstan', pp. 340–2; Finberg, *Lucerna*, pp. 111–12, and *The Early Charters*, pp. 17–18.

[125] Letter to Prince Edward, Duke of Cornwall, in 1352 (ed. Hingeston-Randolph, *The Register of John*, I.75): 'Et en meisme lesglise de Seynte Berione est escript en lur veyl Myssal coment Levesqe Descestre, Willeam, la dedya, et excomenga touz ceaux qe feissent encountre la franchise Seynte Berione, et la prist especialment en la proteccion de la Esglise Dexcestre. Et, moun treshonure Seignur, mout me mervaille qe len vous aad enfourme qe le Roi Adelstan founda cele Chapelle. Qar si len regarde bien les Cronicles len trovera qil ne tient rien en Cornwaille ne outre la Ryvere de Thamer. Et pur ceo fist il enclore la Vylle Dexcestre et fist le Chastel.'

[126] No proof exists that the latter was employing the charter. In the letter to which the above is a reply, Edward wrote that Æthelstan had founded the free chapel of St Buryan 'plus de quatre centz et quarrante et oet ans passez' (*ibid.*, p. 74). If this curiously precise 448 years is taken from 1352, the result is too early for Athelstan: however, *408* years exactly suits the date borne by the charter. For Grandisson's account to the bishop of Worcester of the basis for the royal claim, not mentioning the charter, see *ibid.*, p. 73.

[127] 'Lentrisidyn' in the second set of bounds must bear the name of Tresidder, a nearby farm (see Gover, 'The Place-names of Cornwall', p. 621); the second part of 'mankependoun' in the first set of bounds is almost certainly *pendour*, 'water's head'; 'Treikyn (alternative reading 'Treikyu'), one of the seven places, may be the 'Trelcewe' recorded among possessions of the College of St Buryan in the Chantry-Certificate of 1549 (Henderson, 'Ecclesiastical Antiquities', I.62j and cf. p. 64). The letters *r* and *n*, *l* and *i* are prone to confusion by untutored readers of Insular script but are distinctive in the later English scripts. In a forgery, the subscriptions, which abound in misreadings of þ as *h*, etc., could have been taken from unrelated Anglo-Saxon documents, but the bounds apply to St Buryan.

[128] See pp. 83–4 below. Wendy Davies, who pointed these out to me, endorsed the judgment of the charter given at the outset of this paragraph, in private communication (1975).

religious house which will owe service of prayer promised him by the clerics. It did not establish that house, and yet conveyed the property upon which the foundation stood. The land is said to be 'in loco qui dicitur Ecclesia Sancte Beriane', which renders *Ecglosberria*, the name of the manor recorded as held by the canons of St Berriona in Domesday Book.[129] Thus we see the significance of the St Buryan charter to our study: the interpretation argued here is that is represents a re-endowment by the new political power of an *existing* establishment,[130] comprising a group of clerics serving the church, and possessing the lands, of their saint.[131]

Our attention turns now to the *Landochou* charter, which allows a glimpse of what the Celtic monastery called *Docco* had become by the mid-tenth century. The charter exists in a copy made *ca* 1305 in connexion with a legal dispute over special obligations of Plympton Priory toward *Lanow* (viz., *Landochou*) church.[132] It records a grant of land by King Edgar, and was drawn up in 961 × 963.[133] The arguments for the document's authenticity advanced by W. M. M. Picken have been endorsed by Wendy Davies who, familiar from her examination of Celtic diplomatic material with grants of property to saints rather than living recipients and with blanket or vague immunity clauses, has dismissed his worries that the charter is defective on these points.[134] Its authenticity and integrity are accepted here.

In the *Landochou* charter, the disposition reads as follows:[135]

Wherefore I, Edgar, by divine disposition king of the Anglo-Saxons, have given for the love of God to those two saints Dochou and Cywa into eternal inheritance some parts of land, that is, the measure of two *mansae* in [at?] the *monasterium* which is

[29] Exon., fo 207r, *Eglosberrie* in Exch., fo 121r.
[30] Cf. Henderson, *Essays*, p. 96: 'The charter was really a protection against spoliation rather than a gift'.
[31] Beyond female sex and an Irish connexion, nothing is really known about St Buryan. The name is on the list in the Vatican MS. Reg. lat. 191 (Olson & Padel, 'A tenth-century list', pp. 34 and 48). See Dalton & Doble, *Ordinale*, I.10 (cf. Doble, *The Saints of Cornwall*, III.80) and Leland, *Itinerary* (ed. Smith, I.189).
[32] London, Public Record Office, MS. C47/52/1/1, m.3 (ed. Picken, 'The "Landochou" charter').
[33] *Ibid.*, pp. 40–1.
[34] *Ibid.*, pp. 39–42; Wendy Davies in private communication (1975). The charter-bounds also display appropriate tenth-century spellings (especially 'þuern' for *guern*; cf. Jackson, *Language and History*, pp. 388–9).
[35] 'Quapropter ego Eadgar diuina dispensacione rex Ongilsaxonum partes aliquas terre, hoc est mensura duarum mansarum in monasterio quod ab incolis Landochou uocitatur, istis duobus sanctis Dochou et Cyp[for þ]a pro Dei amore in eternam hereditatem largitus sum cum omnibus ad se rite pertinentibus, campis, siluis, pascuis, riuolis [*sic*], fluminibus, pratis, ea condicione ut habeant eam terram liberam sine fine, precipiendo precipio, in nomine Omnipotentis Dei ut ad monasterium sancti Dochou et sancte Cypa prefata terra reddatur ubi reliquie eorum piissimorum patroniorum honorifice obseruantur.' In the manuscript, 'Ea [*sic*] condicione' begins a new section.

called by the inhabitants Landochou, with all things rightly pertaining to these. fields, forests, pastures, streams, rivers, meadows, with this condition, that they shall hold this land limitlessly free. By [so] ordering I order in the name of Omnipotent God that the aforesaid land be given to the *monasterium* of St Dochou and St Cywa where the relics of these most pious patrons are honourably venerated.

The final portion warrants explanation as to the purpose of thus rephrasing the grant. The king first says that he *has given* the land with its appurtenances to the two saints; then, on the basis of this grant, he *orders* that the land *be given* to the *monasterium* of those saints, their resting place. Thus, the earthly recipient of the grant is specified. This last section would appear to be intended as a clarification of the bequest to the saints.[136]

The early monastery called *Docco* in the *Vita (Prima) Sancti Samsonis* is unquestionably in the background of the religious house of the charter. 'Dochou' shows the expected linguistic change from 'Docco';[137] the 'monastery which is called Docco' of the *uita* is practically equivalent to, if not a translation of, an earlier form of *Landochou*; and the location of the place in the charter, present-day St Kew near the north Cornish coast and the Camel estuary, is appropriate for the monastery at which Samson arrived from Wales. Whether the tenth-century *monasterium* was still what could be described as a communal monastery or had become an endowed group of clerics is not known. Note that this charter, too, is a grant to an existing religious house of its nuclear lands.[138]

The link which we can make between the evidence of the *Vita Sancti Samsonis* and that of the *Landochou* charter is very important, documenting as it does one instance of an expected phenomenon – the persistence and patronage of early Cornish religious houses under Anglo-Saxon rule. This is helpful to our analysis not only of the St Buryan charter but throughout the chapter as we work backward from later collegiate churches to predicate early monasteries in Cornwall. Nor is the subsequent history of *Landochou* without interest. It did not long remain in the possession of the saints, for as *Lannohoo*, etc., in Domesday Book it is a royal manor.[139] Yet in the earlier twelfth century part of the manor was given back with the

---

[136] The different interpretation given by Picken, 'The "Landochou" charter', p. 41 based upon his view mentioned in n. 138 below, is unnecessary to explain the meaning of the passage.

[137] Jackson, *Language and History*, pp. 572–3.

[138] The bounds present great difficulties but permit the conclusion on topographic grounds that, if the site of the parish-church lay within the area bounded, the latter must have covered a sizable portion of the present parish of St Kew. A difference concerning the location of the early monastery called *Docco* exists between the writer, who favours the site of the parish-church, and Picken, who puts it at the farm called Lanow, postulating a shift to the former place before the time of the *Landochou* charter. A Latin- and ogom-inscribed memorial stone (Macalister, *Corpus*, I.462, no. 484) was found near the church, and the development of a secular barton of Lanow may be explained by subsequent manorial history.

[139] Exon., fo 101r; see p. 91 below.

church into ecclesiastical hands; from then the church was collegiate and had perhaps been so all along.[140] The continuity at this ecclesiastical site can be seen in others in Cornwall.

The St Buryan and *Landochou* charters have certain points of likeness.[141] These occur in the charters' core, the dispositions, of which an analysis is given here. Both begin 'Quapropter ego', followed by the names of the kings (but with different royal styles). Later, at the end of the description of the property granted, the St Buryan charter has the words 'to the honour of God and blessed Beriana', apparently meant to identify the grantees, and in the *Landochou* charter we find the names of the saintly beneficiaries. Clauses governed by *pro* which give quite different religious motivations for the grants then intervene. The dispositive words which come next are identical in both charters: 'in eternam hereditatem largitus sum'; the appurtenances follow; then, significantly, come the words 'ea uidelicet condicione ut' in the St Buryan charter and 'ea condicione ut' in the *Landochou* charter, introducing general immunity clauses.

Two of these similarities are in points atypical of Anglo-Saxon charters, which in fact have led certain commentators to suspect a forged or defective text.[142] These matters have been alluded to earlier: the granting of land to the saint(s) concerned rather than to their present followers or foundation and the rendering of the immunity clause by means of a simple phrase beginning *ea condicione*. Interesting comments on both have been made by Wendy Davies, viewing them against a different background of charter-material from Celtic regions.[143] Bequest to saints 'is not unknown in Celtic charters' and lack of detailed conditions 'is normal is Celtic charters'. Another feature of the dispositions, the words *largitus sum*, is common in Celtic diplomatic material; it occurs in Anglo-Saxon charters as well, but rarely in those of Æthelstan. Similar to 'libera sit . . . ab omni mundiali censu' in the St Buryan charter are phrases in the charters of *Liber Landauensis* and the Vespasian *Vita Sancti Cadoci* in Wales and of the Cartularies of Redon and Landévennec in Brittany; but such are found also in Anglo-Saxon charters both dubious and apparently authentic.[144] The word *cyrographum* in Æthelstan's signature is also particularly, though certainly not uniquely, associated with the above-mentioned Welsh documents. The sanction of the *Landochou* charter is 'very similar to some Celtic ones'.

[140] Dugdale, *Monasticon*, VI.53; Hingeston-Randolph, *The Registers*, pp. 224–5; Henderson, *The Cornish Church Guide*, p. 93; Maclean, *The Parochial and Family History*, II.84–7.
[141] Picken, 'The "Landochou" charter', p. 38, n. 7.
[142] Rose-Troup, 'St. Buryan Charter', p. 295; Picken, 'The "Landochou" charter', pp. 41–2.
[143] Wendy Davies very kindly supplied me with the following observations in 1975, by the letter cited in nn. 128 and 134 above.
[144] On these points cf. Davies, 'Saint Mary's', pp. 466–70.

The likeness of the St Buryan and *Landochou* charters to other charter-material of Celtic provenance has led Wendy Davies to suggest that a Cornish diplomatic tradition lay in their background.[145] Support for this comes from the similarities between the two charters, which might be expected if they had the proposed common derivation, as well as from two more recent discoveries. One is the pertinence to Cornwall of a charter in which 'Count' Maenchi grants *Lanlouern* to St Heldenus in the reign of Æthelstan; the other is the late record of Æthelstan's charter in favour of the bishopric of St Germans, discussed in section 3 above.[146] In their common feature of a grant 'in diocesim sempiternam/perpetuam', otherwise unknown in Anglo-Saxon charters but present in Breton records, these documents give independent evidence of a Cornish diplomatic tradition. We should note that the donor gives land to a saint. His charter is particularly interesting as recording a bequest by a Cornishman to a Cornish saint, but made under Anglo-Saxon auspices at Athelney (Somerset). It is tempting to regard this as continuing an old practice of recording land-grants, but now performed in accordance with new political factors. One may speculate for a moment about how usages of a Cornish diplomatic tradition could have found their way into Anglo-Saxon charters – through models provided by existing documents; or through information otherwise known or passed on to those drafting the charters concerning the suitability and desirability of bequests to saints and of certain phrases.[147] In any case, there is good evidence here for the making of written records of the estates of early Cornish religious houses.[148]

Otherwise, the material considered in this section has suggested the existence of an early monastery at St Buryan. It also has a broad significance in outlining the pattern for survival of the early monasteries in Cornwall, in altered forms and conditions, into later periods in which they have left some written trace.

[145] From parallels among diplomata from other Celtic regions, Davies has postulated a 'definable pre-conquest Celtic diplomatic tradition' (see *ibid.*, especially pp. 462, 473 and 485; cf. her '*Liber Landavensis*', especially pp. 346–7, 351, and – most importantly – 'The Latin charter tradition'.

[146] See pp. 63–4 and the reference in n. 58 above. The property and recipient of 'Count' Maenchi's charter (Sawyer, *Anglo-Saxon Charters*, p. 353, no. 1207) have been identified respectively as Lanlawren in the parish of Lanteglos by Fowey and St Hyldren, patron of the nearby church of Lansallos, possibly on this evidence of landholding the site of an early monastery.

[147] For a fragment of evidence for written Old Cornish in the background of an Anglo-Saxon charter, see Padel, 'Cornish language notes', pp. 58–9.

[148] The practice is attested by the ninth century in Wales by the charters in the Lichfield Gospels and in Brittany by Uurmonoc, *Vita Sancti Pauli Aureliani*, § 19.

6. A NOTE ON ST NEOT

Asser, in his *De Rebus Gestis Alfredi*, wrote 'and now also St Niot rests in the same place', when referring to the church of St Gueriir in Cornwall where King Alfred was cured.[149] Later hagiography of Neot avers that he was an English saint who founded a monastery in Cornwall.[150] Charles Henderson has shown that, on the contrary, the patron and eponym of St Neot in Cornwall was a Cornish saint identified with an English name-sake.[151] Some of his arguments for this are weak,[152] but the presence of 'Sanctus Anietus' among the tenants of Cornish lands in the *Inquisitio Geldi* – supported by the saint's name 'Niet' in the slightly later Exeter Domesday Book and *Niet* or *Niot* in vernacular place-names for the Cornish site from Domesday Book to modern times – is compelling evidence that we are dealing with a saint different from the English Neot.[153]

It is hardly possible to determine how the identification of the Cornish saint with Neot, patron of the church of St Neots in Huntingdonshire, came

[149] § 74 (ed. Stevenson, *Asser's Life*, p. 55): 'Sed quodam tempore, diuine nutu, antea, cum Cornubiam uenandi causa adiret, et ad quandam ecclesiam orandi causa diuertisset, in qua sanctus Gueriir requiescit *et nunc etiam Sanctus Niot ibidem pausat*, suatim utens – erat enim sedulus sanctorum locorum uisitator etiam ab infantia, orandi et eleemosynam dandi gratia – diu in oratione tacita prostratus, ita Domina misericordiam deprecabatur, quatenus omnipotens Deus pro sua immensa clementia stimulos praesentis et infestantis infirmitatis aliqua qualicunque leuiori infirmitate mutaret, ea tamen condicione, ut corporaliter exterius illa infirmitas non apparet, ne inutilis et despectus esset'. Stevenson thought, unnecessarily, that the italicised passage was an interpolation: *ibid.*, pp. xlix, xcvii–xcviii, cii, 296–7; cf. Whitelock, *The Genuine Asser*, p. 12, n. 3. But this view has been rejected by Gransden, *Historical Writing*, p. 49, n. 52. 'Gueriir' is otherwise unknown; there is no reason to reject him as a Cornish saint, although scribal error is a possibility (cf. Stevenson, *Asser's Life*, p. 296; Doble, *S. Neot*, p. 4; and Charles Henderson, *apud* Doble, *ibid.*, pp. 39–40). On all this see Michael Lapidge, *apud* Dumville & Keynes, *The Anglo-Saxon Chronicle*, XVII.lxxvi.

[150] See Stevenson, *Asser's Life*, pp. 256–61, and Doble, *S. Neot*, pp. 1–39.

[151] *The Cornish Church Guide*, p. 149, and 'East Cornwall', p. 417; cf. Doble, *S. Neot*, p. 2.

[152] 'Celtic' features which Henderson found in legends of the saint, the existence of his holy well and of tenth- and eleventh-century free-standing stone crosses at St Neot in Cornwall, may all reflect the character not of the saint but of the environment in which his legend and foundation developed. These features nevertheless illustrate no lack of homogeneity of saint or foundation with undeniably Celtic counterparts.

[153] In hagiographical works the name is always spelled *Neotus*, and St Neots in Huntingdonshire (see below) has consistent place-name forms in *Ne-* with the sole exception of St Nyot's in 1329 (Mawer & Stenton, *The Place-names of Bedfordshire and Huntingdonshire*, p. 265). Asser's phrase about 'Niot' is specific to Cornwall.

about. The origin of the monastery at the place just mentioned is unclear[154] and the legend of its patron-saint contradictory, Neot being presented as a contemporary both of tenth-century Glastonbury figures and of King Alfred, whom he predeceases (before 878).[155] Perhaps the story of the translation of the saint's relics from the Cornish to the Huntingdonshire site is connected with conflicting claims, between the monasteries of St Neots and Crowland about possession of the relics of Neot, which arose in the period around 1000.[156] In any case, Anglo-Saxon penetration of Cornwall found an existing cult of a local saint Aniet, Niet, or Niot, and at some stage the identification was made.

We are able to bring to the discussion a piece of evidence which Charles Henderson did not know. On the Brittonic list of saints' names in the Vatican codex, Reginensis latinus 191, is probably 'Nioth', equivalent to the name given by Asser.[157] This document presents exactly the situation in which one would expect to find the Cornish saint, and is thus another factor in discrediting what has been the usual view of St Neot and his foundation in Cornwall. In doing so, the foregoing discussion has prepared the way for consideration within the next section of whether the landholding collegiate church of *Nietestou* in Cornwall, recorded in Domesday Book, represents a devolved early Cornish monastery.

7. DOMESDAY BOOK

Domesday Book shows the existence in Cornwall in the second half of the eleventh century of a number of landholding religious establishments, most if not all of them collegiate churches. Before we examine these through the relevant entries and consider what they represent within the ecclesiastical history of Cornwall, a word about source-material is in order. Cornwall is

---

[154] See Stevenson, *Asser's Life*, pp. 297–8, and Doble, *S. Neot*, pp. 25–7.

[155] The Alfred connexion is particularly obscure, and the passage in Asser's text may even be its source.

[156] See Ordericus Vitalis, *Historia Ecclesiastica*, IV (ed. & transl. Chibnall, *The Ecclesiastical History*, II.342–3); and Doble, *S. Neot*, p. 34; cf. Stevenson, *Asser's Life*, pp. 298–9. Spooner, *St. Neot*, p. 17, observes that the disputed removal of the relics out of Cornwall may be only an 'echo' of the real conflict between St Neots and Crowland. Doble, *S. Neot*, p. 14, makes a compelling suggestion that the homily *Of Seinte Neote* (see n. 88 above), which gives the legend of Neot in the earliest known form (Stevenson, *Asser's Life*, p. 258), was written at Crowland.

[157] See p. 56 above. 'Nioth' may possibly be 'Rioth' (cf. Olson & Padel, 'A tenth-century list', pp. 49–50). Doubt arises because of a rightward upstroke from the base of the second minim of the *n*; however, it should be remarked that, although *n* and *r* are liable to confusion in the script of the list, the upstroke of the letter in question is unlike those of letters *r* on the list, being indefinite in contrast to the deliberateness of the latter, and otherwise the letter has the form of *n* rather than *r*.

dealt with in both the Exchequer and Exeter versions of Domesday Book, the latter being a first-draft summary of returns for southwestern England, the basis in a fair copy for the Exchequer Domesday.[158] Entries in the Exeter Domesday sometimes give more information and have better name-forms than those in the Exchequer version,[159] and the former are usually given preference in the following discussion. Reference will also be made to materials included within the Domesday *Liber Exoniensis*: accounts of the geld-inquest pertaining to a period either shortly before or contemporary with Domesday Book proper,[160] lists of hundreds, accounts of lands illegitimately possessed (*terrae occupatae*), and a small number of fief-summaries.

The manor of *Sanctus Germanus*[161] was held by the bishop of Exeter, but in it the canons of St Germanus had twelve of the total of twenty-four hides.[162] It is of course to be identified with St Germans, where the later history of landholding makes clear the locations of the bishop's and canons' portions: significantly, the church and its immediate environs lay wholly within the canons' land.[163] These canons are a survival of the bishopric of Cornwall, which was superseded in 1050 by the see of Exeter. To the latter came the church, clerical community, and domain of St Germanus. It has already been shown in section 3 that their tenth-century *monasterium* of Lanalet (at St Germans) continued an establishment older than Æthelstan's bishopric of Cornwall, and suggested that this had been an early Cornish monastery.[164]

The existence of a collegiate church of St Petroc at Bodmin is shown by references to *Sancti Petrochi canonici* and *presbiteri de Bomene* holding certain estates.[165] No other ecclesiastical tenant had a larger number of

---

[158] See Finn, *Domesday Studies*, with historiographical discussion on pp. 3–6.

[159] Differences in Exeter and Exchequer Domesday data are tabulated by R. W. Finn *et al.*, 'Comparison'.

[160] Finn, *Domesday Studies*, pp. 97–123.

[161] Exon., fos 199v–200r (main entry), 201r (account of usurped lands at the end of bishop of Exeter's fief), 507r (*Terrae Occupatae*); Exch., fo 120v (main entry as *aecclesia Sancti Germani* and an account of usurped lands).

[162] Exon., fo 199v: 'In ea sunt XXIIII hide: de his habent Canonici sancti Germani XII hide que nu[m]quam reddiderunt Gildum pro II hidis'; Exch., fo 120v: 'Ibi sunt XXIIII hidae. Ex his XII hidae sunt canonicorum quae nunquam geldauerunt, et aliae XII hide sunt episcopi et geldabant pro II hidae tempore Regis Eduuardi.'

[163] Henderson, *Records*, pp. 7–8, 12–13, 25–8, 43. The conjecture by Ravenhill, 'Cornwall', p. 301, n. 1, is unwarranted. The division of the manor is generally traced to its acquisition by the bishop of Exeter (Pedler, *The Anglo-Saxon Episcopate*, pp. 108–9; Henderson, *Records*, pp. 8 and 25, and *The Cornish Church Guide*, pp. 70–1).

[164] Pp. 60–6 above.

[165] The former occur in entries for *Languihenoc* and *Rieltona* (see next note), the latter in entries for *Holecoma* and *Nietona* in Devon (Exon., fos 481v and 483r; Exch., fo 117v).

Cornish manors, although the amount and value of Cornish land in the hands of the bishop of Exeter was much greater. First in the Domesday record comes the home-manor of *Bodmine*, then *Languihenoc*, site of the original monastery of St Petroc in Cornwall at Padstow, then sixteen more estates, and finally notice of ten additional properties which had been usurped from Petroc.[166] The distribution of these lands can be seen on Map N.

With one exception, the other collegiate churches in Domesday Cornwall had a single property apiece. The canons of St Achebrannus held *Lannachebran*,[167] situated at present-day St Keverne on the Lizard Peninsula of southwestern Cornwall. The canons of St Probus held *Lanbrabois*,[168] at Probus in the interior of southern Cornwall. The canons of St Carentoch held *Langorroc*,[169] at Crantock on the central-north coast of Cornwall. The canons of St Stephen held *Lanscauetona*, at St Stephens by Launceston, midway on the eastern border of Cornwall.[170] The canons of St Pieranus held *Lanpiran*, from which, however, two manors had been taken away.[171] One of these receives no further mention, but the other appears among the lands of the usurping count of Mortain as *Tregrebri*, said to be appropriately 'de honore sancti Peranni'.[172] The nucleus of *Lanpiran* would have been at St Piran's Oratory, or perhaps by then at the nearby church-site beside the stone-cross mentioned in n. 209 below, in Perranzabuloe parish on the central-north coast. We know from the geld-accounts that St Pieranus had property in *Stratona* Hundred farther to the north. There *Tregrebri* has been plausibly identified as *Tregenver*, a defunct farmstead at Trethevy in

[166] Exon., fos 202r–205r, and Exch., fos 120v–121r (main entries); Exon., fos 111v, 112r, 241v, and Exch., fos 120v, 123v (usurped properties and one owing the saint a customary rent); Exon., fos 507v–508r (*Terrae Occupatae*); fo 528v (fief-summary); fos 72r–73r (geld-accounts) and see also fo 63v.

[167] Exon., fo 205v, Exch., fo 121r; Exon., fo 72r (geld-accounts). 'Achobran' is on the list in Vatican MS. Reg. lat. 191 (Olson & Padel, 'A tenth-century list', pp. 34 and 47–8). See Doble, *Saint Perran*.

[168] Exon., fo 206r, Exch., fo 121r as *Lanbrebois*; Exon., fo 75r (geld-accounts). In the place-name *-bois* indicates a Celtic patron-saint rather than a Roman St Probus, for the nominative case-ending *-us* would not have been retained in the vernacular. The saint appears as *Propus* on the vernacular list in Vatican MS. Reg. lat. 191 (Olson & Padel, 'A tenth-century list', pp. 34 and 51–2). There was a *Lanprobi* in Somerset.

[169] Exon., fo 206r, Exch., fo 121r. See pp. 93 and 98 below and Doble, *Saint Carantoc*.

[170] Exon., fo 206v, and Exch., fo 120v; Exon., fo 73r (geld-accounts). To a Cornish place-name comprising *lan* plus saint's name, Old English *tun* has been added; see Gover, 'The Place-names of Cornwall', p. 145. For transference of this place-name from St Stephens to the present Launceston see Henderson, *The Cornish Church Guide*, pp. 113, 115, 180.

[171] Exon., fos 206v–207r, Exch., fo 121r; Exon., fo 72v (geld-accounts). *Pierguin* on the list in Vatican MS. Reg. lat. 191 may be the saint concerned (Olson & Padel, 'A tenth-century list', pp. 34 and 52–3). See Doble, *Saint Perran*.

[172] Exon., fo 240v; Exch., fo 123v, reads 'Haec terra est de possessione Sancti Pieran'.

the coastal parish of Tintagel.[173] Mention is made not only of canons of St Pieranus but also of their dean, who was owed a customary payment from the detached manors. The canons of St Berriona held *Ecglosberria*.[174] They would be successors to the clerics of Æthelstan's charter, their manor a continuation of the property which it conveyed 'in loco qui dicitur Ecclesia Sancte Beriane'; and the suggestion has been made that this was a grant of a pre-existing estate to a pre-existing religious body.[175] Finally, the priests or clerics of St Nietus held *Nietestou*.[176] The use here of *presbiteri* or *clerici* rather than *canonici* stands out in the Domesday account of Cornish ecclesiastical landholders, but its significance is uncertain.[177]

Then there are a few Cornish landholding ecclesiastical establishments for which collegiate status is not indicated by a mention of groups of canons or priests but remains a distinct possibility. One of them, dedicated to St Michael, held the manor of *Treiwal*.[178] This is to be identified with Truthwall in Ludgvan parish on the mainland opposite St Michael's Mount. The Mount, assumed to be the site of the church mentioned in the Exchequer entry, is not recorded in Domesday Book; unsuited to large-scale cultivation, it would have received support from nearby *Treiwal*. The manor is said to have been held at the end of Edward's reign by Brismar who, in an entry for a usurped portion thereof, is called *sacerdos*.[179] Did he constitute the whole

---

[173] Henderson, 'East Cornwall', pp. 527—8; Oliver Padel has located this place at O.S. grid-reference SXO85887.

[174] Exon., fo 207r, Exch., fo 121r as *Eglosberrie*; Exon., fo 72r (geld-accounts).

[175] See p. 81 above.

[176] Exon., fo 124v, and Exch., fo 121r (main entries); Exon., fo 230v, and Exch., fo 124r (usurped property); Exon., fo 72r (geld-accounts).

[177] Note the interchangeability of canons and priests with reference to St Petroc's community holding estates in Cornwall and Devon respectively (see p. 87 above).

[178] Exon., fo 208v, and Exch., fo 120v (main entries); Exon., fo 258v, and Exch., fo 125r (usurped property of *Treuthal* (= *Treiwal*); Exon., fo 508r (*Terrae Occupatae*); Exon., fo 72r (geld-accounts). There is a dubious charter in which Edward the Confessor grants 'Sanctum Michaelem qui est iuxta mare' to Mont Saint-Michel in Normandy (Sawyer, *Anglo-Saxon Charters*, p. 317, no. 1061, and see also Hull, *The Cartulary*, pp. x–xiii and 61). Even if the charter is genuine, the tenure was short-lived, for the Domesday manor was held at the end of Edward's reign by a Cornish establishment, not the Norman abbey. Compare the Exon. heading 'Terra Sancti Michahelis de Cornugallia' with others for Cornish houses, viz. 'Terre Sancti Petrochi de Cornugallia' and 'Terre Sancti Pierani in Cornugallia', and compare also entries for Devon possessions of Mont Saint-Michel (Exon., fos 96v, 194v, 195v, Exch., fos 100r, 104r) and for a landholding Shropshire church of St Michael (Exch., fo 252v); on the pre-Conquest tenure see also Taylor, *The Celtic Christianity*, pp. 148–54.

[179] Exon., fo 258v. In the entry under *Terrae Occupatae* this land is said to have been 'in dominicatu sancti' at the end of Edward's reign, leaving no doubt that Michael was indeed in possession at this time. For an explanation, see p. 94 below.

of the establishment? Up to a point the situation at *Nietestou* was similar: entries for a usurped portion of that manor give the pre-Conquest tenant as Godric *presbyter*; yet we know that at that time the manor as a whole was held by priests in plurality.[180] The Exchequer entries for the initial manor of St Petroc at *Bodmine* and *Treiwal* are alike in that the tenant is given as the church of the saint, and canons or priests are not mentioned. These parallels show that we need not reject the idea that the church of St Michael was collegiate. The use of *ecclesia* in reference to St Michael's, otherwise employed in the Exchequer Domesday for substantial establishments, often abbeys, and in Cornwall only for the important collegiate church of St Petroc, might suggest more than a simple church of one priest or a hermitage at St Michael's Mount. Or perhaps, since its manor had been seriously despoiled by the count of Mortain, a collegiate establishment had declined or become defunct. Turning to another ecclesiastical landholder, we see that this fate may also have befallen the unspecified establishment of St Constantinus, whose tenure of an unnamed property in *Winnentona* Hundred was barely maintained against the count's encroachment.[181] The estate is to be identified as sited at Constantine churchtown, formerly *Langustentyn*.[182]

Whereas canons or priests are conspicuous by their absence from Domesday entries for the lands of St Michael and St Constantinus, ecclesiastical landholders are normally expressed as saints, not religious communities, in the geld-accounts for Cornwall. There St Che and St Goranus appear as tenants-in-chief in *Tibestena* Hundred.[183] In Domesday Book their properties are secularised: one is the manor of *Landighe* at the site of Old Kea in Kea parish in southern Cornwall,[184] while St Goranus would have held the land later called Langoron or *Langoran* at Gorran in southern Cornwall,[185] an estate apparently submerged in the Domesday manor of *Lantien*.[186] In favour of the existence of collegiate churches of St Che and St Goranus, as well as of St Michael and St Constantinus, is the collegiate status of the other eight Cornish ecclesiastical landholders.

180 See n. 176 for references.
181 Exon., fo 207r, Exch., fo 121r; Exon., fo 72r (geld-accounts). See p. 92 below.
182 Gover, 'The place-names of Cornwall', p. 501; Henderson, *A History*, pp. 44–5, 146. See Doble, *The Saints of Cornwall*, II.15–24.
183 Exon., fo 72r.
184 Exon., fo 254v, Exch., fo 124v, held of the count of Mortain by a sub-tenant, and before the Conquest by Ailsi. The place-name comprises *lan*, hypocoristic *to* ('thy'), and the saint's name (Gover, 'The Place-names of Cornwall', p. 457). See Doble, *Four Saints*.
185 Gover, 'The Place-names of Cornwall', p. 398. The patron-saint's name occurs as *Guron* on the list in Vatican MS. Reg. lat. 191 (Olson & Padel, 'A tenth-century list', pp. 34 and 60–1). Cf. the second *Vita Sancti Petroci*, § 19, where he is clearly identified with the Bodmin hermit.
186 Present-day Castle, near Lantyan. Henderson, 'The ecclesiastical history', p. 181.

A loose end to tie up is the honour of St Cheus to which belonged the manor of *Tremaruustel* in Domesday Book.[187] The saint's name is the same as that of the landholding saint in the geld-accounts mentioned above. It is not impossible that tiny *Tremaruustel* could fit, along with *Landighe*, into the total geld-free hidage of St Che in *Tibestena* Hundred.[188] Yet in Exeter Domesday *Tremaruustel* occurs in a section of east Cornish manors; unless a mistake has been made, it does not belong in southerly *Tibestena* Hundred. W. M. M. Picken has instead rather convincingly identified the manor with Treroosel in St Teath parish, a few miles from the site of the 'monasterium Sancti Dochou et Sancte Cywa' of King Edgar's charter.[189] It is the latter saint, Picken has maintained, whose name has been mistakenly written 'Chei' in Domesday Book, Che of the geld-accounts being a different patron-saint of a different establishment.[190] The honour of St Cheus must then go back to tenurial arrangements before St Dochou and St Cywa lost title to the home-manor of *Landochou* which, as mentioned previously, appears as the royal manor of *Lannohoo* in Domesday Book, held by Harold at the end of Edward's reign.[191] From *Lannohoo* had been taken away the manors of *Pondestoch* and *Sanguinas*, names which as Poundstock and St Gennys designate churchtowns quite far to the east along the north coast. These properties were not part of the estate of *Landochou* as granted in Edgar's charter, and whether they represent old holdings of the *monasterium* there or acquisitions of its secular successors is not known. Yet it is tempting to see the establishment of St Dochou and St Cywa, like those of St Pieranus and St Petroc, holding a spread of lands along the north coast of Cornwall.

---

[187] Exon., fo 245v: 'hec mansio est de honore sancti Chei'; Exch., fo 125r, is corrupt.

[188] *Tremaruustel* was assessed at two geld-acres, for which no geld was recorded. The Cornish geld-acre was one-third virgate, and there were four virgates in a hide (Ravenhill, 'Cornwall', p. 306). The geld-accounts give only the sum of geld-free hides of each tenant-in-chief in each hundred without reference to individual estates. From the half hide of St Che less two-thirds virgate of *Tremaruustel*, one-and-one-third virgates would remain. In Domesday Book *Landighe* was assessed at one hide and rendered geld for one virgate. The discrepancy could reflect some difference between the geld-account and Domesday Book properties, but figures in these sources often do not tally.

[189] 'The manor'.

[190] His ingenious explanation of how the names were confused (*ibid.*, pp. 228–9) is unfortunately based on an incorrect reconstruction of the saint's name as **Kyw*, whereas it was Cywa, the *vernacular* form in the *Landochou* charter. Later forms support this: see Gover, 'The Place-names of Cornwall', p. 117. This name, as Ciguai, is possibly on the list in Vatican MS. Reg. lat. 191 (Olson & Padel, 'A tenth-century list', pp. 54–5). Cf. Loth, *Les Noms*, *s. n.* 'Civoa pour Kiwa' on p. 23, and 'Languivoa' on p. 74, as against 'Keẘ' on p. 22; Doble, *The Saints of Cornwall*, IV.108; Dalton & Doble, *Ordinale*, IV.3. Confusion of the name of the saint in a form like **Chiuua* or **Cheuua* with *Cheus* seems quite conceivable.

[191] Exon., fo 101r, Exch., fo 120r (main entries); Exon., fo 238r, Exch., fo 123v (usurped properties); Exon., fo 507r (*Terrae Occupatae*).

Our survey of Cornish religious foundations recorded as holding lands in Domesday Book is now complete. A universal feature is the total exemption of their lands from the payment of geld. Usually the manors are said never to have rendered geld; in a few cases this is expressed in terms of liberty or immunity.[192] The property of St Constantinus had lost this privilege.[193] Also, geld is said to have been paid only *ad opus ecclesie* from the manor of *Languihenoc*,[194] only to the saint or the church in the blanket-statement covering all the lands of St Petroc, and to St Michael from the usurped portion of his manor. Perhaps in these instances geld which would normally have gone to the king had been granted to the ecclesiastical establishments instead,[195] but more likely 'geld' is used here in a broader sense to refer to customary payments – formerly owed to the saints – which are generally recorded for usurped manors. The geld-free ecclesiastical manors of Cornwall are highly unusual in Domesday Book, and attention can particularly be drawn in this respect to the large body of exempt estates of the canons of St Petroc. It was ordinary practice for only a part of a manor to be subject to payment of geld, the balance being demesne which was exempt.[196] The geld-accounts reckon all geld-free lands, including those of the Cornish saints, as demesne, and the passage about St Constantinus (quoted in note 193 below) seems to reflect the same concept. Instead, the perpetual geld-free status of estates of Cornish religious houses represents a special ecclesiastical privilege, as the above-mentioned references to immunity or liberty confirm, rather than merely that all the land of the manors was fiscal demesne.[197] This privilege was not shared by Cornish possessions of the only two external ecclesiastical tenants, the bishop of Exeter and the abbot of Tavistock.[198] It looks like a survival from before the time when Cornwall

---

[192] Exon., fo 206v, Exch., fo 121r (*Lanpiran*); Exon., fo 207r, Exch., fo 121r (*Ecglosberria*); Exon., fo 202r, Exch., fo 120v (St Petroc's manor of *Rieltona*).

[193] Exon., fo 207r: 'Sanctus Constantinus habet dimidam hidam terre que tempore regis Eduuardi fuit inmunis ab omni seruitio, sed postquam comes accepit terram semper reddidit Gildum iniuste ut terra uillanorum'.

[194] Exon., fo 202r.

[195] So Finn, *An Introduction*, p. 254, a passage highlighting the atypicality of the geld-exemption in Cornwall.

[196] That is, 'fiscal demesne', through changes over time not always the same quantity as 'manorial demesne'; see Finn, *Domesday Studies*, pp. 111–14.

[197] The latter phenomenon is otherwise unknown in Cornwall, and is perhaps not relevant in the cases in question, wherein occasionally part of a manor is specified as demesne (for example, *Rieltona*) or a distinction is drawn between the canons' and villeins' land (for example, *Lanpiran*): this seems a discrepancy of another order than the difference between fiscal and manorial demesne noted above.

[198] In one of the bishop's Cornish manors, *Sanctus Germanus*, his portion paid geld on two of the twelve hides, but the twelve hides of the canons' portion (in a typical phrase for Cornish religious houses) 'numquam reddiderunt Gildum' (Exon., fo 199v).

was absorbed into Wessex, a deep-rooted immunity from secular exaction, which was respected when the Anglo-Saxon geld was levied.[199]

Another feature common to almost all the Cornish collegiate churches and unspecified ecclesiastical establishments of Domesday Book and the geld-accounts is possession of an estate bearing the name of the landholding saint. Each of these property-names is in fact the name of a religious centre within the land designated. The properties must have contained, probably with enlargements, the original endowments of the foundations which still possessed them. Continuity is also suggested by many of the place-names themselves. It is not uncommon for Cornish places of worship designated by *lan* plus a personal name to be dedicated to a saint of a different name: this is true of about half the parish-churches with *lan*-names in Cornwall.[200] Yet there is only one instance of the phenomenon among the places considered here: *Languihenoc*, the second manor listed among the lands of Petroc, site of the first Cornish foundation attributed to the saint and of a parish-church dedicated to him. Otherwise we have *Lannachebran, Lanbrabois, Langorroc,*[201] *Lanscauetona, Lanpiran, Langustentyn, Landighe,* and *Langoran,* in all of which *lan* is combined with the name of the patron-saint who had title to the lands. A reasonable explanation of why the eponym and dedication differed is replacement of the cult of one saint by another. The unusually high coincidence of these two factors in connexion with properties of Cornish saints whose title was recognised in Domesday

[199] A not unrelated and unusual feature of material relating to Cornwall in *Liber Exoniensis* concerns the lands of Petroc. In the geld-accounts, which are grouped by hundreds, the final Cornish section reads, 'Sanctus Petrochus habet XXX hidas terre que numquam gildauerunt' (Exon., fo 73r). Interlined above 'Rieltone hundret' on the first list of Cornish hundreds (Exon., fo 63v) are the words 'Sancti Petrochii'. The territory of Petroc and of *Pautona* Hundred made up the later hundred of Pyder, a name which may derive from Petroc (Henderson, *Essays,* p. 120; Picken, 'The Names', pp. 37–8; Oliver Padel commented favourably in private communication in 1977 that 'a name spelt *Petroc* in Old Cornish, and latinised as *Petrocus,* would have been pronounced in the vernacular, at any date from the fifth century until the language died, as /pedr/-, not /petr/-'). The system of hundreds seems to break down here in an interesting way. *Languihenoc,* a coastal enclave belonging to Petroc within the hundred of *Pautona,* is a clear anomaly. The saints holding (in Domesday Book) the geld-free manors of *Langorroc* and *Lanpiran,* enclaves within Petroc's lands, are unmentioned in the geld-accounts. Yet the situation may have been nothing more unusual than what Finn described here: 'In Somerset many of the lands of the bishop of Wells are not dealt with under the geld-account Hundreds in which they lie, but in a separate section described as "part of the land of Bishop Giso which belongs to the honour of his bishopric" (78b) and also as his "Hundred" (81b). It might be, however, that the bishop had for the convenience of all concerned obtained the privilege of having the greater part of his lands dealt with as a whole for purposes of taxation, which might prove economical of time and effort' (*Domesday Studies,* pp. 102–3).

[200] Padel, 'Cornish language notes', pp. 15–27.

[201] Probably containing a hypocoristic form of St Carentoch (*ibid.,* p. 17).

Book and the geld-accounts is to be expected. Here the foundations were not small-scale and obscure, as many a *lan* must have been, but important and well established, with clear house-traditions of their saints to whose activities their origins were in general traced back through a continuous existence of religious observance and privileged proprietorship.

All of the Cornish ecclesiastical establishments in Domesday Book had held their lands at the end of Edward's reign, with two apparent exceptions. *Lanbrabois* is assigned to King Edward himself, and *Lanscauetona* to Earl Harold.[202] Yet these manors share the geld-free status of their counterparts; they had never paid geld, a claim which extends back at least into Edward's time.[203] Their names are those of the religious houses to which they belonged at the time of the Domesday inquest. There is no indication that these collegiate churches were post-Conquest foundations, and *Lanscauetona*, reported to be suffering despoliation by the count of Mortain, could hardly have originated in a recent endowment.[204] Neither religious house is attested before the Conquest, but Probus appears on the list of saints in the Vatican codex, Reginensis latinus 191, in the tenth century, and an abbreviated ancestral form of *Lanscauetona* is found on coins minted there in the period 979 × 985.[205] The obvious question in the circumstances is why the manors came after the Conquest to the canons of St Probus and of St Stephen rather than to the king. In fact, Cornish entries in Domesday Book can sometimes be seen to have named the sitting tenant, the person with effective control, of manors in Edward's time.[206] The most promising explanation of the pre-Conquest tenure of *Lanbrabois* and *Lanscauetona* is that they were being in some sense administered or farmed by Edward the Confessor and Harold respectively. Like the other Cornish collegiate bodies, with entries which the items in question resemble in every other way, the canons of St Probus and of St Stephen had pre-Conquest title to their Domesday manors.

We have now to consider what these collegiate churches, and unspecified religious establishments which may also have been collegiate, in the second half of the eleventh century represent in terms of Cornish ecclesiastical development. Evidence discussed previously – in the third chapter – has shown that there were early monasteries in the region. This suggests

[202] No pre-Conquest tenant is given for the latter in Exchequer Domesday.

[203] The geld-exemption for *Lanpiran*, *Ecglosberria*, and *Rieltona* (see n. 192) is specifically applied to Edward's time.

[204] As in many holdings of Cornish religious establishments, its value is said to have been higher 'quando comes accepit'. In what circumstances the count had 'received' the manor is uncertain, but cause of its loss in value is given in the transference of its market to the castle in the adjacent comital manor of *Dunheuet*.

[205] North, *English Hammered Coinage*, I.115, 110, and pl. X, no. 24.

[206] For example, *Treiwal*, the Domesday manor of St Michael, which together with a usurped portion was held before the Conquest by Brismar the priest; yet in *Terrae Occupatae* the usurped manor is said to have been 'in dominicatu sancti' at the end of Edward's reign (Exon., fo 508r).

continuity from the Celtic past for the Cornish ecclesiastical establishments of Domesday Book and the geld-accounts, which with one exception are dedicated to Celtic saints. The devolution of early monasteries into groups of clerics attached to a church is well attested in Wales and Scotland,[207] although it does not follow that all clerical bodies had once comprised abbot, monks, and rule devoted to seeking christian perfection apart from society.

A highly unsatisfactory alternative to a hypothetical early monastic background for the Cornish sites is foundation as minster-churches under English auspices. It is not that Cornish saints ceased to be patronised with the assimilation of Cornwall into Wessex; on the contrary, we have seen that Dochou and Cywa, Berian, Petroc, and Hyldren benefited from veneration forthcoming from the English and/or continuing among the Cornish. Yet it required very considerable patronage to create the picture of ecclesiastical foundations and landholding provided by Map N, particularly that block of ecclesiastical land, southwest of Bodmin, containing collegiate churches of Pieranus and Carentoch and several manors of Petroc. And there are indications that despoliation of Cornish ecclesiastical landholders did not begin with the Norman conquest. Usurpation of land of St Petroc by Earl Harold is mentioned in Domesday Book[208] and the bequest to Dochou and Cywa had been secularised. The *Tiwærnhel* charter of A.D. 960 indicates Anglo-Saxon encroachment on property of Pieranus if not of Petroc,[209] and charters of 967, 977, and 1059, if they are genuine, suggest the same against the canons of St Achebrannus.[210] The conclusive argument against the Cornish churches' origin as minsters in the Anglo-Saxon period is provided by the distribution of manors of Cornish ecclesiastical establishments shown on Map N. These are located mostly toward the west and especially along the mid-section of the north coast of Cornwall, but also thinly in the east and north where English settlement was most intensive and influence most readily exerted. Only *Lanscauetona*, by reason of dedication and situation, was

---

[207] See Lloyd, *A History*, I.205–7; Cowley, *The Monastic Order*, pp. 3–6; Addleshaw, *The Pastoral Structure*, pp. 24–7; and especially Cowan, 'The development', pp. 44–7, of great help to the present study, in which consideration has been given to the relationship of Celtic, English, and Norman factors in ecclesiastical/monastic development.

[208] Exon., fo 204v; Exch., fo 121r.

[209] Sawyer, *Anglo-Saxon Charters*, p. 227, no. 684. The charter-bounds can be sufficiently traced to show that the estate covered the area of Domesday *Lanpiran* and three of Petroc's manors: *Tiuuarthel* itself, *Car gau*, and *Lancichuc*. The surviving free-standing stone-cross associated with St Pieran's establishment is almost certainly one of the charter's boundary-points.

[210] *Ibid.*, nos 755, 832, and 1027, respectively. Between the southeastern bounds of *Lesmanaoc*, granted in the first charter, and the eastern bounds of *Trefualoc*, granted in the others, there is little room for coastal property of *Lannachebran*. *Lesmanaoc* means 'monkish court' or more likely 'court of the Meneage', a regional name denoting 'monkish (land)', for which see the Appendix, below, pp. 108–9.

95

perhaps the site of foundation of a new minster.[211] The spread of sites along the north coast and the scatter in the south is instead an expected pattern from the evidence of the early saints' Lives examined previously, of which the first *Vita Sancti Petroci* is perhaps contemporary with the sources considered here; but the Breton *uitae* are considerably earlier and products of a different environment.

We can work backward with some confidence from the evidence of Domesday Book to the existence of early Cornish monasteries of St Germanus, St Petroc, St Achebrannus, St Probus, St Carentoch, St Pieranus, St Berriona, and St Nietus. It supplies good forms of the names of several: *Lannachebran, Lanbrabois, Langorroc, Lanpiran*, and presumably *Ecglosberria*.[212] There were probably other early monasteries – of St Constantinus called *Langustentyn*, St Che called *Landighe*, and St Goranus called *Langoran*. Another may have existed which bore a name combining *lan* and a personal name which is either Stephen or similar enough to be identified with Stephen. As for the local ecclesiastical establishment of St Michael which held *Treiwal* from a centre presumed to be on nearby St Michael's Mount, this too could have been a monastic foundation, although veneration of that saint is unlikely to have been earlier than the eighth century.

Domesday Book sets out information about the landed property of these ecclesiastical establishments in the second half of the eleventh century, and we may in closing take a quick look at that record. The estates, which except for *Lanbrabois* and some manors of Petroc are all said to be suffering from despoliation by the count of Mortain, tend to be small but not of a uniform assessment, most falling within the range one-half to three hides. A few manors of Petroc and the canons' portion of *Sanctus Germanus* are, for Cornwall, relatively well endowed. In general, the estates display the relatively high figures for sheep and pasturage characteristic of the economy of Domesday Cornwall;[213] these probably represent a long-term pattern. Two features of tenure and distribution stand out: the tendency for religious houses to hold a spread of estates along the north coast manifested by the canons of St Petroc and St Pieranus and to some extent by the *monasterium* of *Landochou*; and the overwhelming preponderance of the collegiate church

---

[211] It would seem that collegiate churches of Celtic origin could be easily absorbed into the English system characterised by minsters, with which they could be identified. Probably this occurred in Cornwall, which the profession of Kenstec shows at least in part incorporated within English ecclesiastical organisation in the mid-ninth century.

[212] Whereas *lan*, 'sacred enclosure', can certainly designate the monastic enclosure and surrounding land, *eglos* could, but need not, be late and indicate a late origin for what it designates (Padel, 'Cornish language notes', pp. 23–7). It also might be somehow connected to another factor in respect of which the establishment is exceptional among those considered here: dedication to a female saint.

[213] Ravenhill, 'Cornwall', pp. 330–3, 338–9; Darby, 'The South-western counties', pp. 386–7.

of St Petroc over other local ecclesiastical establishments as a landholder. The latter could be explained by the earlier presence of bishops there. We are hampered in our understanding of both by not knowing when the additional estates were acquired.[214] Despite such limitations, Domesday Book – with its regular reference to pre-Conquest tenure – and related materials like the geld-inquest provide a body of extraordinarily important evidence unparalleled in any other Celtic region in the period; and in ecclesiastical matters if not others this record relates to the Celtic past.

8. RECORDS OF THREE PRIORIES IN CORNWALL

By 1100 most of the Cornish ecclesiastical establishments which have been considered in this chapter were in secular hands, with only the communities at Bodmin, St Germans, Launceston, and St Buryan retaining their independence. Yet in the early twelfth century some were given back to ecclesiastics and in a few cases continued or were refounded as collegiate churches. Both conditions apply to the church of SS. Dochou and Cywa, given (as alluded to above) by King Henry I to Exeter Cathedral and passed on to Plympton Priory,[215] and the churches of St Probus, also given by Henry to Exeter,[216] and St Carentoc, bestowed by William, count of Mortain, on Montacute Priory about 1110 and coming eventually to the bishop of Exeter.[217] The churches of St Pieran and St Niet were granted respectively by Henry I to Exeter Cathedral and by Count William to Montacute Priory like the above, but they were no longer collegiate.[218]

Against this background of ecclesiastical continuity will be examined in this final section of the chapter three post-Conquest houses in Cornwall which lack documentation in Domesday or earlier materials but have Celtic associations. These, it is suggested, either continue or were fittingly established on the traditional site of older and ultimately monastic foundations. They would thus be nearly analogous to the church of SS. Dochou and Cywa, no longer an independent landholder at the time of the Domesday survey, and only figuring therein as the remembered 'honour of St Cheus', but deriving nonetheless from an early monastery.

The very small Cornish priories of St Carroc, Lammana, and St Anthony in Roseland were respectively dependencies of the Cluniac priory of Montacute in Somerset, the Benedictine abbey of Glastonbury in Somerset,

---

[214] The suggestion by Henderson that some were obtained at the expense of other religious houses should be borne in mind (*The Cornish Church Guide*, p. 26, and see also his *Essays*, pp. 120–2).

[215] See above, p. 83, n. 140 for references.

[216] Henderson, 'The ecclesiastical history', pp. 411–12.

[217] *Ibid.*, pp. 106–7.

[218] *Ibid.*, pp. 398–9, and *The Cornish Church Guide*, p. 149.

and the Augustinian priory of Plympton in Devon. Both St Carroc and Lammana were located in southeastern Cornwall where Domesday records show a cluster of manors held by secular lords of King Edward's time (see Map N); these lands came to the counts of Mortain. By the mid-twelfth century Montacute Priory had been given what is referred to in King Henry II's confirmation of the bequest as *Sanctus Carrocus*.[219] The grant did not represent appropriation of a parish-church, but rather concerned a place now known as St Cadix, within a mile – and for topographic reasons inevitably within the parish – of the church of St Veep.[220] We cannot tell if a foundation of St Carroc existed here at the time of the grant; however, with respect to the localisation of the saint's name the case is different. The saint might be the Carroc or Carreuc who has a few dedications in Brittany,[221] or Carentoc with the hypocoristic name probably seen in *Langorroc*,[222] or a purely local figure. In any case, the dedication is exceedingly unlikely to have been made in an Anglo-Norman context.[223] Even if the name designated an estate and nothing more at the time of the grant, it implies the earlier existence of an ecclesiastical establishment there.

Turning to the priory of Lammana, we find the earliest evidence in 'Lamane',[224] entered last among the possessions of Glastonbury Abbey in

[219] See Holmes *et al.*, *Two Cartularies*, pp. 123–4 (English translations only): Dugdale, *Monasticon*, V.167 (*inspeximus* of I Henry IV), reading in part 'et in Cornubia Sanctum Cairocum cum omnibus appendiciis suis; ecclesiam de Alternona, ecclesiam Sancti Neoti, ecclesiam Sancti Karentoci et ecclesiam de Lerchi, et Pennard cum appendiciis suis'. 'Sanctus Carrocus' (emending from the Montacute Cartulary) looks like an estate-name. In the Cartulary it is found neither in earlier documents nor associated with the initial endowment of Montacute (Holmes *et al.*, *Two Cartularies*, pp. 119–28). On the priory of St Carroc, of obscure origin and not documented as such a priory before the end of the twelfth century, see Knowles & Hadcock, *Medieval Religious Houses*, pp. 97, 102, 481; Henderson, *The Cornish Church Guide*, pp. 197–8; Oliver, *Monasticon*, p. 69; and for the most extensive coverage, Henderson, 'East Cornwall', pp. 556, 560–2, 566 (his reference on p. 560 to the grant by Count William *ca* 1100 of the 'Prioratus de Sancto Carroco' is undocumented and misleading, however). On Montacute Priory, founded by Count William or more probably his predecessor Count Robert, see Knowles & Hadcock, *Medieval Religious Houses*, p. 101.

[220] This church was in the patronage of the lords of Manely until appropriated to Montacute in the thirteenth century, its revenues coming then or later to the dependent priory of St Carroc (Henderson, *The Cornish Church Guide*, p. 197, and 'East Cornwall', pp. 556 and 560). Cf. Gover, 'The Place-names of Cornwall', p. 301.

[221] Loth, *Les Noms*, p. 19.

[222] As above, n. 201.

[223] The practice of identifying obscure local with 'universal' saints operated here with SS. Ciricus (Cyrus, Ciricius, etc.) and Julitta associated by the thirteenth century with the church of St Veep. The original saint's name nevertheless persisted in connexion with the priory and its site, arriving by identification with the much better known St Cadog at the present curious form 'St Cadix'.

[224] Dugdale, *Monasticon*, I.36–8.

1144 and 1168. Specific information about the nature of this possession is first provided by a charter drawn up around 1200 which records that[225]

. . . I Hastutus [for 'Hasculfus'] son of Iohannes de Solenneio, have granted and by the present charter have confirmed to God and the church of the Blessed Virgin Mary of Glastonbury and to the convent of the same place the whole island of St Michael of Lammana with all its appurtenances, both lands and tithes, which they hold from the ancient gift of my predecessors . . .

There follows an immunity-clause, an additional grant of tithes of the donor's demesne of *Portlo* and rights of jurisdiction in the monks' court, and prohibition of interference in Lammana by the donor's bailiffs or servants. The first two witnesses to the charter, 'Helya tunc eiusdem priore, at eius socio monacho Iohanne', indicate that Lammana was a priory.[226]

The Celtic association of this establishment lies in the place-name, of which the earliest forms are *Lamane*, *Lammana* and *Lamana*. It should be a name in *lan*, with a second element beginning with *m-*, where for ease in pronunciation *-nm-* has been reduced to *-mm-* or *-m-*; no other explanation suggests itself.[227] The second element may be *managh*, 'monk', used as a personal name or commemorating an anonymous monastic (eremitic?) figure,[228] or a personal name Mana.[229] Note that it is not the *lan* of St Michael:[230] the place-name derives from religious activity on the site before

---

[225] '. . . ego Hastutus filius Iohannis de Solenneio concessi et presenti carta confirmaui Deo et ecclesiae beatae Uirginis Mariae Glaston. et eiusdem loci conuentui totam insulam Sancti Michaelis de Lammana cum omnibus pertinentiis suis, et terris, et decimis, quam ab antiquo dono praedecessorum meorum tenent . . .' (Oliver, *Monasticon*, p. 70, from Adam of Damerham, *Historia de Rebus Gestis Glastoniensibus*, ed. Thomas Hearne [Oxford 1727], II.599). Members of the de Soleigny family held in the previous and succeeding century the important and erstwhile comital manor of Fawton some miles to the north of Lammana (Henderson, 'East Cornwall', p. 516).

[226] On Lammana see Knowles & Hadcock, *Medieval Religious Houses*, p. 69; Oliver, *Monasticon*, p. 70; Henderson, *The Cornish Church Guide*, p. 184; Lewis, "*Ab Antiquo*"; Henderson, 'East Cornwall', pp. 515–22; Adams, 'Catalogue of Mediaeval Cornish Chapels', nos 305 and 306.

[227] Gover, 'The Place-names of Cornwall', p. 299; cf. p. 471 (Lamorran). Henderson, 'The ecclesiastical history', pp. 139–40, cited a name Lamana designating property not far from Cury parish church in southwest Cornwall.

[228] Henderson, *The Cornish Church Guide*, p. 184, and 'East Cornwall', pp. 239 and 516; Lewis, "*Ab Antiquo*", p. 14; cf. Loth, *Les Noms*, pp. 87–8, and Padel, *Cornish Place-name Elements*, pp. 156–7, *s.v. manach*. A St Manacus is patron of Lanreath church, over five miles northwest of Lammana; and St Manac(c)a is patron of Manaccan (earlier *Managhan*) church in southwest Cornwall.

[229] Gover, 'The Place-names of Cornwall', p. 299; Loth, *Les Noms*, pp. 87 and 10. Of possible interest is a 'Well in Well Lane (part of Lammana)' according to Lewis ("*Ab Antiquo*", p. 8) 'said to have been dedicated to S. Anne'; the chapel on nearby old Looe bridge was dedicated to St Anne.

[230] Cf. *Lanvyhaill*, the Cornish name for St Michael Caerhays (Gover, 'The Place-names of Cornwall', p. 414).

Michael became associated, or at least assumed a paramount position, in the cult there, and it suggests an ecclesiastical establishment of considerable antiquity.

As with St Carroc, the origin of the dependent priory of Lammana is obscure. It is unlikely to have been a pre-Conquest possession of the important abbey of Glastonbury and yet to have gone unnoticed in the Domesday inquest. An interesting comparison can be made with Glastonbury's other dependent priory, Bassaleg in Monmouthshire, of which the donation by Robert de Haya in 1116 is known through a surviving charter.[231] Bequest by a secular landholder at about this time is what one would expect for Lammana. The ends of the priories of Bassaleg and Lammana were very similar indeed: under Abbot Michael of Glastonbury both were farmed out in the mid-thirteenth century.[232] And we may observe that Bassaleg had formerly been a Welsh collegiate church, the sort of background proposed here for Lammana.[233]

Written sources provide further information of significance for our enquiry about Lammana. What is re-granted by the charter of ca 1200 quoted above is an island, 'totam insulam Sancti Michaelis de Lammana' – on which the existence of a religious establishment is a safe inference since Lammana had been a Glastonbury possession for some time – and mainland-property for that establishment's support. In later documents the situation is more complex. A charter drawn up about forty years afterwards gives the abbot of Glastonbury licence to put to farm 'the church and island of Lammana, the aforesaid churches, lands, and possessions of the same place, with appurtenances'.[234] A contemporary document concerning a tithe-dispute refers to 'the church of the island and the chapel of Lammana',[235] terminology giving superior status to the former. In the 'Placita de aduocacione ecclesie de Lamana' from near the end of the century, recorded in the cartulary of Launceston Priory, the holdings of Glastonbury at Lammana are said to have comprised a messuage and carucate 'in Lamana', the capella de Lamana, 'quandam insulam cum

---

[231] Knowles & Hadcock, *Medieval Religious Houses*, p. 59.

[232] Adam of Damerham, *Historia de Rebus Gestis Glastoniensibus* (ed. Hearne, II.518); John of Glastonbury, *Cronica sive Antiquitates Glastoniensis Ecclesie*, § 116 (ed. & transl. Carley & Townsend, *The Chronicle*, pp. 218, 219).

[233] Knowles & Hadcock, *Medieval Religious Houses*, p. 467.

[234] 'Concessimus . . . imperpetuum plenam licentiam et liberam potestatem ponendi ecclesiam et insulam de Lammana, praefatas ecclesias, terras, et possessiones eiusdem loci, cum pertinentiis, ad firmam . . .' (Oliver, *Monasticon*, p. 70, from Adam of Damerham, *Historia* [ed. Hearne, II.604]). As there has been a previous reference to holdings of the abbot and convent of Glastonbury, 'terris et possess-ionibus suis de Lammana, cum pertinentiis', but to no churches but that of Glastonbury, the passage is confusing, but the writer certainly meant to indicate the presence of more than one church at Lammana.

[235] Adam of Damerham, *Historia* (ed. Hearne, II.603): 'cum quidem indempnitate ecclesiae de insula et capellae de Lammana . . . sine aliquo praeiudicio dictarum ecclesiae de insula et capellae de Lammana'.

capella Sancti Michaelis in eadem insula iuxta Lamana', the great tithes 'dicte terre de Lamana' and of part of the demesne of Portlooe, and revenues belonging *ad dictas capellas*.[236] The phrase, 'a certain island with the chapel of St Michael in the same island next Lamana', clearly distinguishes between the place called Lammana and the island. The name has continued to be applied to the mainland one-half mile opposite the island, where the Tithe Award of 1839 records the hamlet of *Lemain* and a field called *Lemain Park*. On the other hand, names in the form 'island of Lammana' occur in mid-sixteenth-century documents concerning the chantry established and maintained by secular heirs to Glastonbury's possession,[237] and in later deeds.[238] One of the chantry-certificates explicitly sites the chantry-chapel on the island, as might be expected of the successor to the priory-church.[239]

The foregoing shows that post-Conquest religious activity focused on the island but leaves in doubt whether the earliest associated religious feature, the place-name Lammana, or to be exact the site of the *lan* which it designated, belongs to the island or the mainland opposite. The first point suggests that we may be working back to an early monastery on an island off the coast of Cornwall and corresponding to the island-monasteries in other Celtic regions. However, a different explanation can be proposed for the importance of the island and indeed for the foundation of the priory: this is yet another island of St Michael, with a priory established in

[236] Fos 181r–182r, transcribed by Henderson in 'East Cornwall', p. 517; also with subsequent references to 'praedictas terras de Lamana et insulam que est dedicata ut dicitur' and to Glastonbury rights 'de Lamana et in insula predicta'.

[37] Chantry-certificates nos 9/15, 15/82 and 10/16 (ed. Snell, *Documents*, pp. 47–8). Cf. Maxwell Lyte, *Calendar of the Patent Rolls preserved in the Public Record Office, Edward VI*, II.40. In 'Extract from Roll of Fees Paid to Members of Suppressed Chantries and Religious Houses out of the Exchequer' is mentioned the free chapel of 'Justus de la Mayne' (Snell, *Documents*, p. 56), with the incumbent the same as for the 'Isle of Lamayne' in certificate 10/16. This could be a unique reference to a Celtic patron-saint for Lammana corresponding to St Just with three dedications elsewhere in Cornwall, but it is far more likely to derive from palaeographical confusion, for example of abbreviated forms of *Ins*ula and *Ius*tus.

[38] Adams, 'Catalogue of Mediaeval Cornish Chapels', no. 305.

[39] Chantry-certificate no. 15/82: 'The chauntrye called Lamane ffounded by the late Erle of Exeter to ffynde a pryste for ev' to celebrate holye servyce in A chappell edyfyed in a lyttle Ilande'. Documentary evidence regarding function and relationship of the two chapels is usually ambiguous. The mainland chapel may have been a chapel of ease (Lewis, *"Ab Antiquo"*, p. 13). Possibly significant of the primacy of the island as a religious *locus* is that, whereas the site of the mainland-chapel was eventually forgotten, the island stayed in popular lore as the goal of a traditional crossing on Good Friday. The extent to which this is related to the Cornish practice of 'trigging' for shellfish on that day is unclear; of course tides are especially low at that time of year. (See the letter of C. K. C. Andrew, *apud* Lewis, *The Child Christ*, pp. 19–20, and Lewis, *"Ab Antiquo"*, p. 27; cf. Courtney, *Cornish Feasts*, p. 25.) Picken, 'Light on Lammana', has now corroborated the island-focus of the priory.

imitation of Mont Saint-Michel, St Michael's Mount, or both. Doubtless the dedication to Michael arose from that background, but the place-name Lammana (as we have seen) suggests earlier roots of religious activity.

The exact attribution of Lammana is thus of some importance. Possibilities include that it designated an unrelated and perhaps quite insignificant religious site on the mainland and was adopted for convenience to name the island, or that an early monastery spread its buildings, lands, and name over both the island and adjacent mainland. Original application of Lammana to the island cannot be proven. It is in fact first documented as 'insula Sancti Michaelis de Lammana' in the charter, but the appellation could have been taken from a mainland-site, with *de Lammana* in fact equivalent to *iuxta Lammana*. The parallel reference to the island *ca* 1490 as 'Insula Sancti Michaelis de Loo', and its present name Looe Island, show just such a borrowing.[240] There were, however, circumstances conducive to transference of the name Lammana from the island and/or its restriction to the mainland. The lands appurtaining to the island, as confirmed in the charter of *ca* 1200, are referred to in the later 'Placita de aduocacione' as the 'land(s) of Lamana', from an indigenous place-name, or the name of the island, or (as is very likely) from the name of the priory. This is the document which distinguishes *Lamana* from the island. It specifies tithes 'dicte terre de Lamana' and that the vicar of Talland had cure of souls 'de omnibus hominibus habitantibus in terris de Lamana'; the island is not mentioned in these respects.[241] Under such conditions, especially in a century which saw disputes over the tithes and advowson of Lammana, strong forces would have operated to concentrate attention on the mainland-property. Furthermore, archaeological excavation has revealed considerable development of the mainland-portion of the priory-estate, where the chapel and other structures have been found, and it may be that for reasons of convenience much of the activity of the priory came to take place there.[242] The likely use of the mainland-chapel as a chapel of ease would also fit the pattern of convenience. As attention focused on the mainland, the name Lammana came to be applied there exclusively, while the island was thought of as a nearby appendage. Preconditions for this hypothesis have

---

[240] Gover, 'The Place-names of Cornwall', p. 298.
[241] For the reference, see n. 236. Although the entire Lammana property, island and mainland, is said in this document, the chantry-certificates, and the item from the Patent Rolls cited in n. 237 to be within the parish of Talland, the island came down into modern times as extra-parochial (not included in the Tithe-Award of 1839; see Wallis, *The Cornwall Register*, p. 386). Cf. the chantry-certificates as in n. 237, and the Terrier of 1727 in which the vicar of Talland describes mainland Lammana as a parish at some time incorporated into Talland (Henderson, 'East Cornwall', p. 515).
[242] See C. K. C. Andrew, *apud* Adams, 'Catalogue of Mediaeval Cornish Chapels', no. 306; 'R. I. C. Department of Excavations: Papers relating to the Excavation of Pre-Norman Chapel and Medieval Priory at Lammana, near Looe', unpublished manuscript at the Royal Institution of Cornwall Museum, Truro.

been shown to exist sufficiently that the original application of the place-name Lammana to the island should in no wise be ruled out.

Looe Island, lying just off the coast of southeastern Cornwall (with which it was very probably connected at low tide in the earlier middle ages),[243] was the site of the priory of Lammana and is promising as the site of an early monastery of Lammana. The excavations on the mainland, albeit incompletely reported, do not appear to have produced evidence of early mediaeval activity; archaeological investigation of the island, on which a piece of imported Mediterranean pottery has been found, should be a high priority.[244]

The priory of St Anthony in Roseland emerges from a background different from that of the two sites which we have been considering. It lay within the great block of land in episcopal hands which comprised the adjacent Domesday manors of *Trigel* (Tregaire) and *Treliuel* (Treliever) in southern Cornwall. From the former, Robert, bishop of Exeter, gave *ca* 1140 to the Augustinian priory of SS. Peter and Paul at Plympton in Devon 'the church of St Antoninus, king and martyr, and the church of St Just, martyr, with lands, tithes, liberties, and all their appendages'.[245] This is a standard description of appropriation of a parish-church to a religious house. St Anthony in Roseland was the site of a priory dependent on Plympton in the reign of Henry III.[246] It came to possess the entire, albeit diminutive, parish of St Anthony (of 753 acres), but whether this came with the original grant to Plympton or piecemeal later is uncertain, as is the date of foundation of the dependent priory.[247]

St Anthony in Roseland is dedicated, as will not be immediately apparent, to a local saint who has another dedication at St Anthony in Meneage and a holy well at Ventontinny in Probus parish: all are situated around the Fal waterway in southern Cornwall.[248] In the Vatican codex, Reginensis latinus 191, the saint appears as 'Entenin' in a group of patrons of the four churches of the Roseland Peninsula plus adjacent Ruan Lanihorne. The geographical correlation of names on the list, most marked at this point, permits us to infer with confidence the existence by the tenth century of some sort of ecclesiastical establishment on the site of the later priory.

The suggestions that early monasteries lie in the background of the priories of St Carroc, Lammana, and St Anthony in Roseland are made

---

[43] Cf. Bond, *Topographical and Historical Sketches*, p. 29, on conditions in the early nineteenth century.

[44] See p. 42 above.

[45] 'Et in Cornubia ecclesiam sancti Antonini regis et martyris, et ecclesiam sancti Iusti martyris, cum terris, decimis, libertatibus, et omnibus appendiciis suis, quae Robertus episcopus primus eis dedit' (confirmation by Henry II, *ca* 1180; ed. Dugdale, *Monasticon*, VI.54, and Oliver, *Monasticon*, p. 135).

[46] *Liber Feodorum* (ed. Maxwell Lyte, I.548 and 573).

[47] See Henderson, 'The 109 ancient parishes', pp. 18–25, and Knowles & Hadcock, *Medieval Religious Houses*, pp. 143 and 172.

[48] See Olson, 'Saint Entenyn'.

in similar circumstances. Such dependent priories were not common: Montacute Priory had five, one each in the counties of Cornwall, Devon, Dorset, Somerset, and Monmouthshire;[249] Glastonbury Abbey had two, as we have seen; and Plympton Priory had one each in Cornwall and Devon.[250] We may ask why small religious houses were founded at the places which we have been considering. The foundation of the priories of St Carroc, Lammana, and St Anthony in Roseland is obscure: documents show by what point they were in existence and with more or less certainty in what period the lands on which they stood had been acquired by the mother-house. In the context of Anglo-Norman Cornwall the sites are isolated. There is sufficient indication of some sort of pre-Conquest ecclesiastical establishment at each, which contributed a dedication and/or place-name to the priories. The absence of landholding ecclesiastical communities or saints for these places in Domesday Book and related material may of course be the result of secularisation of their properties. The area of southeast Cornwall where St Carroc and Lammana are located was perhaps under special secular pressure; the newly recognised tenth-century charter on behalf of St Hyldren shows property of one Cornish saint in the same area, and this was not recorded after the Conquest.[251] It would be surprising if a pre-Conquest religious house of St Anthony in Roseland had persisted as an independent landholder amid the bishop's estates. Private motivation in foundation and endowment of ecclesiastical establishments is hardly assessable, but one factor in some benefactions appears to be (as we have seen) a sense that, where an ecclesiastical community had existed in the past, it is fitting that it should continue to do so, or at least that its endowment should remain with the Church. With this in mind, the proposal is made that the priories of St Carroc, Lammana, and St Anthony in Roseland may have been successors to earlier religious communities. Doubt remains regarding the scale on which religious life was ever practised at these places, and it may be that they had an eremitic rather than cenobitic past. Nevertheless, they warrant consideration as promising sites for early monasteries in Cornwall.

From material examined in this chapter a number of early monasteries can be inferred with some confidence. At one point the existence of the monastery called *Docco*, mentioned in the *Vita (Prima) Sancti Samsonis*, is reinforced by the tenth-century re-endowment of *Landochou*. This in turn provides important support for arguments that the Cornish ecclesiastical communities recorded in Domesday Book represent devolved early monasteries. The analogy can be extended to other Cornish sites where, although other explanations are possible, an early monastic interpretation is best.

[249] Knowles & Hadcock, *Medieval Religious Houses*, pp. 96–103.
[250] *Ibid.*, p. 166.
[251] See pp. 84 and 64 above.

V

CONCLUSION

The monastic movement reached the British Isles around A.D. 500. There is reason to think that it took root in Cornwall so early, but not that Cornwall was ahead of the other Celtic regions in this respect. Indications are that early monasticism in Cornwall derived principally from south Wales.

In its wake the movement left monasteries which can be identified in Cornwall. To the ninth century at the latest belong the monastery called *Docco* (St Kew) and the southern Cornish monastery (probably St Sampson, Golant) at which the author of the *Vita (Prima) Sancti Samsonis* had resided. The existence of early monasteries of *Lan Wethinocke* (Padstow), *Langorroc* (Crantock), *Lanpiran* (St Piran's Oratory, Perranzabuloe), *Lannachebran* (St Keverne), and *Lanalet* (St Germans) is open to the question only of whether any might have been Cornish clerical rather than monastic communities from the beginning; otherwise, doubts begin to enter with *Lanbrabois* (Probus), *Ecglosberria* (St Buryan), St Neot, and *Lammana* (Looe Island or adjacent mainland), but do not become significant until *Dinuurrin* (Bodmin?), *Lanscauetona* (St Stephens by Launceston), *Langustentyn* (Constantine), *Landighe* (Old Kea), and *Langoran* (Gorran), and more especially St Carroc (St Cadix, Veep), St Anthony in Roseland, the *domus* of Sitofolla (Paul?), and St Michael's Mount. This brings us to a total of twenty sites, shown on Map A.

A number of features of early Cornish monasteries have emerged. Names in *lan* originally referred to the sacred monastic enclosure but were extended to designate the estate upon which the monastery was situated. Judging from the evidence of Domesday Book and the geld-accounts, these estates were protected by powerful immunities from secular imposts. The monasteries appear to have kept written record of their landed possessions, as witness traces of a Cornish – and even specifically ecclesiastical – diplomatic tradition in charters for *Landochou*, St Buryan, and St Germans. St Samson's monastery in Cornwall had a record of its founder. Early mediaeval Cornwall has been seen to be linked in ecclesiastical culture with Brittany (and through Brittany with the rest of the west European continent), with Wales, and increasingly with Anglo-Saxon England. While Cornwall in the first millenium A.D. can hardly be termed rich in culture of any kind, its early monasteries were not isolated from contact with other regions.

In the area of monastic practice and organisation there is little to proffer besides veneration of the founding saint, and the role of the founder's kin in Samson's Cornish monastery. The early monasteries of Cornwall clearly ended up as groups of priests serving and sharing the lands and revenues of a church. A resident bishop was a feature of the monasteries (or minsters) of *Dinuurrin* and *Lanalet* in the mid-ninth century and the second quarter of the tenth, respectively. Neither place gives its name to the diocese of Cornwall in the Anglo-Saxon ecclesiastical documents which we possess. There were not necessarily bishops in these two places at the same time, although – if we assume *Dinuurrin* to be Bodmin – the clergy of St Petroc appear to have been continuing to press some old claims in the tenth century, and a retrospective claim of high antiquity was made for the bishops of Cornwall resident at St Germans.

Overall, Cornwall displays a concentration of the sites in question along the north coast, and a scatter of them about the south coast. Ten to twenty monasteries is not a large number, especially when compared with the plethora of early ecclesiastical sites represented by churches, chapels, and place-names in Cornwall. The discrepancy could suggest that there was a strong eremitical cast to the monastic movement in Cornwall, which left the countryside dotted with minor religious settlements. Alternatively, the non-monastic clerical component in the Church in early mediaeval Cornwall may have been greater than is usually allowed, having been overshadowed in our sources by articulate and interesting monastic tradition.[1]

The foregoing discussion raises the question of whether all early monasteries in Cornwall have been accounted for in this study. The answer is negative. The necessary criterion for a site to be considered here has been evidence of the existence of an early religious community. As a result, the sites identified here are only those which were sufficiently well established and/or located away from areas of maximum pressure of acquisitive landholders for such evidence to survive. On the other hand, a group of monks living an ordered existence under an abbot in a defined settlement endowed with lands privileged with immunities, who kept records and were in receipt of popular veneration, might be expected to survive (or at least not disappear without trace) if conditions were at all favourable. Therefore a great increase in the number of known early monastic sites in Cornwall is not to be anticipated. In this way it can be concluded that this study has identified and discussed those Cornish sites for which there is firmest evidence of the existence of early monasteries.

Further study of these sites may point out other characteristic early monastic features which can then be sought elsewhere in Cornwall. Already a promising beginning has been made with the discovery of what may be a section of the *uallum monasterii* at Padstow, with noting of shrinking cemeteries, a phenomenon which may be related to the existence of a

---

[1] Cf. Thomas, 'Hermits'.

monastic enclosure,[2] and with recognition of the significance of privileged sanctuaries as perhaps also connected with the monastic enclosure.[3] By these continuing investigations, to which should be added selection of some known monastic site for competent archaeological excavation, it should be possible to build on the basic understanding of Cornish monasticism set out in this study.

[2] See MacDonald, 'Two major early monasteries', pp. 52–7. Cornish sites include Crantock, St Stephens by Launceston, and perhaps St Buryan and St Neot: see Olson, 'Crantock'.

[3] The anomalousness of Cornwall's privileged sanctuaries at Padstow, St Buryan, and Probus is apparent from Cox, *The Sanctuaries*, especially pp. 214–26: he does not include the sanctuary of St Keverne; cf. Charles Henderson, *apud* Doble, *Saint Perran*, pp. 63–5.

APPENDIX

The Meneage is a region in southwestern Cornwall corresponding to no known civil or ecclesiastical unit.[1] The name derives from *manahoc*, an adjective meaning 'monkish' with which 'land' is apparently to be understood.[2] A charter dated 967 records the grant of *Lesmanaoc* by King Edgar to his vassal Wulfnoth Rumuncant.[3] This name, now Lesneage in St Keverne parish, is compounded of the secular element *lis* or *les*, 'court' or 'chief place', and *manahoc* to give either the rather odd 'monkish court' or more likely 'court of the Meneage'.[4] Certainly the Meneage is referred to as a region in a charter of the mid-twelfth century at the latest, in which Mont Saint-Michel received from Robert, count of Mortain, along with St Michael's Mount and other bequests, certain properties in *Amanech* or *Manech*.[5] It has continued to designate a region down to the present. Henderson defined the Meneage geographically as 'the parishes of St. Keverne, St. Anthony, Manaccan, St. Martin and the eastern part of St. Mawgan'.[6]

The original extent of the region is debatable. One view would see 'Meneage' as in some monastic past having come to designate a more or less defined region, where properties and parishes of a later period could be designated as 'in Meneage'. In another and more likely view, 'Meneage' formerly named an area smaller than its later extent, but in time came to be applied more widely in a proprietary and parochial context. The association

---

[1] Charles Henderson, *apud* Doble, *Saint Perran*, p. 60.

[2] Gover, 'The Place-names of Cornwall', p. 541, supplemented for me by Oliver Padel.

[3] Birch, *Cartularium*, III.473–4, no. 1197 (cf. Sawyer, *Anglo-Saxon Charters*, p. 242, no. 755). The document is in script of the third quarter of the eleventh century, and Chaplais, 'The authenticity', pp. 13–14, had some doubts about whether it is a copy of a genuine charter. In favour of authenticity is the unusual feature of a recipient with both an English and a Cornish name, paralleled in the tenth-century Lamorran charter which Chaplais (*ibid.*, p. 14) found unobjectionable. Even should the charter be spurious, the name *Lesmanaoc* must go back to a time, certainly not after the Conquest, when the place was the *lis* of the district.

[4] Gover, 'The Place-names of Cornwall', p. 555, for the latter. Cf. Henderson, 'The ecclesiastical antiquities', pp. 269–70.

[5] 'dedi et dono in Manech tres acras terre Traaraboth uidelicet Limanech, Trequauers, Carmelel' (ed. Hull, *The Cartulary*, p. 1).

[6] Henderson, 'The ecclesiastical antiquities', p. 262. These parishes are in Kerrier Hundred, south of the Helford River.

of component lands in a manor might have resulted in the application of 'Meneage' to them all, whereas only some, perhaps in particular the barton and demesne, had originally been considered to lie within the region. A number of the Meneage churches have patron-saints with dedications elsewhere in Cornwall: St Anthony (also in Roseland), St Martin (also by Looe), St Mawgan (also in Pyder). There was need to distinguish between these, and recourse may have been had to a convenient nearby regional name.[7] Thus there is a very real possibility that the land which was monkish was only a part of the area which came to be known as the Meneage, and the best indication of its location is the vicinity of Lesneage.

Existence of a region designated as 'monkish' implies the existence of a landholding monastery or monasteries. Thomas Taylor argued that the monastery in question was a Celtic establishment on St Michael's Mount.[8] Granted that the post-Conquest priory there held land in the region, one can only agree with Henderson that Taylor's ideas regarding a Celtic monastery on the Mount rest upon insufficient evidence.[9] Henderson suggested that the Meneage 'in the Celtic period seems to have belonged to a group of small monastic communities',[10] in which he would certainly have included St Keverne and Manaccan and perhaps St Anthony in Meneage.[11] An alternative explanation of the Meneage offered here is that the monkish land belonged entirely to the monastery of *Lannachebran* at St Keverne. The canons of St Achebrannus represent the only landholding religious house in Kerrier Hundred at the time of the Domesday survey. Its survival suggests the importance of the foundation. Widespread landholdings of St Petroc and traces of those of St Pieranus and probably St Kew are documented in Domesday Book; there is no reason why St Achebrannus should not have once possessed their like. As mentioned above,[12] we may have evidence of the despoliation of this saint's lands in the royal grants of Lesneage and mainly contiguous properties in the second half of the tenth century.

[7] The earliest name-forms, see Gover, 'The Place-names of Cornwall', associating these places with the Meneage, are *Ecclesia Sancti Antonini in Manahec* in 1269 (p. 541), *Seynt Mowgan in Maneke* in 1422 which was *Ecclesia Sancti Maugani in Kerier* in 1316 (p. 570), and *Seynt Marten in Meneag* in 1558 for which an earlier place-name was *Dydemin* (p. 567). References to 'Constantine in Meneage' are twice documented (deeds of 1509 and 1527, for which see Henderson, *A History*, pp. 1 and 189; cf. Doble, *The Saints of Cornwall*, III.18). Henderson, holding the first of the above-mentioned views, was cautious about accepting the correctness of an association which would extend the ancient area of monkish land across the Helford River into Constantine parish. The other view would see this as a natural extension of the aforementioned process of parish-identification, distinguishing the place in question from the sub-parish of St Constantine (with its famous holy well) in the parish of St Merryn on the north coast of Cornwall.

[8] Taylor, *The Celtic Christianity*, p. 157, and see also pp. 143, 145, 147, 160, 168.

[9] 'The ecclesiastical antiquities', p. 217; cf. p. 270.

[10] *The Cornish Church Guide*, p. 90; cf. p. 21.

[11] *Ibid.*, pp. 90, 129, and 'The ecclesiastical antiquities', p. 14, respectively.

[12] See p. 95.

BIBLIOGRAPHY

ADAMS, J. H. 'Berry Tower, Bodmin', *Devon and Cornwall Notes and Queries* 28 (1959–61) 243–6 *and* 29 (1962–4) 125 *and* 304

ADAMS, J. H. 'Catalogue of Mediaeval Cornish Chapels' (unpublished manuscript in the Institute of Cornish Studies, Pool, Redruth)

ADDLESHAW, G. W. O. *The Pastoral Structure of the Celtic Church in Northern Britain* (York 1973)

ALCOCK, L. 'A reconnaissance excavation at South Cadbury Castle, Somerset, 1966', *Antiquaries Journal* 47 (1967) 70–6

ALCOCK, Leslie *Dinas Powys. An Iron Age, Dark Age and Early Medieval Settlement in Glamorgan* (Cardiff 1963)

ALCOCK, L. 'Excavations at South Cadbury Castle, 1967: a summary report', *Antiquaries Journal* 48 (1968) 6–17

ALCOCK, L. 'Excavations at South Cadbury Castle, 1968: a summary report', *Antiquaries Journal* 49 (1969) 30–40

ALCOCK, L. 'Excavations at South Cadbury Castle, 1969: a summary report', *Antiquaries Journal* 50 (1970) 14–25

ALCOCK, L. 'Excavations at South Cadbury Castle, 1970: a summary report', *Antiquaries Journal* 51 (1971) 1–7

ANDREW, C. K. C. 'Lammana, near Looe', *Devon and Cornwall Notes and Queries* 19 (1936/7) 145–6

ANON. 'Proceedings at the meetings of the Archaeological Institute Feb. 2, 1849. "Antiquities and Works of Art Exhibited"', *Archaeological Journal* 6 (1849) 81

ANON. 'Proceedings at the meetings of the Archaeological Institute Dec. 6, 1850. "Antiquities and Works of Art Exhibited"', *Archaeological Journal* 7 (1850) 403

ASHBEE, P. 'Excavations at Bar Point, St. Mary's, Isles of Scilly, 1977' *Cornish Archaeology* 17 (1978) 134

ASHE, Geoffrey (ed.) *The Quest for Arthur's Britain* (London 1968)

BARLEY, M. W., & HANSON, R. P. C. (edd.) *Christianity in Britain 300–700. Papers presented to the Conference on Christianity in Roman and Sub-Roman Britain held at the University of Nottingham 17–20 April 1967* (Leicester 1968)

BARTON, K. 'Excavations at Hellesvean, St. Ives, in 1957', *Proceedings of the West Cornwall Field Club* 2 (1956–61) 153–5

BERGIN, O. J., *et al.* (edd.) *Anecdota from Irish Manuscripts* (5 vols, Halle a.S. 1907–13)

BEST, R. I., *et al.* (edd.) *The Book of Leinster, formerly Lebar Na Núachongbála* (6 vols, Dublin 1954–83)

BIELER, Ludwig, & BINCHY, D. A. (edd. & transl.) *The Irish Penitentials* (Dublin 1963)

BINCHY, D. A. (ed.) *Corpus Iuris Hibernici* (6 vols, Dublin 1978)

BINCHY, D. A. 'Patrick and his biographers, ancient and modern', *Studia Hibernica* 2 (1962) 7–173

BINCHY, D. A. 'The pseudo-historical prologue to the *Senchas Már*', *Studia Celtica* 10/11 (1975/6) 15–28

BIRCH, Walter de Gray (ed.) *Cartularium Saxonicum: a Collection of Charters relating to Anglo-Saxon History* (3 vols, London 1885–93)

BLAIR, J. 'Secular minster churches in Domesday Book', in *Domesday Book. A Reassessment*, ed. P. [H.] Sawyer (London 1985), pp. 104–42

BOGHOLM, N., *et al.* (edd.) *A Grammatical Miscellany offered to Otto Jespersen on his Seventieth Birthday* (Copenhagen 1930)

BOLLANDUS, J., *et al.* (edd.) *Acta Sanctorum quotquot toto orbe coluntur, vel a Catholicis Scriptoribus celebrantur* (Antwerp 1643– [in progress])

BOND, Thomas *Topographical and Historical Sketches of the Boroughs of East and West Looe, in the County of Cornwall; with an Account of the Natural and Artificial Curiosities and Picturesque Scenery of the Neighbourhood* (London 1823)

BOON, Amand, & LEFORT, L. T. (edd.) *Pachomiana Latina. Règle et Épitres de S. Pachome, Épitre de S. Théodore et 'Liber' de S. Orsiesius. Texte latin de S. Jérôme* (Leuven 1932)

BOWEN, E. G. *Saints, Seaways and Settlements in the Celtic Lands* (2nd edn, Cardiff 1977)

BOWEN, E. G. *The Settlements of the Celtic Saints in Wales* (2nd edn, Cardiff 1956)

BROMWICH, R. 'The character of the early Welsh tradition', in *Studies in Early British History*, ed. N. K. Chadwick (Cambridge 1954; rev. imp., 1959), pp. 83–136

BROMWICH, Rachel (ed. and transl.) *Trioedd Ynys Prydein: The Welsh Triads* (2nd edn, Cardiff 1978)

BRUCE-MITFORD, R. L. S. 'A Dark-Age settlement at Mawgan Porth, Cornwall', in *Recent Archaeological Excavations in Britain*, ed. R. L. S. Bruce-Mitford (London 1956), pp. 167–96

BRUCE-MITFORD, R. L. S. (ed.) *Recent Archaeological Excavations in Britain. Selected Excavations 1939–1955 with a Chapter on Recent Air Reconnaissance* (London 1956)

BULLEID, A., & MORLAND, J. 'The Mound, Glastonbury. Report of the Excavation Committee', *Proceedings of the Somersetshire Archaeological and Natural History Society* 72 (1926) 52–4

BU'LOCK, J. D. 'Early Christian memorial formulae', *Archaeologia Cambrensis* 105 (1956) 133–41

BURKITT, F. C. 'St. Samson of Dol', *Journal of Theological Studies* 27 (1925/6) 42–57

BURROW, I. C. G. 'Tintagel – some problems', *Scottish Archaeological Forum* 5 (1973) 99–103

111

BUTCHER, S. A., & NEAL, D. S. 'Samson, Isles of Scilly', *Cornish Archaeology* 10 (1971) 94–5

CABROL, Fernand, & LECLERCQ, H. (edd.) *Dictionnaire d'archéologie chrétienne et de liturgie* (15 vols in 30, Paris 1907–53)

CARLEY, James P., & TOWNSEND, D. (edd. & transl.) *The Chronicle of Glastonbury Abbey. An Edition, Translation and Study of John of Glastonbury's Cronica sive Antiquitates Glastoniensis Ecclesie* (2nd edn, Woodbridge 1985)

CATLING, R. M., & ROGERS, J. P. *G. H. Doble: a Memoir and a Bibliography* (2nd edn, Exeter n.d.)

CHADWICK, Nora K. *Early Brittany* (Cardiff 1969)

CHADWICK, N. K. 'Early culture and learning in North Wales', in *Studies in the Early British Church*, ed. N. K. Chadwick (Cambridge 1958), 29–120

CHADWICK, N. K. 'St. Ninian: a preliminary study of sources', *Transactions of the Dumfriesshire and Galloway Natural History and Antiquarian Society*, 3rd S., 27 (1948/9) 9–53

CHADWICK, Nora K. (ed.) *Studies in Early British History* (Cambridge 1954; rev. imp., 1959)

CHADWICK, Nora K. (ed.) *Studies in the Early British Church* (Cambridge 1958)

CHADWICK, Nora K. *The Age of the Saints in the Early Celtic Church* (London 1961; rev. imp., 1963)

CHAPLAIS, P. 'The authenticity of the royal Anglo-Saxon diplomas of Exeter', *Bulletin of the Institute of Historical Research* 39 (1966) 1–34, reprinted with addenda in the author's *Essays in Medieval Diplomacy and Administration* (London 1981)

CHIBNALL, Marjorie (ed. & transl.) *The Ecclesiastical History of Orderic Vitalis* (6 vols, Oxford 1969–80)

COLGRAVE, Bertram (ed. & transl.) *Two Lives of Saint Cuthbert: a Life by an Anonymous Monk of Lindisfarne and Bede's Prose Life* (Cambridge 1940)

COURTNEY, M. A. *Cornish Feasts and Folklore* (Penzance 1890)

COWAN, I. B. 'The development of the parochial system in medieval Scotland', *Scottish Historical Review* 40 (1961) 43–55

COWLEY, F. G. *The Monastic Order in South Wales, 1066–1349* (Cardiff 1977)

COX, J. Charles *The Sanctuaries and Sanctuary Seekers of Mediæval England* (London 1911)

COX, James Stevens *Government of the Town* (Ilchester 1956)

CROFTS, C. B. *A Short History of St. Buryan* (Camborne 1955)

CROFTS, C. [B.] 'King Athelstan and the parish of St. Buryan', *Devon and Cornwall Notes and Queries* 23 (1947–9) 337–42

CROFTS, C. B. 'St. Buryan. An attempt to restore and identify the charter place names', *Devon and Cornwall Notes and Queries* 24 (1950/1) 6–9

CUISSARD, C. (ed.) 'Vie de Saint Paul de Léon en Bretagne d'après un manuscrit de Fleury-sur-Loire conservé à la bibliothèque publique d'Orléans', *Revue celtique* 5 (1881–3) 413–60

DALTON, J. N., & DOBLE, G. H. (edd.) *Ordinale Exon. (Exeter Chapter MS. 3502 collated with Parker MS. 93)* (4 vols, London 1909–40)

DARBY, H. C., & FINN, R. W. (edd.) *The Domesday Geography of South-west England* (Cambridge 1967)

DARBY, H. C. 'The South-western counties', in *The Domesday Geography of South-west England*, edd. H. C. Darby & R. W. Finn (Cambridge 1967), pp. 348–92

DAVID, Pierre *Études historiques sur la Galice et le Portugal du VIe au XIIe Siècle* (Lisbon 1947)

DAVIES, Wendy *An Early Welsh Microcosm. Studies in the Llandaff Charters* (London 1978)

DAVIES, W. '*Liber Landavensis*: its construction and credibility', *English Historical Review* 88 (1973) 335–51

DAVIES, W. 'Saint Mary's Worcester and the *Liber Landavensis*', *Journal of the Society of Archivists* 4 (1970–3) 459–85

DAVIES, W. 'The Celtic Church', *Journal of Religious History* 8 (1974/5) 406–11

DAVIES, W. 'The Latin charter-tradition in western Britain, Brittany and Ireland in the early mediaeval period', in *Ireland in Early Mediaeval Europe*, edd. D. Whitelock *et al.* (Cambridge 1982), pp. 258–80

DAVIES, Wendy *Wales in the Early Middle Ages* (Leicester 1982)

DAVIES, W. H. 'The Church in Wales', in *Christianity in Britain 300–700*, edd. M. W. Barley & R. P. C. Hanson (Leicester 1968), pp. 131–50

DE LA BORDERIE, Arthur Le Moyne, *et al.* *Histoire de Bretagne* (6 vols, Rennes 1896–1914)

DELEHAYE, H. [Review of R. Fawtier, *La Vie de Saint Samson* (1912)], *Analecta Bollandiana* 32 (1913) 362–4

DESHUSSES, Jean (ed.) *Le Sacramentaire Grégorien: ses principales formes d'après les plus anciens manuscrits* (2 vols, Fribourg en Suisse 1971/9)

DE SMEDT, C. (ed.) 'Vita S. Winwaloei primi abbatis Landevenecensis, auctore Wurdestino', *Analecta Bollandiana* 7 (1888) 167–264

DE VOGÜÉ, Adalbert *La Communauté et l'abbé dans la Règle de Saint Benoît* ([Tournai] 1961)

DEXTER, T. F. G. 'St. Piran. A Study in Celtic Hagiology and in Cornish Church History' (unpublished MS. in the Royal Institution of Cornwall Library, Truro)

DEXTER, T. F. G. 'St. Piran's Oratory: an attempt to trace its history and to show that it was a mediaeval pilgrim shrine', *Journal of the Royal Institution of Cornwall* 20 (1915–21) 358–73

DOBLE, Gilbert H. *A History of the Church and Parish of Saint Meubred, Cardynham* (Long Compton 1939)

DOBLE, Gilbert H. *Four Saints of the Fal: St. Gluvias, St. Kea, St. Fili, St. Rumon* (Exeter 1929)

DOBLE, G[ilbert] H. (ed. D. S. Evans) *Lives of the Welsh Saints* (2nd edn, Cardiff 1984)

DOBLE, G[ilbert] H. (ed.) *Pontificale Lanaletense (Bibliothèque de la Ville de Rouen A.27. Cat. 368). A Pontifical formerly in use at St Germans, Cornwall* (London 1937)

DOBLE, Gilbert H. *Saint Carantoc, Abbot and Confessor. Patron of Crantock, Cornwall, and of Llangranog, Cardigan* (2nd edn, Long Compton 1932)

DOBLE, Gilbert H. *Saint Gerent (Gerendus, Gerens)* (Long Compton 1938)

DOBLE, Gilbert H. *S. Neot. Patron of St. Neot, Cornwall, and St Neot's, Huntingdonshire* (Exeter [1929])

DOBLE, Gilbert H. *Saint Patern, Bishop and Confessor, Patron of Llanbadarn* (Lampeter 1940)

DOBLE, Gilbert H. *Saint Perran, Saint Keverne and Saint Kerrian* (Long Compton 1931)

DOBLE, Gilbert H. *Saint Petrock, Abbot and Confessor* (3rd edn, Long Compton 1938)

DOBLE, Gilbert H. *Saint Samson in Cornwall* ([Wendron 1935])

DOBLE, Gilbert H. (ed. D. Attwater) *The Saints of Cornwall* (5 vols, Truro 1960–70)

DU CANGE, Charles *Glossarium Mediae et Infimae Latinitatis* (2nd edn, 2 vols, Niort 1884/7)

DUINE, F. 'La vie de Saint Samson à propos d'un ouvrage récent' *Annales de Bretagne* 28 (1912/13) 332–56

*DUINE, F. 'Mémento des sources hagiographiques de l'histoire de Bretagne', *Mémoires de la Société archéologique d'Ille et Vilaine* 4 (1917/18) 245–457

DUINE, F. *Origines bretonnes. Étude des sources. Questions d'hagiographie et Vie de S. Samson* (Paris 1914)

DUINE, F. [Review of T. Taylor, *The Celtic Christianity of Cornwall* (1916)], *Annales de Bretagne* 31 (1915/16) 575–6

DUINE, F. 'S. Samson évêque de Dol: quelques objections à une réponse', *Annales de Bretagne* 35 (1921–3) 171–86

DUINE, F. *Saints de Domnonée. Notes critiques* (Rennes 1912)

*DUINE, F. (ed.) 'Vie antique et inédite de S. Turiau évêque-abbé de Bretagne', *Bulletin et mémoires de la Société archéologique du Département d'Ille-et-Vilaine* 41 (1912/13) 1–48

DUMVILLE, D. N. 'Sub-Roman Britain: history and legend', *History* N.S., 62 (1977) 173–92

DUMVILLE, David [N.] & KEYNES, S. (gen. edd.) *The Anglo-Saxon Chronicle. A Collaborative Edition* (23 vols, Cambridge 1982– [in progress])

DUMVILLE, D. N. 'The historical value of the *Historia Brittonum*' *Arthurian Literature* 6 (1986) 1–26

DUNNING, G. C. 'The Prehistoric Society, The Devonshire Association, The Devon Archaeological Exploration Society: a report of the conference held at Exeter September 23rd to 26th, 1949', *Archaeological News Letter* 2 (1949/50) 110–16

EHWALD, Rudolf (ed.)   *Aldhelmi Opera* (Berlin 1913–19)

EVISON, Vera I., *et al.* (edd.)   *Medieval Pottery from Excavations. Studies presented to Gerald Clough Dunning, with a Bibliography of his Works* (London 1974)

EWERT, A. (ed.)   *The Romance of Tristran by Beroul* (2 vols, Oxford 1939/70)

FAWTIER, Robert (ed.)   *La Vie de Saint Samson: Essai de critique hagiographique* (Paris 1912)

FAWTIER, R.   'Saint Samson, abbé de Dol: réponse à quelques objections', *Annales de Bretagne* 35 (1921-3) 137-70

FINBERG, H. P. R.   *Lucerna. Studies of Some Problems in the Early History of England* (London 1964)

FINBERG, H. P. R.   *The Early Charters of Devon and Cornwall* (2nd edn, Leicester 1963)

FINBERG, H. P. R.   *West-Country Historical Studies* (Newton Abbot 1969)

FINN, R. Welldon   *An Introduction to Domesday Book* (London 1963)

FINN, R. W., *et al.*   'Comparison of Exeter and Exchequer versions', in *The Domesday Geography of South-west England*, edd. H. C. Darby & R. W. Finn (Cambridge 1967), pp. 395-428

FINN, R. Welldon   *Domesday Studies. The* Liber Exoniensis (London 1964)

FÖRSTER, M. (ed.)   'Die Freilassungsurkunden des Bodmin-Evangeliars', in *A Grammatical Miscellany offered to Otto Jespersen*, edd. N. Bøgholm *et al.* (Copenhagen and London 1930), pp. 77-99

FÖRSTER, M.   'Die Heilige Sativola oder Sidwell. Eine Namenstudie', *Anglia* 62 [N.F., 50] (1938) 33-80

*FOWLER, P. J., *et al.*   *Cadbury Congresbury, Somerset, 1968: an Introductory Report* (Dorchester 1970)

FOX, A.   'Some evidence for a Dark Age trading site at Bantham, near Thurlestone, S. Devon', *Antiquaries Journal* 35 (1955) 55-67

FOX, A.   'Twenty-fifth report on the archaeology and early history of Devon', *Report and Transactions of the Devonshire Association for the Advancement of Science, Literature and Art* 93 (1961) 61-80

GOVER, J. E. B.   'The Place-names of Cornwall' (unpublished typescript, 1948, deposited in the Royal Institution of Cornwall Library, Truro)

GOVER, J. E. B., *et al.*   *The Place-names of Devon* (2 vols, Cambridge 1931/2)

GRANSDEN, Antonia   *Historical Writing in England* c. *550 to* c. *1307* (London 1974)

GRIERSON, Philip   *English Linear Measures: an Essay in Origins* (Reading 1972)

GROSJEAN, P. (ed.)   'Édition et commentaire du *Catalogus sanctorum Hiberniae secundum diversa tempora* ou *De tribus ordinibus sanctorum Hiberniae*', *Analecta Bollandiana* 73 (1955) 197-213 *and* 289-322

GROSJEAN, P. (ed.) 'Vies et miracles de S. Petroc', *Analecta Bollandiana* 74 (1956) 131–88 *and* 470–96

GUILLOTEL, H. 'Les origines du ressort de l'évêché de Dol', *Mémoires de la Société d'histoire et d'archéologie de Bretagne* 54 (1977) 31–68

GUTHRIE, A. 'Dark Age sites at St. Ives', *Proceedings of the West Cornwall Field Club*, N.S., 1 (1952–6) 73–4

GUTHRIE, A. 'Hellesvean Dark Age house', *Proceedings of the West Cornwall Field Club*, N.S., 2 (1956–61) 151–3

HADDAN, Arthur West, & STUBBS, W. (edd.) *Councils and Ecclesiastical Documents relating to Great Britain and Ireland* (3 vols, Oxford 1869–78)

HAMLIN, A. 'A *chi-rho*-carved stone at Drumaqueran, Co. Antrim', *Ulster Journal of Archaeology*, 3rd S., 35 (1972) 22–8

HANSON, R. P. C. *Saint Patrick, His Origins and Career* (Oxford 1968)

HARDEN, D. B. (ed.) *Dark-Age Britain. Studies presented to E. T. Leeds* (London 1956)

HARMER, F. E. (ed. & transl.) *Select English Historical Documents of the Ninth and Tenth Centuries* (Cambridge 1914)

HAYES, J. W. *Late Roman Pottery* (London 1972)

HEARNE, Thomas (ed.) *Adami de Domerham Historia de Rebus Gestis Glastoniensibus* (2 vols, Oxford 1727)

HEARNE, Thomas (ed.) *Joannis Lelandi Antiquarii de Rebus Britannicis Collectanea* (3rd edn, 6 vols, London 1774)

HENCKEN, H. O'Neill *The Archaeology of Cornwall and Scilly* (London 1932)

HENDERSON, Charles (ed. G. H. Doble) *A History of the Parish of Constantine in Cornwall* (Long Compton 1937)

HENDERSON, Charles 'Antiquities' (unpublished manuscripts in the Royal Institution of Cornwall Library, Truro)

HENDERSON, C. G. 'Concerning Bodmin Priory', *103rd Annual Report of the Royal Cornwall Polytechnic Society*, N.S., 8 pt. 3 (1936) 27–39

HENDERSON, Charles 'East Cornwall' (unpublished manuscript in the Royal Institution of Cornwall Library, Truro)

HENDERSON, Charles 'Ecclesiastical Antiquities' (unpublished manuscripts in the Royal Institution of Cornwall Library, Truro)

HENDERSON, Charles *Essays in Cornish History* (Oxford 1935)

HENDERSON, Charles, & COATES, H. *Old Cornish Bridges and Streams* (London 1928)

HENDERSON, Charles *Records of the Church and Priory of St. Germans in Cornwall* (Long Compton 1929)

HENDERSON, Charles *The Cornish Church Guide and Parochial History of Cornwall* (n.p. 1925)

HENDERSON, C. 'The ecclesiastical antiquities of the 109 parishes of west Cornwall', *Journal of the Royal Institution of Cornwall*, N.S., 3 pt. 2 (1957–60) 211–382

HENDERSON, C. 'The ecclesiastical history of the four western hundreds', *Journal of the Royal Institution of Cornwall*, N.S., 3 pt. 4 (1957–60) 383–497

HENDERSON, C. 'The ecclesiastical history of the 109 western parishes of Cornwall', *Journal of the Royal Institution of Cornwall*, N.S., 2 pt. 4 (1953–6) 105–210

HENDERSON, C. 'The 109 ancient parishes of the four western hundreds of Cornwall; to wit – Penwith; Kirrier; Powder and Pyder', *Journal of the Royal Institution of Cornwall*, N.S., 2 pt. 3 (1953–6) 1–104

HENDERSON, Charles 'Topography' (unpublished manuscripts in the Royal Institution of Cornwall Library, Truro)

HENDERSON, Mary 'A Survey of Ancient Crosses of Cornwall. 1952–1983' (unpublished typescript deposited in the Royal Institution of Cornwall Library, Truro)

HINGESTON-RANDOLPH, F. C. (ed.) *The Register of John de Grandisson, Bishop of Exeter, (A.D. 1327–1369)* (3 vols, London 1894–9)

HINGESTON-RANDOLPH, F. C. (ed.) *The Registers of Walter Bronescombe (A.D. 1257–1280), and Peter Quivil (A.D. 1280–1291), Bishops of Exeter, with Some Records of the Episcopate of Bishop Thomas de Bytton (A.D. 1292–1307); also the Taxation of Pope Nicholas IV A.D. 1291 (Diocese of Exeter)* (London 1889)

HOLMES, T. S., *et al.* (edd.) *Two Cartularies of the Augustinian Priory of Bruton and the Cluniac Priory of Montacute in the County of Somerset* (London 1894)

HOSKINS, W. G. *The Westward Expansion of Wessex* (Leicester 1960)

HÜBNER, Emil (ed.) *Inscriptiones Hispaniae Christianae* (2 vols, Berlin 1871/1900)

HUGHES, K. 'The Celtic Church: is this a valid concept?', *Cambridge Medieval Celtic Studies* 1 (1981) 1–20

HUGHES, Kathleen *The Church in Early Irish Society* (London 1966)

HULL, P. L. (ed.) *The Cartulary of St. Michael's Mount (Hatfield House MS. no. 315)* (n.p. 1962)

JACKSON, Kenneth *Language and History in Early Britain. A Chronological Survey of the Brittonic Languages, 1st to 12th C. A.D.* (Edinburgh 1953)

JAMES, E. 'Ireland and western Gaul in the Merovingian period', in *Ireland in Early Mediaeval Europe*, edd. D. Whitelock *et al.* (Cambridge 1982), pp. 362–86

JENNER, H. 'The Bodmin Gospels', *Journal of the Royal Institution of Cornwall* 21 (1922–5) 113–45

JENNER, H. 'The Lannaled mass of St. Germanus in Bodl. MS. 572', *Journal of the Royal Institution of Cornwall* 23 (1929–32) 477–92

JENNER, H. 'The manumissions in the Bodmin Gospels', *Journal of the Royal Institution of Cornwall* 21 (1922–5) 235–60

KEMBLE, John M. (ed.) *Codex Diplomaticus Aevi Saxonici* (6 vols, London 1839–48)

KENNEY, James F. *The Sources for the Early History of Ireland:*

117

Ecclesiastical. An Introduction and Guide (New York 1929; rev. imp., by L. Bieler, 1966)

KENT, T. 'Antiquities in the neighbourhood of Padstow', *Journal of the British Archaeological Association* 4 (1848) 392–5

KER, N. R. *Catalogue of Manuscripts containing Anglo-Saxon* (Oxford 1957)

KERSLAKE, T. 'The Celt and the Teuton in Exeter', *Archaeological Journal* 30 (1873) 211–25

KEYNES, Simon *The Diplomas of King Æthelred 'the Unready' 978–1016. A Study in their Use as Historical Evidence* (Cambridge 1980)

KNOWLES, David *From Pachomius to Ignatius. A Study in the Constitutional History of the Religious Orders* (Oxford 1966)

KNOWLES, David, & HADCOCK, R. N. *Medieval Religious Houses: England and Wales* (2nd edn, London 1971)

KNOWLES, David *The Monastic Order in England. A History of its Development from the Times of St. Dunstan to the Fourth Lateran Council 940–1216* (2nd edn, Cambridge 1963)

LAING, Lloyd *The Archaeology of Late Celtic Britain and Ireland c. 400–1200 A.D.* (London 1975)

LAPIDGE, Michael, & HERREN, M. (transl.) *Aldhelm: The Prose Works* (Ipswich 1979)

LAPIDGE, M. (ed.) 'The cult of St Indract at Glastonbury', in *Ireland in Early Mediaeval Europe*, edd. D. Whitelock et al. (Cambridge 1982), pp. 179–212

LATHAM, R. E. *Revised medieval Latin Word-list from British and Irish Sources* (London 1965; rev. imp., 1980)

LECLERCQ, H. 'Chrisme', in *Dictionnaire d'archéologie chrétienne et de liturgie*, edd. F. Cabrol & H. Leclercq (15 vols in 30, Paris 1907–53), I.1481–1534

LEEDS, E. T. 'Excavations at Chun Castle, in Penwith, Cornwall', *Archaeologia* 76 [2nd S., 26] (1926/7) 205–40 *and* 81 (1931) 33–42

LE MEN, [R.-F.-L.], & ERNAULT, E. (edd.) 'Cartulaire de Landévennec', in *Mélanges historiques, choix de documents* (5 vols, Paris 1873–86), V.533–600; reprinted in *Britannia Christiana: Bretagne monastique* 5 (1985)

LEROQUAIS, V. *Les Pontificaux manuscrits des bibliothèques publiques de France* (4 vols, Paris 1937)

LEWIS, H. A. *"Ab Antiquo". The Story of Lammana (Looe Island). Dedicated to Prior Helyas (1200) and all his Predecessors* (St. Martin's [1946])

LEWIS, H. A. *The Child Christ at Lammana. A Legend of Looe and Talland* (n.p. n.d.)

LIEBERMANN, F. (ed.) *Die Heiligen Englands; angelsächsisch und lateinisch* (Hannover 1889)

LLOYD, John Edward *A History of Wales from the Earliest Times to the Edwardian Conquest* (3rd edn, 2 vols, London 1939)

LOT, Ferdinand *Mélanges d'histoire bretonne (VIe–XIe siècle)* (Paris 1907)

LOTH, J. 'La vie la plus ancienne de St. Samson abbé-évêque de Dol d'après des travaux récents', *Revue celtique* 39 (1922) 301–33 *and* 40 (1923) 1–50

LOTH, J. 'La vie la plus ancienne de Saint Samson de Dol d'après des travaux récents: remarques et additions', *Revue celtique* 35 (1914) 269–300

LOTH, J. 'Les anciennes litanies des saints de Bretagne', *Revue celtique* 11 (1890) 135–51

LOTH, J. *Les Noms des saints bretons* (Paris 1910)

MAC AIRT, Seán, & MAC NIOCAILL, G. (edd. & transl.) *The Annals of Ulster (to A.D. 1131)* (2 vols, Dublin 1983–)

MACALISTER, R. A. S. (ed.) *Corpus Inscriptionum Insularum Celticarum* (2 vols, Dublin 1945/9)

MACDONALD, A. 'Two major early monasteries of Scottish Dalriata: Lismore and Eigg', *Scottish Archaeological Forum* 5 (1973) 47–70

MACLEAN, John *The Parochial and Family History of the Deanery of Trigg Minor, in the County of Cornwall* (3 vols, London 1873–9)

MACQUEEN, John *St. Nynia: a Study of Literary and Linguistic Evidence* (Edinburgh 1961)

MAWER, A., & STENTON, F. M. *The Place-names of Bedfordshire & Huntingdonshire* (Cambridge 1926)

MAXWELL LYTE, H. C. (ed.) *Calendar of the Patent Rolls preserved in the Public Record Office, Edward VI, A.D. 1547–1553* (6 vols, London 1924–9)

MAXWELL LYTE, H. C. (ed.) *Liber Feodorum. The Book of Fees commonly called Testa de Nevill. A.D. 1198–1293* (3 vols, London 1920–31)

MAYR-HARTING, Henry *The Coming of Christianity to Anglo-Saxon England* (London 1972)

MIGNE, J.-P. (ed.) *Patrologiae [Latinae] Cursus Completus . . .* (221 vols, Paris 1844–64)

MILES, H., *et al.* 'Excavations at Killibury Hillfort, Egloshayle 1975–6', *Cornish Archaeology* 16 (1977) 89–121

MILES, H., & MILES, T. 'Trethurgy', *Current Archaeology* 4 (1973) 142–7

MOHRMANN, Christine *The Latin of St. Patrick* (Dublin 1961)

MOMMSEN, Theodor (ed.) *Chronica minora saec. IV. V. VI. VII.* (3 vols, Berlin 1891–8)

MORRIS, J. 'The dates of the Celtic saints', *Journal of Theological Studies*, N.S., 17 (1966) 342–91

NAPIER, A.S., & STEVENSON, W.H. (edd.) *The Crawford Collection of Early Charters and Documents now in the Bodleian Library* (Oxford 1895)

NASH-WILLIAMS, V. E. (ed.) *The Early Christian Monuments of Wales* (Cardiff 1950)

NIERMEYER, J. F. (ed.) *Mediae Latinitatis Lexicon Minus* (Leiden 1954–76)

NORTH, J. J.   *English Hammered Coinage* (2 vols, London 1960/3)

OLIVER, George   *Monasticon Dioecesis Exoniensis, being a Collection of Records and Instruments illustrating the Ancient Conventual, Collegiate and Eleemosynary Foundations, in the Counties of Cornwall and Devon, with Historical Notices, and a Supplement, comprising a List of Dedications of Churches in the Diocese, an Amended Edition of the Taxation of Saint Nicholas, and an Abstract of the Chantry Rolls* (Exeter 1846)

OLSON, B. L., & PADEL, O. J. (edd.)   'A tenth-century list of Cornish parochial saints', *Cambridge Medieval Celtic Studies* 12 (1986) 33–71

OLSON, [B.] L.   'Crantock, Cornwall, as an early monastic site', in *The Early Church in Western Britain and Ireland*, ed. S. M. Pearce (Oxford 1982), pp. 177–85

OLSON, [B.] L.   'Saint Entenyn', *Cornish Studies* 3 (1975) 25–8

PADEL, O. J.   'Beroul's geography and patronage', *Reading Medieval Studies* 9 (1983) 84–94

PADEL, O. [J.]   'Cornish language notes', *Cornish Studies* 1 (1973) 57–9; 2 (1974) 75–8; *and* 4/5 (1976/7) 15–27

PADEL, O. J.   *Cornish Place-name Elements* (Nottingham 1985)

PADEL, O. J.   'The Cornish background of the Tristan stories', *Cambridge Medieval Celtic Studies* 1 (1981) 53–81

PADEL, O. J.   'Two new pre-Conquest charters for Cornwall', *Cornish Studies* 6 (1978) 20–7

PAGE, William (ed.)   *The Victoria History of the Counties of England: Cornwall* (2 vols, London 1906)

PEARCE, S. M.   'The dating of some Celtic dedications and hagiographical traditions in south western Britain', *Report and Transactions of the Devonshire Association for the Advancement of Science, Literature and Art* 105 (1973) 95–120

PEARCE, Susan M. (ed.)   *The Early Church in Western Britain and Ireland. Studies presented to C. A. Ralegh Radford arising from a Conference Organised in his Honour by the Devon Archaeological Society and Exeter City Museum* (Oxford 1982)

PEARCE, Susan   *The Kingdom of Dumnonia. Studies in History and Tradition in South-western Britain A.D. 350–1150* (Padstow 1978)

PEDLER, E. H.   *The Anglo-Saxon Episcopate of Cornwall; with Some Account of the Bishops of Crediton* (London 1856)

PETER, T. C.   'St. Piran's Old Church', *Journal of the Royal Institution of Cornwall* 16 (1904–6) 133–43

PICKEN, W. M. M.   'Light on Lammana', *Devon and Cornwall Notes and Queries* 35 (1982–6) 281–6

PICKEN, W. M. M.   'St. German of Cornwall's Day', *Devon and Cornwall Notes and Queries* 27 (1956–8) 103–7

PICKEN, W. M. M.   'The "Landochou" charter', *apud* W. G. Hoskins, *The Westward Expansion of Wessex* (Leicester 1960), pp. 36–44

PICKEN, W. M. M.   'The manor of Tremaruustel and the Honour of St. Keus', *Journal of the Royal Institution of Cornwall*, N.S., 7 (1973–6) 220–30

PICKEN, W. M. M.   'The names of the hundreds of Cornwall', *Devon and Cornwall Notes and Queries* 30 (1965–7) 36–40

PLAINE, F. B. (ed.)   'Vita S. Brioci episcopi et confessoris ab anonymo suppari conscripta', *Analecta Bollandiana* 2 (1883) 161–90

PLAINE, F. B. (ed.)   'Vita Sancti Pauli episcopi Leonensis in Britannia minori, auctore Wormonoco', *Analecta Bollandiana* 1 (1882) 208–58

PLUMMER, Charles (ed.)   *Two of the Saxon Chronicles Parallel, with Supplementary Extracts from the Others. A Revised Text on the Basis of an Edition by John Earle* (2 vols, Oxford 1892/9; rev. imp., by D. Whitelock, 1952)

PLUMMER, Charles (ed.)   *Vitae Sanctorum Hiberniae partim hactenus ineditae* (2 vols, Oxford 1910; rev. imp., 1968)

POLLARD, S. H. M.   'Neolithic and dark age settlements on High Peak, Sidmouth, Devon', *Proceedings of the Devon Archaeological Exploration Society*, N.S., 23 (1966) 35–59

POULIN, J.-C.   'A propos du diocèse de Dol: Saint Samson et la question des enclaves', *Francia: Forschungen zur westeuropäischen Geschichte* 6 (1978) 610–15

POULIN, J.-C.   'Hagiographie et politique. La première Vie de Saint Samson de Dol', *Francia: Forschungen zur westeuropäischen Geschichte* 5 (1977) 1–26

POWELL, T. G. E.   *The Celts* (London 1958)

RADFORD, C. A. R., & SWANTON, M. J.   *Arthurian Sites in the West* (Exeter 1975)

RADFORD, C. A. R.   'Excavations at Glastonbury Abbey, 1956', *Antiquity* 31 (1957) 171

RADFORD, C. A. R.   'Glastonbury Abbey', in *The Quest for Arthur's Britain*, ed. G. Ashe (London 1968), pp. 119–38

RADFORD, C. A. R.   'Imported pottery found at Tintagel, Cornwall. An aspect of British trade with the Mediterranean in the early christian period', in *Dark-Age Britain*, ed. D. B.Harden (London 1956), pp. 59–70

RADFORD, C. A. R.   'Report on the excavations at Castle Dore', *Journal of the Royal Institution of Cornwall*, N.S., 1 (1946–52), appendix (1951) 1–119

RADFORD, C. A. R.   'Romance and reality in Cornwall', in *The Quest for Arthur's Britain*, ed. G. Ashe (London 1968), pp. 75–100

RADFORD, C. A. R.   'The Celtic monastery in Britain', *Archaeologia Cambrensis* 111 (1962) 1–24

RADFORD, C. A. R.   'The Church in Somerset down to 1100', *Proceedings of the Somersetshire Archaeological and Natural History Society* 106 (1961/2) 28–45

RADFORD, C. A. R.   'The church of Saint Germans', *Journal of the Royal Institution of Cornwall*, N.S., 7 (1973–6) 190–6

RADFORD, C. A. Ralegh   *The Early Christian Inscriptions of Dumnonia* (Pool 1975)

RADFORD, C. A. R.   'The later pre-Conquest boroughs and their defences', *Medieval Archaeology* 14 (1970) 83–103

RADFORD, C. A. Ralegh *Tintagel Castle* (2nd edn, London 1939)

RADFORD, C. A. R. 'Tintagel in history and legend', *Journal of the Royal Institution of Cornwall* 25 (1937–42), appendix (1942) 25–41

RADFORD, C. A. R. 'Tintagel: the castle and Celtic monastery. Interim report', *Antiquaries Journal* 15 (1935) 401–19

RAHTZ, P. 'Castle Dore - a reappraisal of the post-Roman structures', *Cornish Archaeology* 10 (1971) 49–54

RAHTZ, P. 'Excavations on Glastonbury Tor, Somerset, 1964–6', *Archaeological Journal* 127 (1970) 1–81

RAHTZ, P. 'Irish Settlements in Somerset', *Proceedings of the Royal Irish Academy* 76 C (1976) 223–30

RAHTZ, P. 'Monasteries as settlements', *Scottish Archaeological Forum* 5 (1973) 125–35

RAHTZ, P. 'Pottery in Somerset, A.D. 400–1066', in *Medieval Pottery from Excavations*, edd. V. I. Evison *et al.* (London 1974) pp. 95–126

RAHTZ, P. A. 'Sub-Roman cemeteries in Somerset', in *Christianity in Britain, 300–700*, edd. M. W. Barley & R. P. C. Hanson (Leicester 1968), pp. 193–5

RAINSBURY DARK, K. 'The plan and interpretation of Tintagel', *Cambridge Medieval Celtic Studies* 9 (1985) 1–17

RAVENHILL, W. L. D. 'Cornwall', in *The Domesday Geography of South-west England*, edd. H. C. Darby & R. Welldon Finn (Cambridge 1967), pp. 296–347

RICHTER, Michael (ed.) *Canterbury Professions* ([London] 1973)

ROBINSON, J. Armitage *The Saxon Bishops of Wells. A Historical Study in the Tenth Century* (London [1918])

ROLLASON, D. W. 'Lists of saints' resting-places in Anglo-Saxon England', *Anglo-Saxon England* 7 (1978) 61–93

ROSE-TROUP, F. 'St. Buryan charter', *Devon and Cornwall Notes and Queries* 18 (1934/5) 294–9

ROSITZKE, Harry August (ed.) *The C-Text of the Old English Chronicles* (Bochum-Langendreer 1940)

RUTHERFORD, Anthony 'The *Historia Brittonum*: Some Sources and Analogues' (unpublished M.Litt. thesis, University of Edinburgh 1974)

RYAN, John *Irish Monasticism: Origins and Early Development* (Dublin 1931; 2nd edn, Shannon 1972)

SAUNDERS, A. D., *et al.* 'Lydford Castle, Devon', *Medieval Archaeology* 24 (1980) 123–86

SAUNDERS, C. 'The excavations at Grambla, Wendron 1972: Interim report', *Cornish Archaeology* 11 (1972) 50–2

SAWYER, P[eter] H. *Anglo-Saxon Charters. An Annotated List and Bibliography* (London 1968)

SAWYER, Peter [H.] (ed.) *Domesday Book. A Reassessment* (London 1985)

SELKIRK, A., & SELKIRK, W. 'Lundy', *Current Archaeology* 1 (1967/8) 196–202

SHARPE, R. 'Some problems concerning the organization of the Church in early medieval Ireland', *Peritia: Journal of the Medieval Academy of Ireland* 3 (1984) 230–70

SIMS-WILLIAMS, P. 'Gildas and the Anglo-Saxons', *Cambridge Medieval Celtic Studies* 6 (1983) 1–30

SMITH, J. M. H. 'The "archbishopric" of Dol and the ecclesiastical politics of ninth-century Brittany', *Studies in Church History* 18 (1982) 59–70

SMITH, Lucy Toulmin (ed.) *The Itinerary of John Leland in or about the years 1535–1543* (5 vols, London 1906–10)

SNELL, Lawrence S. *Documents Towards a History of the Reformation in Cornwall* (3 vols, Exeter 1953–60)

SPOONER, B. C. *St. Neot* (n.p. n.d.)

STENTON, F. M. *Anglo-Saxon England* (3rd edn, Oxford 1971)

STEVENSON, William Henry (ed.) *Asser's Life of King Alfred together with the Annals of Saint Neots erroneously ascribed to Asser* (Oxford 1904; rev. imp., by D. Whitelock, 1959)

STOKES, Whitley [S.] (ed. & transl.) *Félire Óengusso Céli Dé. The Martyrology of Oengus the Culdee critically edited from Ten Manuscripts* (London 1905)

STOKES, Whitley [S.], & O'DONOVAN, J. (edd. & transl.) *Sanas Chormaic. Cormac's Glossary* (Calcutta 1868)

STOKES, W[hitley] S. (ed.) *Three Irish Glossaries . . .* (London 1862)

TAYLOR, Thomas *The Celtic Christianity of Cornwall. Divers Sketches and Studies* (London 1916)

THOMAS, Charles *A Provisional List of Imported Pottery in Post-Roman Western Britain and Ireland* (Pool 1981)

THOMAS, C. 'Are these the walls of Camelot?', *Antiquity* 43 (1969) 27–30

THOMAS, Charles *Christian Antiquities of Camborne* (St Austell 1967)

THOMAS, C. 'East and West: Tintagel, Mediterranean imports and the early Insular Church', in *The Early Church in Western Britain and Ireland*, ed. S. M. Pearce (Oxford 1982), pp. 17–34

THOMAS, C. 'Evidence for post-Roman occupation of Chun Castle, Cornwall', *Antiquaries Journal* 36 (1956) 75–8

THOMAS, Charles *Exploration of a Drowned Landscape. Archaeology and History of the Isles of Scilly* (London 1985)

THOMAS, Charles *Gwithian: Ten Years' Work (1949–1958)* (Camborne 1958)

THOMAS, C. 'Hermits on islands or priests in a landscape?', *Cornish Studies* 6 (1978) 28–44

THOMAS, C. 'Imported Late-Roman Mediterranean pottery in Ireland and western Britain: chronologies and implications', *Proceedings of the Royal Irish Academy* 76 C (1976) 245–55

THOMAS, C. 'Imported pottery in Dark-Age western Britain', *Medieval Archaeology* 3 (1959) 89–111

THOMAS, C., et al. 'Lundy, 1969', *Current Archaeology* 2 (1969/70) 138–42

THOMAS, C. 'Parish churchyard, Phillack', *Cornish Archaeology* 12 (1973) 59

THOMAS, C. 'Post-Roman rectangular house plans in the South-west: some suggested origins', *Proceedings of the West Cornwall Field Club*, N. S., 2 (1956–61) 156–61

THOMAS, C. 'Rosnat, Rostat, and the early Irish Church', *Ériu* 22 (1971) 100–6

THOMAS, Charles (ed.) *Rural Settlement in Roman Britain. Papers given at a C. B. A. Conference held at St. Hugh's College, Oxford, January 1 to 3, 1965* (London 1966)

THOMAS, C. 'Settlement-history in early Cornwall: the antiquity of the hundreds', *Cornish Archaeology* 3 (1964) 70–9

THOMAS, C. 'The character and origins of Roman Dumnonia', in *Rural Settlement in Roman Britain*, ed. C. Thomas (London 1966), pp. 74–98

THOMAS, Charles *The Early Christian Archaeology of North Britain* (London 1971)

THOMAS, A. C. 'The end of the Roman South west', in *The Roman West Country*, edd. K. Branigan & P. J. Fowler (Newton Abbot 1976), pp. 198–213

THOMAS, C. 'The Irish settlements in post-Roman western Britain: a survey of the evidence', *Journal of the Royal Institution of Cornwall*, N.S., 6 (1969–72) 251–74

THOMAS, C. 'The occupation of May's Hill and its dating – a note', *Cornish Studies* 11 (1983) 78–80

THOMPSON, E. A. 'Britonia', in *Christianity in Britain, 300–700*, edd. M. W. Barley & R. P. C. Hanson (Leicester 1968), pp. 201–5

THORN, Caroline, *et al.* (edd.) *Domesday Book: Cornwall* (Chichester 1979)

THORN, Caroline, *et al.* (edd.) *Domesday Book: Devon* (2 vols, Chichester 1985)

TIERNEY, J. J. 'The Celtic ethnography of Posidonius', *Proceedings of the Royal Irish Academy* 60 C (1959/60) 189–275

TROLLOPE, E. 'Roman remains in the vicinity of Padstow, Cornwall', *Archaeological Journal* 17 (1860) 311–16

USSHER, W. A. E., *et al.* (edd.) *The Geology of the Country around Bodmin and St. Austell with Notes on the Petrology of the Igneous Rocks by J. S. Flett. Explanation of Sheet 347* (London 1909)

VIVES, D. José (ed.) *Inscripciones cristianas de la España romana y visigoda* (2nd edn, Barcelona 1969)

VOGEL, Cyrille, & ELZE, R. (edd.) 'Le Pontifical Romano-Germanique du dixième siècle', *Studi e Testi* 226 and 227 (1963) and 269 (1972)

WADE-EVANS, A. W. (ed. & transl.) *Vitae Sanctorum Britanniae et Genealogiae* (Cardiff 1944)

WALLIS, John *The Cornwall Register; Containing Collections relative to the Past and Present State of the 209 Parishes, forming the County, Archdeaconry, Parliamentary Divisions, and Poor Law Unions of*

Cornwall; to which is added, a Brief View of the Adjoining Towns and Parishes in Devon, from Hartland to Plymouth (Bodmin 1847)

WARNER, Rubie D.-N. (ed.) *Early English Homilies from the Twelfth Century MS. Vesp. D. XIV* (London 1917)

WHITAKER, John *The Ancient Cathedral of Cornwall historically surveyed* (2 vols, London 1804)

WHITELOCK, Dorothy (transl.) *English Historical Documents c. 500–1042* (2nd edn, London 1979)

WHITELOCK, Dorothy, *et al.* (edd.) *Ireland in Early Mediaeval Europe. Studies in Memory of Kathleen Hughes* (Cambridge 1982)

WHITELOCK, Dorothy *The Genuine Asser* (Reading 1968)

WILSON, D. M., & HURST, J. G. 'Medieval Britain in 1956. Cornwall: Island of Teän, Scillies', *Medieval Archaeology* 1 (1957) 147

WILSON, D. M., & HURST, J. G. 'Medieval Britain in 1957. Somerset: Glastonbury', *Medieval Archaeology* 2 (1958) 188–9

WILSON, D. M., & HURST, J. G. 'Medieval Britain in 1962 and 1963. Somerset: Cannington', *Medieval Archaeology* 8 (1964) 237

WILSON, D. M., & MOORHOUSE, J. 'Medieval Britain in 1970. Somerset: Congresbury, Cadbury Camp', *Medieval Archaeology* 15 (1971) 133

WILSON, P. A. 'St. Ninian and Candida Casa: literary evidence from Ireland', *Transactions of the Dumfriesshire and Galloway Natural History and Antiquarian Society*, 3rd S., 41 (1962/3) 156–85

INDEX

Note: entries beginning with 'St' refer to Cornish place-names.

132

St Anthony in Roseland 103, 105, 109
  priory of 51, 97–8, 103–4
St Breocke 29
Saint-Bricuc 29
St Buryan 78–80, 84, 97, 105, 107nn;
  see also charters, Anglo-Saxon;
  Ecglosberria
St Cadix 98n, 105
St Carroc, priory of 51, 97–8, 100,
  103–4
St Constantine, St Merryn 109n
St Davids 32n
St Germans 35–6, 51, 53, 60–6, 87, 97,
  105; *see also bishops, bishoprics*;
  charters, Anglo-Saxon
St Keverne 88, 105, 107n, 108, 109
St Kew 14, 82, 105
St Martin by Looe 109
St Martin in Meneage 108–9
St Mawgan in Meneage 108–9
St Mawgan in Pyder 109
St Merryn 43, 109n
St Michael Caerhays 42; *see also*
  Lanvyhaill
St Michael of Lammana, island of,
  priory of: *see Lammana*
St Michael's Mount 89–90, 96, 102,
  105, 108, 109
  priory of 109
St Minver 43n, 44
St Neot 51, 70, 85–6, 105, 107n; *see*
  also Nietestou
St Neots, Hunts. 85–6
St Piran's Oratory 35–6, 43, 88, 105
St Sampson, Golant 12, 13–14, 105
saints
  cult of, veneration of 12, 18, 24, 26,
    60–2, 65, 68–9, 70, 71, 74, 82, 86,
    88n, 90, 95, 96, 100, 106
  customary payments to 88n, 92
  dedications to (patron-saints) 6, 12,
    18, 25–6, 28–9, 34, 53n, 56–60, 64,
    65, 70, 85, 89, 93, 95, 96, 98, 99nn,
    101nn, 102, 103, 104, 109
  feasts of 26, 57, 61
  grants to 78–84, 95
  landholding 58, 59, 77, 78–84,
    87–96 *passim*, 97, 104, 109
St Stephens by Launceston 88, 105,
  107n
St Teath 91
Salomon, Breton ruler 18n

Samson of Dol, St 9–20, 22–3, 27–8,
  29, 48–9, 50, 65, 67, 82
  monastery founded in Cornwall
    by 9–14, 15, 17, 20, 48, 50, 105,
    106
Samson, St, hermit at Padstow 67
Samson, Scilly Isles 42, 45
sanctuaries, privileged 72, 73, 79, 107
Sanctus Carrocus, Sanctus Cairocus (St
  Cadix) 98
Sanctus Germanus (*aecclesia Sancti
  Germani*) 65, 87, 92n, 96
Sanguinas, St Gennys 91
Scilly Isles 42, 45, 46
Scotland 45n, 95
script
  Caroline 57, 66
  Insular 4, 56, 57, 80, 86n
*Secgan be þam Godes sanctum þe on
  Engla lande ærost reston* 25, 70, 71
secularisation of church properties 82,
  91, 95, 97, 101, 104
sees: *see bishops, bishoprics*
Seine, River 12
semita Pauli 21–5
Severn, River 9, 10n
Severn Sea: *see Bristol Channel*
Sherborne, bishop of: *see bishops,
  bishoprics*
shrines 59n
  of Petroc 71
Shropshire 89n
Sidefulla, Sidwell (= ?Sitofolla), St 25
Sitofolla, Sicofolla, St 20–6, 105; *see
  also domus; monasterium* (*-a*)
Somerset 8, 34–5, 37, 44, 45n, 46, 47,
  84, 88n, 93n, 97n, 104
Sourtown 38n
South Cadbury 44
South Hill 12–13, 14, 16–17, 38
Southern Sea: *see English Channel*
Spain, Suevic kingdom in 52n, 59
Stephen, St 88, 94, 96; *see also*
  Lanscauetona
stow 69, 70–1
Stratona Hundred 88
sub-Roman Cornwall 39, 47, 48

Talland 102
Tamar, River 3, 63, 75
Tavistock, abbot of 92
Tean, Scilly Isles 42, 45, 47